James Castrission, 27, worked as an accountant for four years before committing himself to a life of adventure. In 2008, James and his best mate Justin Jones became the first kayakers to cross the Tasman Sea. As well as kayaking, James has led mountaineering expeditions to some of the most challenging peaks around the world, run numerous ultra marathons and sailed to remote destinations across the globe. He is now one of Australia's most sought-after corporate speakers. *Crossing the Ditch* is his first book.

CROSSING
THE DITCH

TWO MATES, A KAYAK,
AND THE CONQUEST OF THE TASMAN

JAMES CASTRISSION

HarperSports
An imprint of HarperCollinsPublishers

Harper_Sports_
An imprint of HarperCollins_Publishers_

First published in Australia in 2009
by HarperCollins_Publishers_ Australia Pty Limited
ABN 36 009 913 517
www.harpercollins.com.au

HarperCollins_Publishers_
25 Ryde Road, Pymble, Sydney, NSW 2073, Australia
31 View Road, Glenfield, Auckland 0627, New Zealand
1–A, Hamilton House, Connaught Place, New Delhi – 110 001, India
77–85 Fulham Palace Road, London, W6 8JB, United Kingdom
2 Bloor Street East, 20th floor, Toronto, Ontario M4W 1A8, Canada
10 East 53rd Street, New York NY 10022, USA

National Library of Australia Cataloguing-in-publication data:

Castrission, James, 1982–
   Crossing the ditch/James Castrission.
   ISBN: 978 0 7322 8859 4 (pbk.)
   Castrission, James, 1982–
   Jones, Justin.
   Sea kayaking – Australia.
   Adventure and adventurers – Australia - Biography.
   Canoes and canoeing – Australia.
   Ocean travel.
   Tasman Sea – Description and travel.
797.12240994

Cover design by Brendon Cook
Front cover image by James Castrission
Back cover image by Ross Land/Getty Images
Typeset in 11.5/16pt Goudy by Kirby Jones
Printed and bound in Australia by Griffin Press
70gsm Classic used by HarperCollins_Publishers_ is a natural, recyclable product made from wood
grown in sustainable forests. The manufacturing processes conform to the environmental
regulations in the country of origin, Finland.

5 4 3 2 1   09 10 11 12

This book is dedicated to the memory of
Andrew McAuley.
Lost at sea, his spirit will live on forever.

"It is not the critic who counts; not the man who points out
how the strong man stumbles, or where the doer of deeds
could have done them better. The credit belongs to the man
who is actually in the arena, whose face is marred by dust
and sweat and blood, who strives valiantly; who errs and
comes short again and again; because there is not effort
without error and shortcomings; but who does actually
strive to do the deed; who knows the great enthusiasm, the
great devotion, who spends himself in a worthy cause,
who at the best knows in the end the triumph of high
achievement and who at the worst, if he fails, at least he
fails while daring greatly. So that his place shall never be
with those cold and timid souls who know neither victory
nor defeat."

THEODORE ROOSEVELT – 26TH US PRESIDENT (1901–09)

CROSSING
THE DITCH

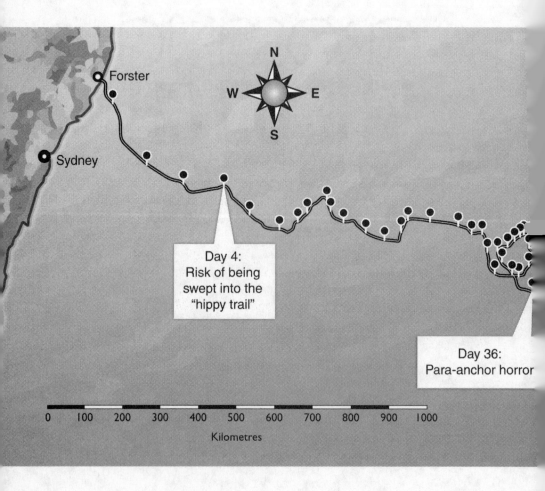

OUR VOYAGE ACROSS THE TASMAN
62 days, 3318 kilometres

Day 46:
Shark attack #1

Day 43:
Christmas Day

Auckland

New Plymouth

CONTENTS

FOREWORD

by DICK SMITH AO, Adventurer

Imagine teaming up with a mate to paddle a small kayak more than 2,000 kilometres across one of the most dangerous seas in the world. You'll be faced with 10-metre seas, gale force winds, exhaustion and the possibility of not coming back.

Why would you ever do it?

James Castrission gives us the answer in one of the greatest adventure stories of the decade.

On 13 November 2007, James and Justin Jones left from Forster, NSW, hoping to become the first to paddle a sea kayak from Australia to New Zealand. On the shore were family and friends, some who were visibly distressed. Only nine months earlier Andrew McAuley, one of Australia's most experienced sea kayakers, had attempted the same crossing and lost his life within sight of New Zealand.

Like many other adventurers, I would have understood if James and Justin had cancelled their expedition. As a 20-year-old Rover Scout, I sailed across the Tasman to Lord Howe Island. Our goal was to attempt climbing Balls Pyramid, one of the world's tallest sea spires. Although our voyage was only a third of the way to New Zealand seasickness plagued most of us, and after 72 hours all we wanted was to step onto land. After that I decided that ocean-based adventuring was not for me.

In June 1993, I crossed the Tasman by balloon from New Zealand to Australia, skimming low over the waves and thankful not to be on the ocean surface. In 2006 I celebrated the 75th anniversary of the first solo flight across the Tasman by repeating Guy Menzies' flight. I knew first-hand what a remote and lonely place the Tasman can be.

When I first heard of James and Justin's plans to "cross the ditch", I had no doubt they'd chosen one of the last great adventures. In an age of guided Mount Everest climbs and tourist trips to the ocean floor, their proposal was a breath of fresh air.

Like many others, they had met at school, enjoyed walking and climbing in the Blue Mountains and dreamed of greater challenges. What set them apart from their schoolmates was that they followed their dreams.

The odds were against them from the start. When James came up with the idea to kayak the Tasman, he'd only spent one day on a yacht – he'd been 13 years old and seasick the whole time. Remarkably, Justin agreed to join him in the tiny sleeping cabin, despite suffering from claustrophobia.

Their trip would be physically demanding, dangerous and the outcome uncertain – a perfect recipe for adventure. It reminded me why I started the journal *Australian Geographic* in late 1985, to encourage the spirit of adventure. I believed then, and still do, that without it, a nation will wilt and wither away.

In the 1980s, the Australian media tended to criticise young people taking risks and extending their boundaries. Fortunately, things have changed. James and Justin drew more than 1.6 million visitors to their expedition website that featured daily reports and photos sent in via satellite phone. Major television and radio stations interviewed them, with no real criticism, and nearly everyone got behind their extraordinary endeavour.

It's not just the media that seems to have matured. The days of "planning an expedition on the back of an envelope" are gone forever. As you read this book, you'll realise the incredible commitment James and Justin made to proper planning, teamwork and reducing the risk of what is, by its very nature, a dangerous undertaking.

Over 18 months they searched out the experts to show them the latest technologies to reduce their risk, indeed make the trip possible. Having the best Global Positioning System and satellite phone was crucial, but as important were the high-nutrient freeze-dried foods and flameless heating pads for cooking. They couldn't carry enough fresh water in their little kayak so they relied on an electric reverse osmosis desalinator. When it failed their trip might have ended but they'd thought to bring a hand-held desalinator as back-up.

Of course they met the naysayers, the experts who said, "I think you're flaming mad!" Some questioned why anyone would endure the amount of hardship they would face. They were considered selfish for the stress they would bring to loved ones. But then adventure is a very selfish pursuit. In his story, James doesn't back away from the fact that it's family and friends who often suffer greater distress than the adventurers themselves.

In the end, after all the planning, discussions of risk profiles, equipment preparation and training, the success of their endeavour came down to one thing – their single-minded desire to succeed. It took them 1.7 million paddle strokes to "cross the ditch", the longest-ever trans-oceanic, two-person kayaking trip in history.

When a big storm hit, they battened down the hatches and rode it out while back home people stayed up all night, checking their progress on the expedition website. James never got over his seasickness nor Justin his claustrophobia. At times it must have been a nightmare.

On day 27, a vast gyre of current pushed them backwards 150 kilometres, yet they refused to give up. They had planned on reaching New Zealand in 45 days at most – they arrived on day 62. Despite the hardships, James writes beautifully of the wonders they encountered as they felt themselves being drawn closer to the natural world around them.

Kingsford Smith flew the first airplane across the Tasman in 1928 to be greeted by some 25,000 people. Nearly 80 years later, in an age when cynics would have us believe adventure is dead, an enthusiastic crowd just as large welcomed James and Justin to New Zealand's shore.

In 2008 James and Justin were awarded the Australian Geographic Young Adventurer of the Year Award. They represent a new generation of adventurers with an exciting future exploring our deep oceans, dwindling icecaps and the limitless expanse of space. This book will give you clues as to what makes them tick.

PREFACE

It was day 36 out on the Tasman. Lying in a dreary, half-drowsy state in the cabin of our kayak *Lot 41*, trying to summon enough energy to wake properly and prepare dinner, a violent set of waves shook us hard. We were pulled through a two-storey wall of water, launched into the air, and spat out the other side. A piercing howl suddenly began reverberating in the cabin. Poking my head outside, I saw in the rapidly fading light that the bridle had wrapped around the rudder, with the full force of the anchor now on it. The seas were massive, with each wave battering the minuscule *Lot 41* and constantly submerging us. The wind was intensifying. It was now dark.

We sat petrified and examined the possibilities, quickly reducing our options to two: the first, to put on all our survival gear, alert our land team and Rescue Coordination Centres on both sides of the Tasman, then ride out the storm – hoping she'd hold up through the night.

The second option was for one of us to swim to the back of the kayak and try to untangle the mess. With the force and speed we were being pulled through the face of these huge waves, this was insanely dangerous. The rudder was chomping up and down like the needle of a sewing machine. The thought of this coming down on top of one of us while struggling to untangle the mess in complete darkness was horrifying. We'd untangled the rudder three weeks earlier when the seas had been infinitely calmer. After that little playful jaunt, my lungs had been half full of water and I was near hypothermic: the confusion that darkness would have added and the aggressive intensity of the frothing cauldron would have made the operation border on suicidal.

If one of us were to go back, it had to be me – there's no way I'd have let my best mate go out there. Fortunately, Jonesy talked me out of it. We made the decision to wait till morning and sort it out when the seas had abated. The screeching continued. It sounded like our kayak was being tortured, like a wounded animal about to be put down. There was no escaping its terrifying howl.

We didn't know what was going to be the first failure point: would it be the rudder breaking off? The bridle breaking? Were the bridle and rudder built strongly enough that the first point of failure would mean the whole back of *Lot 41* being ripped out? The uncertainty would be the hardest part of a torturous night.

This was all a far cry from catching the 7.34am train – all stops from Hornsby on the North Shore line – during my days as an accountant. I remember one particular Monday morning commuting to work, when, staring down at my darkly tanned hands, blood was still seeping from cuts caused by shoving my paws in cracks, rock climbing in the Blue Mountains: it had been an incredible weekend.

The conductor belted out "Next stop Central" and, as I looked up, the pallid, expressionless prisoners began to shuffle towards the carriage door. Their lifeless faces instantly struck a chord with me as I realised I was sitting in a train full of fellow inmates. Each person's tie seemed to symbolise a noose. Of course, a prisoner is a person held captive against their will, but ironically, the only guards administering the years of hard labour were us, the prisoners.

For a long time, I'd done all the things I was meant to do. I'd studied hard at school (well, in my final years at least), shuffled off to university and now I was working as an accountant in a "proper" career, earning a decent wage. I'd already begun to put on the mandatory 1.5 kilograms per year around my waist, and I could see my life unfolding: I'd be a manager in three years' time, get married a couple of years after that, put a deposit on a house, have two children (maybe three, if I was really daring), mow the lawn every Saturday morning like clockwork and then retire at 65. I was dabbling with life; afraid to do what I wanted, yet too afraid to stop. But life had more to offer – I was sure of it.

The 62-day journey by kayak across the Tasman that my best friend Justin Jones and I embarked on in November 2007 was frightening at times – sharks tore at our hull and 30-foot waves crashed over us, and one night we faced the terrifying possibility that the stern of our kayak might be ripped away; that the cabin might well become our coffin. But I've learnt that these fears – real fears – are never as debilitating as the fears of failure, rejection and regret.

When Jonesy and I first thought of the Tasman expedition, the little kid inside me screamed, "Have a go, ya mug." But that voice was fighting 15 years of institutionalisation, so what chance did he have? He'd been taught to silence that voice and do the adult thing. Sticking his neck out in life's stampede meant risking violent decapitation. Who were we to take on the Tasman Sea? I guess one of the primary reasons that inspired us to become the first people to kayak across the Tasman was to conquer those fears.

Adventurers throughout history have struggled to answer the question: why? There's the famous quote by English mountaineer George Mallory – "Because it is there" – while the Australian Antarctic explorer Sir Douglas Mawson said, "If you have to ask the question, you will never understand the answer." By writing this account of our struggle against the Tasman Sea, hopefully I'll be able to give the reader (and maybe myself!) some insights into what motivated a couple of young Aussie blokes who knew nothing about a lot to take on one of the deadliest ocean passages in the world.

1

TEARS, TIGERS AND MEATBALL SANDWICHES

Apparently, when you're two years old, your bones are quite elastic – more like Kevlar than carbon fibre. It's very rare for kids that age to break bones. I somehow succeeded.

Almost from the day I was born, 14 March 1982, I always seemed to have too much energy. My parents had a rough time chasing me around and trying to protect me from myself. They did a pretty good job, though, until I decided it was time for my first BASE jump.

Climbing my first peak – the kitchen bench-top – during a rare moment when my parents had turned their backs, I threw myself off, yelling, "Look at me – I'm Superman!" before thudding into the tiled kitchen floor and bursting into tears.

So I found myself in my first cast – the first of many to come. I didn't let it slow me down, though, and I continued to enjoy the newfound freedom of having just learnt to walk. These adventures resulted in me breaking my cast numerous times, and having to visit the hospital again. But instead of replacing the cast, they'd plaster the outside of it. Within a few months, the cast became too heavy for me to walk or crawl – I was anchored to the living-room floor like a convict attached to a lead ball.

My first nautical experience was when I was five. We were on a family holiday up at Tweed Heads, on the New South Wales–Queensland border, enjoying a calm day at the beach. Chasing a ball that my four-year-old brother Clary had kicked past me, I tripped over a board with a paddle. I'd never seen anything like it before – it was a sit-on-top kayak.

As Clary lost himself in making a sand castle, my interest had been aroused. What *was* that thing? Taking my sister Lil – who was three – back to have a look, I told her I was going to take her for a boat ride. I pulled the kayak into the water and got Lil to sit on the back while I jumped into the seat. My feet flailed horribly short of the rudder pedals as I began to use the two-bladed paddle to propel us out towards the Pacific Ocean.

These were the first strokes I'd ever taken in a kayak … and I loved it. The movement seemed to come to me more easily than walking did. It was fast, fluid and felt so natural – almost like coasting down a big hill on a pushbike. Before long, we were a couple of hundred metres out to sea, with the noise from the people on the beach being lost in the wind. Lil started to get scared and began to cry. "Don't worry – it's all fine, sis," I said in my most reassuring tone. "We'll just go a little further."

Meanwhile, back on the beach, Mum was hysterical. She was jumping up and down, pleading for us to come back in (neither of us had a lifejacket on and Lil didn't know how to swim). I could see Mum in the distance, but I honestly thought she was just waving and saying hello.

Before I could work out what was going on, two lifesavers on board rubber duckies zoomed out to us, knowing we couldn't swim without floaties. Their gestures were smooth and controlled – it was as though they were approaching a bomb – as one of them said calmly, "Now put the paddle down – we're going to pick you up."

"Don't worry about it," I casually replied, "we'll just paddle back."

But they were in no mood to argue, and we were swept up and dumped in the tinnie. The lectures started from the lifeguards about how dangerous our actions had been. I knew that meant I was dead meat when we got to shore.

Mum went berserk. It took me quite a few years to understand why my first kayaking experience wasn't applauded and encouraged by my mother.

At school, I was different right from the start – but in a different way. Early in my first year, I realised what it was. I was sitting in the playground by myself at lunchtime, about to tuck into a sandwich Mum had packed for me, when a group of kids came up to me and started making faces. What had I done?

I sat there as three boys towered above me, with a group of girls standing behind them, giggling. "What's that you're eating, wog boy?" they snarled.

Not knowing what a wog boy was, I replied, "My name isn't wog boy, it's James, and I'm eating a keftethes and eggplant sandwich." (Keftethes are essentially meatballs … with *balls*. They're Greek, with plenty of garlic, onion and oregano, to give them a little kick.)

The kids erupted into laughter, rolling on the pavement. It took them a few moments to gather themselves, and when they sat up they barked, "That hardly looks like food … and *phew* … it stinks."

They started scrunching their noses and dry heaving as though I'd just passed wind. Throwing a few more insults at me, they told me not to come near any of the other kids, then ran off laughing.

I looked down at my keftethes sandwich and didn't know what I'd done wrong. I felt lonely and completely embarrassed. Throwing my lunch in the bin, I ran to the toilets, locked myself in a cubicle and began to cry – although I made sure when someone came in to the urinal, I'd choke back my tears so they didn't hear the sobbing. When the lunchtime bell went, I couldn't muster the courage to leave the toilets. Eventually, though, one of the teachers coaxed me out and back to the classroom.

Mum picked me up from school later on and asked how my day had been.

"Alright," I replied, fixing my gaze out the window.

"Fine – be touchy," said Mum, probably thinking I was just tired.

After a couple of minutes I broke the silence. "Mum, what's a wog boy?"

"What do you mean?" she asked with her stomach churning.

"Well, the other kids won't play with me because they call me a wog boy and because of what I was eating for lunch."

"You poor thing," Mum said tearfully as she pulled the car over to the side of the road and ran her fingers through my neatly parted hair.

"Stop it, Mum, I'm fine," I barked back with all the authority a six year old could muster. But then my face started to go red and tears began to stream. "Mum, I just want to be like all the other kids. Can't you just make me Vegemite sandwiches for lunch on white bread from now on – I don't want any more of that Greek stuff."

That only added to Mum's tears.

We were living in Sydney's North Shore – a predominantly Anglo-Saxon neighbourhood. Wogs, gooks and Indians sometimes felt somewhat unwelcome. At that age, it seemed as if the key to being popular was to have a nice British name and plenty of Old Money.

My grandparents had come to Australia around 1910. My grandpa began working in his uncle's café at the age of eight before he was old enough to run his own. In 1919, he became the co-owner (with his brothers) of the Niagara Café in the small New South Wales town of Gundagai – just down the road from the Dog on the Tuckerbox. The café's crowning moment was in 1942, when Prime Minister John Curtin popped in for steak and eggs on his way back to Canberra. Press clippings and photos of that magical day are still plastered proudly on the walls.

That generation of Greeks worked so hard to set up life in a new country; then the second-generation Greeks in Australia – my parents' era – grew up around the time of the wild years of the 1960s and 1970s. But they floated through this revolution blissfully unaware of the culture that seemed to define the era – ask my parents and their friends about "Purple Haze" by Jimi Hendrix, free love and psychedelic drugs and they have no idea what you're talking about. Frank Sinatra was more their style. Dad has never been drunk in his life: and no, he's not a priest – he's a lawyer.

My grandparents had no formal education, so it was a great honour for them to see their children receive a tertiary education. Success was very important – they defined it by a person's level of education attained and material wealth.

Adventure was not a word in my grandparents' vocabulary. Sure, they'd heard of Edmund Hillary climbing Everest, and Neil Armstrong on the moon, but because they were fighting just to put food on the table for their families, the idea of them being inspired to emulate the great adventurers and explorers was almost laughable.

As the second-generation Greeks started to establish themselves in Australia as hard-working professionals, they began to acquire wealth. The next generation, however – my generation – found ourselves in a situation where our lives seemed pre-defined and pre-established. There was a formula set out and we could see where our lives were heading – which freaked me out a bit.

In my early years at primary school, I found the stuff in the classroom extraordinarily difficult to grasp, but sport came very easily to me. I wasn't too bad at swimming, diving and rugby. The problem I had at school was the constant negative reinforcement my teachers gave me – none of them believed in me. Mum was always encouraging, but even she was occasionally frustrated.

Trying to learn my nine times tables on my way to a diving lesson one day, she had to keep silencing my younger brother and sister for spitting out the answers. I just couldn't do them (especially 9x4, for some reason). Exasperated, Mum pulled the car over and started smacking me.

"I'm trying, Mum, I am. I just can't remember them," I pleaded.

Poor Mum broke down into tears again and replied, "I know … I'm sorry."

As I bumbled through my primary school years in the lowest classes possible, Mum came home after one parent–teacher night with the words of my Year 5 teacher ringing in her ears. He'd told her: "Vivienne, I suggest you get James into the workforce as soon as possible. There's no way he's going to be able to finish school. I'll be impressed if he doesn't end up in jail."

These were harsh words for an 11-year-old kid, and my last parent–teacher interview in the public school system, as my parents moved me to a prestigious private school, Knox Grammar in nearby Wahroonga. Although Knox had a great academic reputation, it was the sport and extra-curricular opportunities that Mum and Dad thought would benefit me.

I repeated Year 5 at Knox and right from day one my teacher Mr Bousie encouraged me, patting me on the back for that try I scored on the weekend, or that catch I'd taken at cricket. Then he masterfully directed that positive energy from the sporting field into the classroom. With a combination of the positive support and acknowledgement of what I was good at, and my realisation of the financial pressure Mum and Dad were under in sending me to a school like Knox, I began to perform.

We never headed on overseas holidays when I was growing up – we didn't have the money. Instead, my parents would bundle us into the family 4WD and we'd head off around Australia. We did heaps of desert trips to the Corner Country – outback New South Wales – my first proper taste of "expeditioning".

Typically, we'd go with four to six other families in 4WDs and spend weeks exploring the central Australian deserts on tracks. Right from those early trips, though (which I enjoyed immensely), I really thought we were bringing city life to the bush, rather than toughing it out and allowing nature to become a part of us. It's difficult to connect with the land when you're thrashing round in a V6 turbo-charged 4WD all day and surrounded by 12V fridges, tables, chairs and lanterns at night.

Even so, these 4WDing trips awoke my adventurous spirit. I'd spend days staring out the window as we bounced along heavily corrugated roads and dirt tracks, dreaming of what Burke and Wills must have gone through. What was life like as an explorer? These outback holidays also gave us plenty of time to roll around in the dirt and just be kids, without all that other materialistic noise that would distract us back home: computer games and videos.

These trips played a pivotal role in bringing Clary, Lil and me closer together. If there were a couple of rocks and sticks on the ground, we could amuse ourselves for hours. Being the oldest, I was the ringleader and they'd usually blindly follow me anywhere – into a creek, up a tree, or sneaking into the crazy neighbour's back yard. If I went, they'd blindly come too (how times have changed!).

Clary was always the more cautious one – the thinker. Often I'd attack things all guns blazing, without properly having thought things through. My brother was much more calculating. It's funny that when Justin and I crossed the Tasman years later, Jonesy played a similar role to the one Clary did when I was a child: I was the natural leader, Justin the natural deputy.

My first job as a kid was working at the local chicken shop for a measly $4.25 an hour. I was 14 and I'll never forget working all the public holidays at Christmas time to pocket a little extra cash. When my payslip arrived, it wasn't time-and-a-half as promised. Angrily, I brought it up with the owner, who basically replied, "Too bad."

I stormed home and decided to contact the Workplace Ombudsman. They offered advice that I could take the shop owner to court over the pay dispute or forget about it. Legal action was a little beyond a 14 year old. It taught me a valuable lesson, though. For as long as I was an employee, I was potentially going to be bullied. Right from a young age I vowed that I'd work to learn, not just for the money.

This idealism was great, but the next summer my best mate Sammy and I wanted to buy a tinnie to go fishing. We had a couple of dollars in our Commonwealth Dollarmite savings account, but not enough to buy a boat. How could two 15 year olds earn that much cash in their summer holidays? We thought long and hard, until Sam suggested we go cotton chipping.

It seemed like a great idea, and once we'd convinced our parents we jumped on a train to Young. I'd seen a few movies and read a couple of novels about what the American Negroes went through as slaves back in the 1800s: cotton chipping gave us a glimpse of what slavery was like.

We were woken at 4am, when a bus would be waiting to take us to the fields. Starting before sunrise we'd bend over with our picks and remove the weeds that grew close to the stem of the cotton. As we walked in a line down these cotton fields, a tyrannical supervisor would march behind us, bellowing if we missed a weed. He was a big man, with a red face and a bloated beer gut. We'd be marched up and down these fields for 12 hours each day and return back to our tent completely shattered at night-time. After a couple of days, our hands bled, our noses peeled from sunburn and our lips were blistered by the wind. It was by far the hardest thing we had ever done – but it made us feel like men.

Returning from this fairly brutal experience, we'd salvaged just enough cash to buy an old rusty trailer, a Quintrex tinnie and a 15-horsepower outboard. This was to be my first proper introduction to the water. Each weekend, one of our parents would drop us down at the closest waterway – the Apple Tree boat ramp down at Bobbin Head – where we'd launch our tinnie. We'd explore the area endlessly, quickly learning where all the best fishing spots and bays to surf recklessly on the back of the tinnie were. As our appetite grew, we pushed further downriver.

Our first overnight experience without parents was quite memorable. Sam, our mate Big Nick (his name was Nick and he was big) and I planned on camping down at Jerusalem Bay, near the mouth of the Hawkesbury River – a whopping 8 kilometres from the boat ramp. On our way there, Big Nick suggested that we head all the way to Pittwater and pick up a case of beer. I thought we already had enough to worry about but quietly obliged. We puttered through the heads in our tinnie, picked up some grog and returned to the bay. We set up Dad's tent on some beautifully flat grass just back from the mangroves and the river. Making a fire, we cooked dinner and drank a couple of cans of VB. We were stoked with ourselves, and, with no parents around, went to bed really late as an act of defiance – 11pm.

So far, so good, but a couple of hours into our kip, the tent began to fill with water.

"Holy shit," Big Nick yelled, "we're sinking."

As we peered out of the tent fly we realised that the tide had risen and was engulfing us, our precious fishing gear, and – worse still – Mum and Dad's prized camping accessories (I knew they'd kill me). We waded through the knee-deep water in our pyjamas, trying to reposition our camp on higher ground as our gear drifted slowly down Jerusalem Bay.

By morning, the tide had ebbed and we found our equipment strewn through the mangroves like cyclone debris. A small, but valuable lesson had been learnt: the sea was boss. Limping back to the boat ramp, with – fortunately – just a couple of saucers and my fishing hat having met a watery grave, we were too proud to tell our parents about the tidal disaster.

Throughout high school, I had to work much harder than the other kids in my classes. It always seemed to take me twice as long as my classmates to do my homework and study, and I'd take five times as long as Jonesy to rote-learn poems for the HSC. At times it was frustrating, but deep down it was satisfying, knowing that while the other kids were technically "smarter", I could match them regardless.

I wasn't a cool kid at school; nor was I a nerd. I seemed to be reasonably well liked and I got along with most people. Jonesy, on the other hand, was quite reclusive, shy and, well … fat. He pretty much hid in the boarding house.

Justin was born in Hornsby Hospital on 20 June 1983. He popped into the world 15 months after me (although it never seemed to be grounds for respecting your elders). Soon after that, the family moved to Indonesia for his dad's work as a geologist.

Indonesia was where his parents had met. His mum, Chintra, grew up in a small fishing village, then left school in Year 10 and started work as a laboratory assistant on Bangka Island, where she met a young Australian scientist, Roderick Jones, who she'd later marry. From an early age, Chintra had been an entrepreneur. At the age of five, she started her first business – delivering cakes on her bicycle. After having three children, she started up some surfwear stores in Indonesia, which, before long, had expanded to 38 surf shops and three department stores. She now runs one of the top four retail outlets in her country. Not bad for an uneducated person from a fishing village.

This success, coupled with being an expat family, brought with it an affluent upbringing for Justin. He lived in Lebong Tandi (a small village hours away from civilisation) with his parents, older brother Andrew and sister Louisa, till he was three. Their home was in a jungle and sometimes he'd wake up in the morning to find tiger footprints outside his bedroom window – it was slightly different from his future home on Sydney's North Shore.

When his family moved to Jakarta, Justin started at the British International School. The exact opposite to me, Jonesy topped all his classes – despite being energetic, loud and having an insatiable appetite for biting people – and loved to read "just for fun". By the age of 11 he'd read *Lord of the Rings* and Bram Stoker's *Dracula* ... twice. In Sydney, I was still stuck on my nine times tables.

Coming to Sydney as a boarder in Year 7 at The King's School in Parramatta, though, his gregarious personality had been left in Indo. He was a bit embarrassed about his Asian background in a very white-bread school, he was underdeveloped physically and he was pretty woeful at sport.

However, he enjoyed school life, instantly taking to the "frat system"; that's where the younger boys have to do whatever the senior students bark at them. One day, some of the seniors told him to pour a bottle of rotten fish oil over Ed – one of the first XV rugby players – and not to return to the boarding house until he did it. Justin followed orders, executed the deed and ran back to safety, where he assumed the Year 12 boys who'd barked out his orders would protect him. He was wrong.

Not long after, a couple of his Year 8 comrades approached him and said, "Ed wants to see you." He walked slowly towards Ed's room, to find the first XV player waiting for him with another bottle of fish oil.

"Drink it," said Ed, matter-of-factly.

Poor Jonesy had no choice. He swallowed a couple of mouthfuls before running to the toilet and vomiting it all up.

The Year 12 guys who put Justin up to this were extremely apologetic and even bought him a pizza to quell the fishy taste. For some reason, Justin loved this "bullying", which he felt bonded the boarders and led to great comradeship.

But Justin didn't need any help from the Year 12s to get himself into trouble. Bored one day in a Year 9 science class, Jonesy spied two cases of wine left over from a staff Christmas party out of the corner of his eye. Together with two of his best mates, they decided that putting a top-secret covert operation together was in order. To cut a long story short, they broke into the lab at night-time and stole the wine. A week later, they got busted when a pair of bottles clinked at an inappropriate time, right in front of a boarding master. Suspension resulted, and his parents decided to pull him out of King's and send him to Knox.

When he arrived at Knox, Justin, a late developer physically, was shy and reserved. As a new boy, he had no friends – or pubes, he confesses; not that I was looking. It wasn't till he was 15 that he started growing any hair other than on his head, which was bad news at an all-boys school with open showers.

He got along well with my brother Clary, though, and they began to play sport together, soon becoming mates. Shortly after, we became Justin's "home family" in Sydney – and that was when our friendship kicked off.

His first year at Knox, he immersed himself in study and topped a few science subjects without receiving a science prize at speech day, due to a technicality (an injustice he still holds close to his heart!). This actually affected him deeply at the time and led to an attitude of "why bother?", as studying soon dropped down his list of priorities.

Justin started spending most weekends with us and coming on family holidays when he wasn't going home to Indonesia. All through school he remained quiet and polite. It wasn't until a couple of catalysts – university and the Murray River expedition – that he started to burst out of his shell.

During our time at school, we were both carrying 25 kilograms more than we are nowadays, mostly around our waists. Voluptuous rolls hid our school belts as we sat studying for hours on end (well, Justin was often doing crosswords and Sudoku). The final two years at Knox were all about burying ourselves in books and forgetting the meaning of the word "exercise".

In my early high-school years I loved my sport; unfortunately, rugby left me with nine broken bones, with the final one resulting in a pretty serious operation where most of the cartilage in my left knee was removed. In the recovery ward, I'll never forget the doc recommending that I never run again – thanks for the pick-me-up after the operation! Actually, the cautiousness he instilled resulted in me focusing my energy on studying, which wasn't a bad thing.

Nearing our final exams and the end of our school days, Justin and I were overweight, socially inept with girls and lacking self-confidence – not a great combination. Struggling to find our position in the world and what role we could play, like so many kids our age we began drinking. At the time it was a brilliant tool in lubricating our awkward social behaviour – especially with females.

Coming from an all-boys school, picking up or even mingling with girls was a bit foreign to us. Those skills had been gifted to the guys in the First XV – they'd been my peers a few years earlier, but my last injury had segregated me from them. At the time, neither of us had a girlfriend, but we had great romantic ideals about how it was meant to happen …

A couple of days after I finished my last HSC exam, I met a gorgeous girl, Jen. It was Melbourne Cup day and I saw her standing on the other side of the room up at the local pub. I had to meet her. Smashing a couple of pints, I built enough confidence to go and introduce myself – this in itself was the scariest thing I'd ever done at the time. The conversation was uncomfortable, forced, and by the end of it, she'd blown my socks off.

Our school formal was approaching and I had no-one to ask. Justin had been set up to go with a girl he didn't know and it looked like I was going down a similar path. My thoughts turned to Jen and I convinced myself I had to invite her. Getting her phone number from one of the guys in the First XV, I nervously scribbled some possible small talk on the back of a beer coaster and gave her a call. Given our initial meeting I was surprised she accepted, but we found ourselves heading off to the formal.

The night was going brilliantly until I saw her dirty dancing with one of the guys I despised most in our year. His hands slithered like snakes over her stunning red dress. I couldn't take it. Running outside, I saw some boarders skolling bottles of red wine and decided to partake myself. A bottle and a half later, I was escorting Jen to the bus for the after-party, and while we were getting on board, my stomach was churning and sweat was starting to prickle on my forehead. This was a feeling I'd become quite familiar with over the coming years – not alcohol-induced but because of my battle with seasickness. It was the early stages of spewing.

Within a few minutes I was choking back the vomit rising into my mouth: it was about to erupt. With no further warning, I started spewing in my seat, to everyone's disgust. I'll never forget looking into Jen's eyes and seeing her disappointment, horror and, worst of all, embarrassment. Crashing off the bus, I passed out in some bushes, leaving Justin to find me hours later. That was that.

I never ended up dating Jen, but somehow, after starting a Commerce degree together at the University of Sydney, we became great friends. And it was at uni that I began to have an insatiable appetite for questioning the framework of society. In my spare time, I immersed myself in authors like Tolstoy, Thoreau and Ayn Rand, and also began enjoying adventure literature. With my learning difficulties as a kid, I don't think I ever read a book for pleasure when I was at school, but these stories of adventure fascinated me. The contrast between sitting in a Microeconomics lecture and dreaming of Scott or Shackleton fighting the elements in Antarctica woke my spirit. These books would help spark something in me that would completely change my life ... not that I knew it yet.

2

"THE MURRAY RIVER, YOU DOOFUS!"

Enough was enough and Jonesy and I had decided we needed to get into shape. As the fat melted off with intense exercise and we slowly got into the outdoors, we began to realise that although we were confused and insecure in our busy – but sheltered – city life, out there bushwalking we were able to discover our core values and principles, as we questioned more and more the world we'd grown up in.

In second year I started boxing regularly. From the moment I first stepped in the ring I loved the sport. Interestingly, the reason I started boxing was because it was one of two sports I just couldn't relate to (the other being soccer – disgraceful for a Greek Australian, I know!). I mean – why would two blokes want to get in the ring and beat the hell out of one another? I was to learn quickly that it was a delicate and skilful art that demanded complete respect.

Boxing three times a week, I soon realised it was a sport that came quite naturally to me, and in my second year I represented Sydney Uni at the Australian University Games (AUG).

Unfortunately, my parents hated boxing and made a one-way deal that if I continued with it, I had to move out of home. Looking at the measly wage I was earning part time as a kitchen hand, there was no way I would've been able to live off that. As a result, I retired from boxing after winning the AUG middleweight title.

The question "what do I want out of life?" started to become a central thought and conversation topic for Justin and myself, especially during those long walks when it seemed natural to contemplate the big issues. We didn't want to have to conform with the world we'd been brought up in, but we didn't have any answers either. We did know, though, that we wanted to spend more and more time bushwalking in the Blue Mountains, which – we identified pretty early on – brought us real happiness.

On one of these walks, a 144-kilometre trek from Katoomba to Mittagong with Justin and two friends named Ben, I turned to the guys as we were clawing our way up the steep Balloon Pass, lathered in sweat, and asked, "What's Australia's longest river?"

"The Murray River, you doofus!" one of the Bens replied. He'd never been one for unnecessary politeness.

"How would you guys like to paddle the length of the Murray this summer?" To this day, I have no idea where the thought came from.

"Don't be stupid, mate, you've never been kayaking before."

"Can't be that hard," I said. "It looks like bushwalking on water."

"Next you're going to say you're Jesus."

When I got home from the trek I opened up the atlas and examined the Murray's meandering path from the Snowy Mountains down to Goolwa at the mouth of the Southern Ocean in South Australia. After a handful of phone calls (to the Murray River registrar, a raft-guiding company on the upper Murray, and a few other paddlers), Justin and I discovered that no-one had ever kayaked the entire length of the river. Our souls were now wide awake – I'm not sure why, but this was something we *had* to do – and immersing ourselves in the project, we quickly got our hands on some big heavy plastic kayaks that would do the job.

True adventure isn't something that can be defined by any one person, but for us it was that burning feeling inside when we were in the outdoors challenging ourselves. Our first couple of paddles around Bobbin Head – where Sam and I had put our little tinnie in the water almost eight years earlier – we felt like explorers. Initially, we said we'd paddle to the other side of the river but we found ourselves travelling a whopping 3 kilometres downstream. We immediately loved the motion of kayaking – it felt so natural.

The Murray River trip, which we dubbed "Kayak for Kids", was the first proper expedition we'd ever organised. Justin, another friend from school, Andrew, and I spent months planning it, raising $10,000 sponsorship and funds for the Starlight Foundation.

On 8 November 2001, we started the 2560-kilometre journey at Thredbo, which we expected to take seven weeks. Little did we know we were heading into one of the hottest summers in years. We bashed through the bush for a couple of days on foot, trying to find the source of the Murray River – Cowombat Flat. When we made it to the source, which began as a trickle no wider than a drainpipe, we started to follow it along its edges.

We found ourselves surrounded by bluffs in scrub that was near impenetrable – at this pace we'd never make it to our rendezvous 40 kilometres downstream, where we were due to pick up our kayaks from my dad and a couple of his 4WDing mates. The only hope we had was to surf on our packs down the ever-growing rapids, which were becoming more intimidating ... enough to throw us around like rag dolls and hold us under for up to 20 seconds at the end of a run. We spent the next three days surfing these rapids, which were Grade 3 at times – really scary.

The water was snowmelt, so it was bloody freezing, and as we hadn't prepared for this, everything in our packs got drenched, including our camera, GPS, sleeping bags, food, and, unfortunately, matches. *Everything*. Each night was spent shivering away in wet thermals hugging each other in the foetal position. It was my first "spooning" experience, and sadly it was far from romantic. Kilometres from civilisation, with the violent white water of the Murray on one side and impregnable scrub on the other, we were terrified.

Eventually, overwhelmingly relieved, we made it to the rendezvous, a week after we'd left Thredbo. We got our kayaks and continued downriver on our Huckleberry Finn adventure. Although we were young, naïve and malleable, and the Murray was proving to be dangerous, we were still loving it.

We'd often stop at towns for supplies and met numerous interesting characters along the way. As we paddled past one particular houseboat, a shirtless bloke started waving his hands about and yelling crazily, "Oi, boys, come over and say hello to Russel!"

Andrew was nowhere to be seen, and Justin and I were both pretty scared. What did this guy want? We gingerly paddled towards him not knowing what to expect, but we quickly found out that the local AM radio station had briefly mentioned our trip, and Russel, whose eyes were hidden by his scuba-mask-Cancer-Council sunglasses, wanted to offer us a bed for the night, a porterhouse steak and a beer. Justin would love to have stopped, but Andrew was keen on pushing another 25 kilometres downriver that evening. Russel handed us a 20-dollar donation and we parted ways.

A little further down the river a bloke named Spike, who let us crash at his caravan park for free, and Bernie and his wife, a couple of the residents, sat with us and gave us a cold VB. Bernie was on his last legs – pancreatic cancer (if he hadn't told us we wouldn't have known it) – and he only had another couple of months to live.

As the summer's heat baked us, we began having to deal with the most difficult issue we had on the expedition – each other. The seed had been planted right at the start and we didn't deal with it sufficiently at the time: our different objectives and agendas for wanting to do the river. Andrew was keen on getting down the Murray as quickly as possible and pushing the mind and body to the limit. Justin, on the other hand, wanted to take his time, enjoy the scenery and the river people and do some fundraising along the way.

This caused enormous tension and bad blood between them. I was left as the middle man with the aim of getting us all down the river safely – either Andrew's or Justin's approach didn't bother me too much. For two reasons, I often found myself siding with Jonesy. Firstly, because he was my best mate, and secondly, because he was the weakest paddler in the group. From the bushwalking we'd done, we learnt to always travel at the speed of the slowest person. On the river, that was Jonesy. He was a slogger – no technique, but he'd push on regardless.

My biggest source of frustration with Justin (which would also come out in the prep for the Tasman) was the lack of training and preparation he'd done. Both Andrew and I had trained hard and worked hard on the logistics, while Jonesy had hardly ever got out on the water. When we did our first decent team paddle, a 40-kilometre round trip from Bobbin Head to Pittwater, he'd lagged significantly, thanks to his lack of training and the big night he'd had the previous evening. His social life took priority over the kayaking.

This lack of training almost ended his Kayak for Kids paddle – and possibly his life – on day 5, when he didn't have enough control over his kayak to avoid a fallen willow tree on the upper reaches of the fast-flowing Murray. Andrew and I steered around it fairly easily, but Justin ploughed straight into it, the flow of the river pinning his kayak about a metre under water. Luckily, he was able to pull himself out before he drowned. It was a frightening experience for us all.

As we continued down the river, the tension between Andrew and Justin crescendoed, to the stage where neither was talking to the other and Justin considered pulling out. It was a vital lesson. When you're on an expedition, everyone needs to be committed to the same objective. The dynamic within a group can have a crucial impact on morale, as well as your ability to push boundaries. With a close-knit team of people you trust, an epic trip is infinitely more manageable.

Paddling in the heat was almost as debilitating as the tension that filled the air. It singed our nostrils and each breath was a brief visit to hell. Then there was the wretched smell – the terrible aroma of dying livestock – that wafted through the heatwaves towards us. Farms were crippled by the raging heat that summer.

All we could do, though, was keep on paddling. By day 32 we were still battling down the Murray, still committed to our bid to become the first people to kayak from source to mouth, with over 1200 kilometres to go.

"Hey, Jonesy," I called out to him that afternoon, "can you imagine paddling a similar distance on the ocean … all the way across to New Zealand … ?"

Justin's look said it all: an empty gaze, one of compassion and sympathy. The heat had got to me, or so he thought. His eyes staunchly peered out from the recesses of his legionnaire's hat. It was worn and ragged with "breathing" holes on the left-hand side and a rim that drooped sadly, revealing a tough life. It proudly fought the harsh rays and provided some respite from the ever-intensifying heat.

After his initial reflection came a muffled reply. "You're crazy."

Before I had time to elaborate, his cadence picked up and all I could see was the uniform flap of his ragged hat; apart from occasional glimpses of a face devoid of expression. I began to question my sanity – had I drunk my three litres of water that day? Despite Jonesy's scepticism, though, I remember, before we returned to Sydney at the end of that journey, a vivid gleam in his eyes. I could tell that a seed had been planted, and it was that subtle glimmer that I'd try to arouse once we were back home.

Seven weeks after finding the source, we arrived together at the mouth of the Murray to the cheers of all our families. Thankfully, Justin and Andrew had put their differences behind them, and on day 49 we paddled to where the river met the ocean. A feeling of pride and contentment welled up inside – something not even winning the under-16 club rugby grand final or managing to do well in my last year at school could match. We weren't surprised to discover that there was no media fanfare to greet our arrival. Just one photographer – from the *Adelaide Advertiser* – was there to record the moment.

Paddling on rivers, bushwalking in the mountains and now organising Kayak for Kids had all played a role for Justin and me in quelling the self-doubt about our place in the world and what we wanted to do with our lives. It also gave me the opportunity to take time out from my family. As I've mentioned, both Mum and Dad are quite traditional folk and they wanted nothing more from their son than to be a partner of a large accounting firm.

We were a middle-class family with two working parents struggling to send their three kids to private schools. Those years around leaving school, Mum and Dad used to argue quite a bit, the fights fuelled by the financial burden of them building a new house. I found myself siding with Mum all the time – in those days, my father seemed quite short-tempered and distant (like most teenagers, I had no trouble seeing the worst in my parents) – which in itself bred tension between me and Dad.

At the same time, I found it difficult to develop any sort of relationship of substance with my mother, because of her reaction to the financial pressures. Most days she was the most caring, loving mother anyone could ask for, but occasionally the situation would get the better of her and she'd snap at me for no apparent reason (that I could see).

Like a lot of young people, I was feeling unloved and unsure of what to do with myself. Adventure provided the stability that I needed. If I hadn't discovered nature at that critical time in my life, I'd hate to see the path it would have led to – unfortunately, alcohol and drug abuse are more common ways for people to curb those feelings bubbling inside.

I started to keep my distance from my family, as well as many of my school friends who'd started partying hard. I was finding solace in nature and comfort in my friendships with outdoorsmen (I'm not being sexist – it was just that they all seemed to be male!), as many of them had similar inner demons nibbling away at them and we'd all instantly forget about these rodents when out playing in the wild.

During these treks, I began thinking about how ironic it was that sometimes those closest to you provided the most resistance to your growth. I remember writing in my diary that it felt like my family never encouraged me whenever I wanted to do something big or change direction in some way. I think people like to keep things as they are – in a constant state – and as soon as we veer off the trodden path, alarm bells start to ring. That's what I felt was going on with my parents anyhow.

Exposure to the wilderness was cleansing, but I became more interested in pushing my boundaries. The bushwalks started to get longer and longer, and Justin and I began taking less gear – often not sleeping – and accessing the remotest areas of the mountains. These tiger walks, as well as 100-kilometre paddles, pushed our minds and bodies beyond what we'd understood was possible.

A classic example was the three peaks walk we did in the Blue Mountains, just out of Sydney. It was an 80-kilometre circuit, mainly off trails and with no sleep, with elevation gain – the cumulative ascents and descents over the course of a trek – of approximately 8000 metres.

Justin's ability to push his body past reason on our third attempt at the three peaks challenge was amazing. We'd been going for 30 hours straight – understandably we were pretty knackered. We were onto the third peak, and making our way up the steep flank of Mount Guongang in the wee hours of the morning. As the spur sharply rolled away, I made my way onto the summit, then sat on the ground waiting for Jonesy, who I thought was right behind me. After 10 minutes I was starting to get pretty concerned and I thought about making my way back down to see what had happened to him. At that moment his head popped up and he slowly made his way towards the summit.

"What happened?" I asked.

Gasping for air, Justin replied, "Sorry, mate, my legs kept on collapsing so I had to crawl."

At that moment, I knew there was no better person with whom to attempt the kayak crossing from Australia to New Zealand. It was that kind of mental tenacity that we'd need to take on the Tasman.

3

CORPORATE JAMES/WEEKEND JAMES

As the intensity of these challenges grew I began to develop a fascination with mountains around the world. I booked myself into a basic mountaineering course over in New Zealand, which was the start of three summers I spent living over there, testing myself and learning valuable lessons.

Over that period I was lucky not to die. Death didn't really worry me: "I nearly died yesterday" was a common diary entry at the time. Despite experiencing some nasty falls, rock slides and avalanches that had swept me down a couple of faces, by some grace of God I survived. Some of my fellow climbers were not so fortunate – in one season in Mount Cook National Park, nine mountaineers died. I'll never forget returning after 10 days in the hills to see four body bags being pulled out of a helicopter. I'd been feeling immortal, but this shook me right out of my complacency.

I was still at uni during these jaunts and after finishing my Commerce degree I started full-time work at one of the "big four" accounting firms. In that first year I learnt heaps about the corporate world, company accounting and how big business operated. I was working as an auditor – one of a team of accountants who'd examine the financial records of big companies to confirm that what they'd recorded was correct.

I soon developed a reputation for working efficiently and quickly, but I hated doing longer hours than I thought were reasonable. Often the main purpose of those extra hours seemed to be to make my manager's utility rates (don't ask) look better. There were too many fun things to do outside the office to make it my life. Again, it was a matter of work to learn, not just for the money.

Most fellow employees understood my work ethic, but every now and then I had an audit with a "long hours" manager. On one particular audit, I'd get up and leave at 7pm every night after having worked an 11-hour day, whether or not other people were still slaving away at their desks. In the third week of the audit I had the inevitable conflict with the manager, who said I wasn't being a team player and that my performance rating was going to be affected. I retaliated that she wasn't resourcing the audit with enough staff, and that everyone else felt the same way as I did, but didn't have the balls to stand up to her. We agreed to disagree.

Those weekends in 2004 were by far the most enjoyable I'd ever had. I began climbing each week with a guy I met at a crag one day, Duncan Hunter (I called him "Yoda", as he was 18 months older than me and clearly much wiser). As a partnership we gelled right from the start, with our similar attitude and motivation ensuring we'd go to the remotest crags with the loosest rock.

We'd drive up to the Blue Mountains on a Friday night in Dunc's old red 1992 Ford Festiva. It was covered in rust, the radio and heater didn't work, and as soon as we tried to go faster than 80 kilometres per hour (only downhill), the steering wheel would shake violently like a bull trying to buck its rider. That didn't worry us at all. We'd be bubbling with excitement and we managed this energy by screaming *"Wee BANG!"*, which acted like the release on a pressure valve.

We'd sleep in our bivy bags in shelters around the mountains and cook out of the back of the car. As our climbing partnership grew, so did our appetite for adventure. We began to prepare to visit some of the most awe-inspiring granite big walls in the world.

Over in California lies Yosemite National Park, where 3000-foot granite cliffs were created millions of years ago by a gradual series of earth upheavals. Today, the valley is respected among climbers as the ultimate big wall climbing destination. It has this reputation because of the stable weather at certain times of the year, the rock is of high quality (it doesn't break or crumble easily), and there's a lifetime of climbing to explore. At the centre of the valley is El Capitan, a completely daunting, vertical 3000-foot face with myriad cracks and fissures leading all the way from base to summit. Parties can spend up to 10 days living on the wall – sleeping in hammocks and climbing tiny cracks to the top. We planned a visit to the big walls in Yosemite Valley for later on in that year.

The stark contrast between the euphoric weekends we were having and my mundane life as an accountant seemed unavoidable. I'd convinced myself that you needed this balance to live a sustainable life. The truth was I was too scared to do anything about it. As the months wore on, the contrast became more and more evident as I began to look around the workplace and see an army of people I didn't want to be anything like.

I was spending 50 hours a week with these people and I knew it was shaping my personality. If they'd seemed to enjoy what they did, it would have been a much more positive environment to work in. Instead, most were stuck in a work pattern that they detested and didn't break because of the fear society had instilled in them: fear of leaving their job, fear of not having a certain income to pay the bills, fear of what those around them might say.

Dunc and I had spent a good six months training for the Yosemite big walls – it was now time to head over. I'll never forget sitting in the bus on my way into the valley, and as we rounded "Oh my God Corner" the full view of El Capitan came into view. It looked like one amazing playground that had all the elements we'd ever dreamt of – a rich sense of climbing history, stunning scenery and such a variety of rock routes and treks that you could spend a lifetime only skimming the surface of its potential.

We started our time in the valley doing some free climbs (that's when a climber only uses their hands and feet to ascend a cliff, rather than artificial aid), then quickly moved on to some of the smaller big walls – Washington Column and Leaning Tower. Each of these steps was to get us ready for an attempt on the Captain. Staring up at her sheer 3000-foot granite walls from the meadows below, we were terrified. It looked blank and impossible. Only on closer inspection could we make out cracks, fissures and features that linked the ground to the summit in over 32 pitches of climbing (a pitch is essentially one rope length).

Convinced that we had the technical skill to climb each pitch, we knew that just getting on El Cap would be a great experience, and that if it got too hard or the weather closed in, we could always bail. With this in mind we started our ascent of the Nose. Pitch by pitch flew by and before we knew it we were 600 metres up the face at our second bivouac (a tiny ledge the size of a poker table that we slept on, with our feet dangling over the void), staring at the intimidating crux of the climb – the great roof.

As Dunc led off, the weather became bitterly cold, and before long we had flakes of snow falling on us. Words from Tom Evans, the resident photographer based down in the meadows, reverberated through our minds: "Just keep going – I hate it when people bail." We slipped our Gore-Tex jackets on and kept plugging away.

Living on a giant granite wall for 72 hours was a far cry from burying myself in a three-day audit, but nothing compared to the lessons that we'd learnt – almost without noticing – down in the meadows. We'd gone through the process of acquiring the necessary skills on smaller challenges by climbing 500-metre cliffs and then progressing to the more daunting 1000-metre faces. We'd had a dream which on the surface seemed impossible, but after inspecting the rock face through a telescope we'd seen a line of weaknesses appear, and decided to give it a go. It was only after this experience that I was able to understand the methodology needed to cross the Tasman. It was actually pretty similar to what I'd learnt bushwalking and kayaking – skills I wasn't picking up as an accountant.

Returning from the States, I found the widening chasm between "Corporate James" and "Weekend James" more and more difficult to manage. We were pushing our boundaries in the outdoors constantly further and I'd distanced myself from my family and the workplace. Adventure had consumed me.

On my final trip to New Zealand I found myself pushing the envelope harder than ever before, soloing dangerous routes and resorting to drinking excessive amounts of alcohol as a means of escaping – evading the fear both of dying in the mountains and being Corporate James. If I kept on this path, I was going to kill myself.

Although I'd climbed quite recklessly all season, there always seemed to be a little voice beating sense into my head if things got too out of control. Towards the end of the trip, I found myself arguing with my climbing partner Johnny near the summit of Malte Brun. He wanted to push on to the summit, but I was keen on retreating. Two hours past our turnaround time, we descended into an ever-building storm, with the occasional avalanche knocking us off our feet.

Trying to fight out of the couloir we were in (which was a funnel for both snow and rocks), I took a 30-foot fall onto an ice screw we'd anchored into the slope. I bounced a couple of times down the steep wall covered in jagged rock and ice and thought I was a goner. As I tumbled, I had a horrifying vision of the screw shattering the surrounding ice and both of us tumbling down the face. My fall was arrested by the rope. Lying upside down, struggling to breathe, it felt like I'd cracked a couple of ribs. Slowly, I began to take short desperate breaths and noticed that a gash on my forehead and leg were dyeing the surrounding snow a thick, vivid red.

Eventually we got down onto the glacier and hid in a crevasse for the evening, as 150-kilometre-per-hour winds ripped through the mountain range. Terrified, we lay in our bivy bags planning our escape back to Mount Cook village the following day. Back in town a couple of days later, feeling incredibly relieved, we drank beer all night until we were kicked out of the pub for leaning over the bar and drinking directly from the tap, Homer Simpson style. It wasn't the classiest end to one of the scariest experiences of my life …

Returning from the trip after countless near misses and having pushed my boundaries further than ever before, I remember staring out the plane window and looking down at the sea. I wrote in my diary: "Currently hovering 36,000ft above the Tasman. Can it be done?"

Twenty-four hours later, I was back at the office, buried in an even-more-terrifying avalanche of paper and figures. For a while, I'd been feeling pretty agitated at the direction my life was taking – another diary entry at the time was that day-to-day life seemed "mundane and pitifully uninspiring. I work a job that I detest." It seemed to sum things up accurately.

Despite that, I was still feeling inspired, because almost as soon as my feet hit the tarmac at Sydney Airport, the adventure bug had begun to attack. I found myself becoming obsessed with the Tasman idea. Whenever I thought about the possibility of that expedition – no-one had ever successfully crossed the ocean by kayak – I almost felt the buzz of an atomic caffeine hit. I was convinced it was time; that we had to give the Tasman a proper go. I had to find out if Jonesy was feeling the same way.

I knew the only person I wanted to do the expedition with was him. We hadn't seen each other much in the previous three years – while I'd been getting more and more into my climbing, Jonesy had been ... well, I wasn't sure what he'd been doing.

"Hey, J, what's been happening?" I tentatively prodded after making the phone call.

"Aw, not much."

"Mate, how'd you like to catch up for dinner?"

Jonesy was suspicious. "What's wrong? You never ask me to dinner."

"Nothing, mate, nothing is wrong ... but there is something I want to talk to you about."

"You're not gay, are you?" he asked.

"F*** off – of course I'm not gay, you idiot." (Not that there was anything wrong with that.)

"Didn't think you were ... just checking."

"Okay, let's do tomorrow night at 7pm."

"Done."

The first thing I noticed as Justin walked into the pizzeria up at Hornsby the following evening was that he was looking slimmer and fitter than ever before. Normally, his cheeks had a decent puff in them and his veranda over the toy shop would have no trouble resting on the table edge.

"Mate, what have you been doing?" I asked him. "You're looking great."

"Been kickboxing five days a week and playing footy."

As he peered through his glasses, I could tell he'd had a couple of big nights. There were bags under his eyes and his normally marble-white sclera were snotty yellow in colour.

"Don't ask," he muttered, before I had the chance to ask. "Had a coupla massive nights."

We occupied ourselves with small talk for a few minutes, but before long Justin said, "Mate, you don't ask me to come to dinner for no reason ... what's up?"

There was a short silence, before I gingerly began. "I've been thinking, mate ..."

"That's a first," Justin jumped in, chuckling.

"Get stuffed," I said, half-exasperated, but smiling. "I'm being serious."

"Two firsts in one night – you're doing well." Justin couldn't stop laughing at himself. He realised he was hilarious. (Not that anyone else did.)

The waitress came over and began to take our orders. As she finished reading the evening's specials, Justin's eyes lit up. "So what's your name?" he asked in a deep voice, staring directly upwards into her eyes.

"Libby," she replied shyly, giving him a slight smile out of the side of her mouth.

"Libby, I'm Justin, pleased to meet you," he blurted confidently. Then shuffling his seat so he wasn't straining his neck as much, he began chatting to her.

He was much more confident than I'd ever seen him. All I wanted to do was talk about the Tasman and he seemed more interested in getting laid.

"Sorry to be rude …" Jonesy was getting into his stride now. "This is my friend Cas – we're having dinner tonight. He's about to tell me that he's coming out of the closet."

I didn't like where this was going, but before I had time to retaliate, Justin thought he needed to clarify. "That's right … he's gay!"

I sat, thinking how well he'd positioned himself here. *Perfect Game. Textbook.* I was boxed out and retaliation would have been childish. (But enjoyable.) I sat there knowing that he'd won the battle, but not the war …

They kept chatting, with Libby giggling constantly. Eventually, she took our orders and headed back to the kitchen. As she walked away I congratulated Jonesy on a well-played game, but reminded him that she looked barely 16.

Shrugging his shoulders and laughing, he replied half-jokingly, "So?"

He'd changed a lot since we'd last spent some decent time together, and I was battling to pierce through the new facade and see the Justin I remembered – which had been those three years earlier on the Murray.

"Back to what I was talking about …" I said in a slightly agitated tone.

"Oh yeah, that."

"Mate, enough beating round the bush. Remember what we talked about on the Murray?" I asked, fiddling with a salt shaker.

I wasn't sure whether Justin could see it coming. "We talked about heaps of stuff, but I think I know where you're going with this," he replied.

"How'd you like to paddle to New Zealand in a kayak?"

The words shot through his facade like a bullet and his face changed instantly.

He stared blankly at me and digested what I'd said. The cat was out of the bag. I sat there nervously, not saying anything. I was totally pumped about the Tasman trip and I was worried he was going to dismiss it as just another stupid idea. I didn't want to do the crossing solo – and I didn't want to do it with anyone else.

Libby brought our garlic bread and a couple of beers to the table. This time, Justin didn't even notice her. She must have felt a little perturbed by this abrupt shift in interest, but I'm sure she could tell we were discussing something important.

Finally, Jonesy broke the silence. "Are you serious, you crazy bastard?"

"Dead serious."

Noticing that he was a little shocked at this unsubtle approach, I retracted a little. "There won't be a better time in our lives to give it a go. I know you want to have a family in a few years – we've got time now. Even if we never get out there and do it because it turns out to be impossible, let's start prodding and start to work out if it is possible."

"How are you thinking we go about it?" he asked. He was still listening, so that was good.

"The first thing is for us to put it all out there by asking all the questions that we've got."

We sat staring at each other like two fighters about to get into the ring. But instead of a referee separating us, there was a super supreme pizza with extra meat (and chilli). As we attacked each slice, we discussed the feasibility of kayaking across the Tasman. Sweat poured off our brows from the chilli, and our hands were clammy – not from the pizza, but from the torrent of scepticism that was flooding our conversation. *Surely*, it was impossible. It took me back to how I'd felt a couple of years earlier staring up at the 3000-foot vertical cliff-face of El Capitan. The blank walls had revealed – eventually – a series of cracks that cleared a path from the base to the summit. But the Tasman looked even more inaccessible.

Looking down at the butcher's paper on the table, we signalled for Libby to come over. One of her fellow waitresses, who'd obviously seen Justin flirting with her earlier, poked her in the ribs and they both started giggling. Nervously looking everywhere but at Jonesy, she walked towards us.

"Libby, would you mind if we borrow your pen?" Justin asked.

"Yeah, sure."

"Thank you."

She walked away, struggling to understand what was going on, as I began scribbling violently on the paper tablecloth. How would we sleep? What would we do with sharks? Container ships? Storms? Excitement flushed through our veins, and before long we were covering the cloth with what seemed like an infinite number of questions. But there were no answers. The closest either of us had ever been to the ocean was a one-day jaunt in a yacht when I was 13.

I'd spewed my guts up all day.

I kept on scribbling down as many questions, thoughts and preliminary concepts as I could, with the pen hardly able to keep up with the words bursting out of our mouths.

Medicine, ocean currents, sleeping arrangements, provision storage, whales, toileting – the brainstorming went on and on and before long the cloth was almost black with writing and sketches.

"What do you think this kayak is going to look like?" asked Jonesy.

"No idea."

In the few white spaces still left on the paper, we started sketching different concepts, the most attractive being a traditional kayak with covers that slid over each cockpit, similar to those on fighter planes. As we consumed a bottle of wine and a few more beers, our confidence grew and our ideas became more and more outlandish.

Without us even realising, the rest of the pizzeria had closed up and the waitresses were mopping the floor.

"Must be time for us to go," I said, maybe stating the obvious.

"Yep, sure is," Justin replied as he signalled for Libby to bring the bill. He signed for the pizza, left a small tip, and without me realising scribbled a note with his phone number on the back: "Call me."

On the way home in the car, Jonesy received a text from her, saying how cute he was and how much she wanted to see him. All in all – great night.

Over the next few days, Justin mulled and mulled over the idea and finally came to a conclusion. "I'm in," he told me over the phone. "The main reason is that I'd struggle looking back at this and always wondering what could have been. Although the cons outweigh the pros 10 to one, I just can't let this opportunity go. Besides, I'm not going to let you have all the fun, mate."

After some more brainstorming sessions we realised it was time to start conducting some research and answering all these questions that we'd raised. This process would end up taking 13 months.

*   *   *

How do you describe Larry Gray? In the early stages of approaching sea kayakers, his name always crept into conversations. He was by far the most experienced and skilful kayaker in Australia, and his resume could fill volumes of an encyclopaedia, with his exploits taking him to untouched coastlines on almost every continent. Descriptions of his grace when paddling sounded more like people talking about an opera or a ballet than an adventurer.

Whenever anyone was describing Larry, they'd normally start with his kayak mastery, then quickly move on to his wildly eccentric personality. Take this: the first time he saw Sydney was when he and his best mate left their home town, Mallacoota, a Victorian coastal town near the New South Wales border, for a bit of a paddle north. A few weeks later they pulled into Sydney Harbour and slept on the steps of the Opera House.

Not long after that, they decided to keep paddling to Papua New Guinea. Larry lived up there for a while, before moving to Greenland to learn the art of kayaking in the country where the craft had originated more than 4000 years ago. Kayaks – or *qajaq*, to use the original Inuktitut term – were developed by indigenous people living in the Arctic regions who used the boats for hunting on inland lakes, rivers and the coastal waters of surrounding oceans. These first kayaks were made from stitched animal skins – such as seal – which were stretched over a wooden frame made from driftwood the Inuit fishermen had collected.

With a few thousand years of knowledge and expertise to tap into, Larry discovered more than a dozen ways to roll a kayak, paddled strokes that had never been seen in the Western world before and mastered the intricacies of kayak design. He brought this knowledge back to Australia, and started designing and constructing a kayak he called the Pittarak, named after a fierce Greenland wind. It is now Australia's premier sea kayak.

We knocked on Larry's door not knowing what to expect. Jonesy and I were wearing suits to make ourselves appear more grown up and more professional – we'd agreed right from the start that in all these initial meetings we'd get dressed up, in the hope that people would take us a little more seriously. The door creaked open.

There was Larry. The first thing that struck me was that the clothes hiding his tanned skin seemed redundant. His baggy T-shirt and faded jeans draped over him uncomfortably and his eyes and hair had a wild look about them. As we engaged in small talk, Larry's pig-dog (it's a dog, but looks more like a pig) ran between his legs and before it had time to escape, Larry clenched his legs together, flipped the dog over and started bouncing it playfully on its back. We were a little surprised, to say the least.

"Larry, stop bouncing the dog," came a female voice.

"Oh, Mary, he loves it though," Larry replied with childlike enthusiasm.

He proceeded to explain that the pig-dog was scared of cats and he was trying to toughen it up. As the bouncing stopped, the dog snapped at his hand, drawing some blood. "Good boy – you'll make a great guard dog one day," was Larry's laconic reply.

Before we sat down to have a chat about our plans, Larry was distracted by the video-editing gear in his office. He showed us some clips from one of his many Greenland expeditions, during which an iceberg collapsed on him and he nearly died, a bearish-looking bloke taught him the art of a "professional trundler" (someone who rolls big rocks down big hills for fun), and he had dinner with a 70-year-old local woman who tried to seduce him, with her husband looking on with pride!

We sat down in his half-renovated kitchen and Larry immediately put into context what the Tasman crossing meant to him.

"The Tasman represents one of the last great firsts of Australian adventure," he told us. "It'll go down as one of the greatest kayak crossings of all time. Any paddler worth a grain of salt has dreamt about it, but no-one has got round to it – for a number of reasons. The biggest one is fear, because the Tasman has a reputation as one of the most unpredictable, violent passages of ocean in the world.

"Here's an idea for some training for you guys," he said with a mad glint in his eye. "Why don't you both jump in a coffin when an east coast low comes across, and I'll push you out off Bondi. Two days later I'll pull you out … if you're alive. That'll give you an idea of what you're going to experience out on the Tasman. Oh … and it'll make great footage too."

We sat there stunned.

"Do you guys actually have any idea what it's like to be stuck in a storm at sea?" he added.

Larry went on to describe the most frightening experience of his life. He was off the coast of Greenland back in the 1980s and the yacht he and the other paddlers were in got hit by a Pittarak. Throughout the night they received knockdown after knockdown. He described what it was like hearing a breaking wave approaching from 300 metres away as it steamed towards your vessel.

We sat there, eyes glazed open, listening to these remarkable stories.

"So have you given any thought to what your kayak is going to look like?" Larry asked eagerly.

"We've got a few ideas …" I began.

Before I had the chance to go any further, he couldn't control himself. He was starting to get excited and began muttering. *Mumble mumble mumble.* We strained to hear him. " … there are so many different concepts that you could run with …" *Mutter mutter mutter*. "… but first … what's a kayak?" he rhetorically asked.

It was slightly agitating as he was clearly speaking to himself and it was hard to decipher what he was saying. Answering his own question, he replied, "At the end of the day a kayak is a small human-powered boat. It typically has a covered deck, and a cockpit covered by a spraydeck. It's propelled by a double-bladed paddle by a sitting paddler."

After Larry gave this definition of what a kayak is, we discussed for a few minutes other factors that might be taken into account. Could we use a sail? Many of the greatest kayak adventures of all time had used sails, but for some reason we were against using one.

In 1928, Franz Romer embarked on the first Atlantic crossing in a Klepper kayak, from Portugal to Puerto Rico. In doing so, he was undertaking the first notable transoceanic kayak expedition. As this expedition relied predominantly on wind power, Franz's adventure was aeons ahead of its time and truly unique: the concept of taking to the ocean in the smallest of crafts – a humble kayak.

Over the next 50 years, a handful of transoceanic attempts were pursued, mostly in Klepper kayaks with slight modifications to the design. Dr Hannes Lindemann used his Atlantic crossing in 1956 to explore the way humans cope with mental strain under extreme conditions. He overcame feelings of panic and suicidal despair by self-hypnosis and a system of "psychohygiene" that he'd developed. Two-and-a-half months alone on the waves, with inadequate food and barely room to stretch his legs, gave him an opportunity to test and improve his methods.

The recommendations that the World Health Organization makes to seafaring nations are based partly on knowledge acquired by Dr Lindemann on his Atlantic crossing. NASA medical specialists also showed an interest in Lindemann's experience – that a human may "fail" sooner than the equipment he uses, whether it's a boat or a spacecraft.

There seemed to be a lot of deviations from Larry's definition of a kayak. For instance, many of the Alaskan aboriginal paddlers, like those on Kodiak Island, used single-bladed paddles and even paddled from a kneeling position, but their boats still seemed to be called kayaks.

Did a kayak need to be Eskimo rollable (righting a capsized kayak by using a funky hip swivel and paddle manoeuvre)? Kleppers were impossible to Eskimo roll, as was the kayak of Andrew McAuley, who had attempted to cross the Tasman in 2007. So maybe not. If you could stand up in a kayak, did this make it not a kayak? Most recreational paddlers could stand up in their kayaks anyway – Larry could do a headstand on the deck of his!

We began to discuss whether a cabin makes a boat not a kayak. Our answer was found by looking at ocean rowing boats, as they all have cabins. We joked that if that meant they weren't "proper rowing boats", then the Atlantic was yet to be rowed, and maybe we should have got out there in a scull then!

A comment made by numerous people after our Tasman crossing, including Paul Caffyn – the first person to kayak around the entire coast of Australia – was that because our boat wasn't a stock-standard kayak, she wasn't a kayak. But what's stock-standard? Who's to define this? If we were to roll out two, 10 or 50 boats identical to ours, would that make her stock-standard? By making a double kayak into a single – which Ed Gillet, who paddled from the west coast of the USA to Hawaii in 1987, and Andrew had done – doesn't this compromise the stock-

standardness of the kayak? Most kayak designers around the world
have patented certain aspects of their designs, which again would
take away from a boat's stock-standard nature, wouldn't it?

Larry had initially seemed quite eccentric to us, but once we
got stuck into the practical issues he certainly knew his stuff, and
we immersed ourselves for the next few hours discussing what
exactly a kayak constitutes. Losing track of time, we suddenly
realised it was 2am.

We ended up agreeing on a fairly liberal definition. As long as
it fitted our risk profile – in other words, if we could fit everything
we needed to fit in – and we had two paddles and a couple of
enclosed pits to paddle in, that was good enough for us. We left
Larry's place in awe of what he'd done in the past, and the
thought occurred to us: Who were we to think we could kayak
across the Tasman?

4

"YOU'RE GOING TO KILL YOURSELF"

We were both dreading telling our parents. We'd thought about that moment for weeks, and on D-Day I couldn't think of anything else. What would be the best way to tell them? Just do it bluntly? Or should I craftily engineer a conversation in which I'd tell them the only thing that made me happy was adventuring, and get them to join the dots? I got some comfort from the thought that they might just dismiss it as "another one of James' stupid ideas".

It was time. At dinner one night, over a bowl of spaghetti bolognaise, I mentioned to my parents I had something important to tell them. Then I blurted it out. "Mum, Dad, I'm planning on kayaking to New Zealand unsupported."

Before I could expand or elaborate, mayhem erupted at the table. Mum started crying and Dad yelled, "You're going to kill yourself, you bloody idiot, it's impossible." In between sobs, Mum, who'd always been so supportive of me, crushed me by saying: "It's a one-way trip … you'll die. I know you want to inspire people, but it's sheer madness. You don't know the first thing about the ocean."

I left the dinner table with questions flooding through my mind. Was I going to kill myself pursuing adventure? Did I take too many risks? Was I acting in an obnoxiously arrogant, selfish way?

The following day, Justin received a phone call from my dad.

"Hello, Justin, John Castrission here," Dad stated matter-of-factly.

"G'day, Mr Cas … what can I do for you?" Jonesy cautiously replied.

Dad went straight to the point. "I need your help. James has got this stupid idea – he wants to kayak to New Zealand. You need to help me talk him out of it … he's going to kill himself."

"I'd love to, Mr Cas, but I'm the other guy going with him," Justin said quietly, waiting for an onslaught similar to the one I'd received the previous evening.

"Don't be bloody stupid, Justin," said Dad. "You've got your whole life in front of you – don't waste it."

"That's exactly why we're doing it now."

There was no understanding on either side and no common ground.

One set of parents informed; one to go …

Justin waited patiently for a couple of weeks for his parents to come to Sydney from their house in Indo before telling them about our plans. Arriving in Kensington, they sat in their main bedroom keen to hear about how uni was going and what Justin was doing with his life.

Unfortunately – from their point of view – he was doing something much more dramatic with his life than they'd imagined.

"Mum, Dad, I'm planning on kayaking to New Zealand," he announced.

Tears immediately began to stream down Justin's mum's face as his dad quietly walked out of the room. "No, Justin, no," his mum spat out as she drummed her fists against his chest. "Don't do it – I don't know how I'm going to handle it." She obviously didn't mean it, but in the heat of the moment, she sobbed, "If you go, never call me Mum again, and if you don't come back I'll kill myself." To Justin, the fists bounced off harmlessly enough, but her words were like daggers – his mum was his biggest idol and inspiration, and to be hurting her like this tore him up. Reduced to tears, Jonesy stormed into the lounge room, where his dad was lying fast asleep on the couch.

After we returned from the Tasman, Justin asked his dad why he'd just silently walked out of the room that night and gone to sleep. A man of few words, he replied, "I knew the grief I was going to go through with your mother over the next few years and I was getting some rest before the storm."

Looking back at our parents' reaction to our Tasman announcement, I guess the issue of who was being the more selfish was a complicated one. Was it them, for not allowing us to be the people we wanted to be? Or was it us, for pursuing our dream, regardless of their fears for our safety?

I started doing bits and bobs of sailing with Andrew, a mate I used to play rugby with, and a few other guys. They'd done a couple of Sydney to Hobart races and seemed to know their stuff. When he was at the helm one day a couple of weeks later as we were sailing around Sydney Harbour, I started quizzing him about the Tasman. After a few succinct replies, he smiled. "Mate, you're best to get in contact with clouds."

I looked skyward.

"No, you twat – Roger Badham. His nickname is 'Clouds'," he laughed as some of the other crew had a wry giggle.

"Oh," I replied feebly.

A couple of days later I gave Roger a call, and although he sounded hesitant, he offered to cook us dinner down at Wollongong where he lived and have a chat. His home was hidden in the dense bushland just up the hill out of the Gong. If he'd wanted, he could have had 180-degree views of the ocean, but as he'd spent his life studying it, he covered up the vista with billowing tropical trees.

Again wearing our suits, we knocked on his front door. He trundled out in an old pair of shorts and a Team New Zealand polo shirt he'd brought back from the recent America's Cup. At first, he was quite reserved and he might as well have told us what he was thinking – his body language seemed to say it all: *Who are these two crazy kids? They've got no hope.*

As we gave a quick summary of what we planned to do, Roger peered just above his spectacles and stared at us. When we'd finished, there was silence. Justin and I glanced at each other uncomfortably, not quite knowing what to say. As I was about to blurt out something like "Um … does your mum call you Roger or Clouds?", he muttered, "I think you're flaming mad."

I'd known it was a bad idea going down there to see him. Now would come the lecture and the "best-of-luck-with-it-all" speech.

Beginning to smile, he added, "In fact, I think you're f***ing insane. But …"

There was a brief pause as he flipped through the first draft of our risk management document, more for effect than to take in what we'd written. "The Tasman is a dangerous place. I've got no idea why anyone would want to endure the hardship of taking her on in a kayak. But now that I've given you that disclaimer, I'm right behind you. I'll help you with the passage planning and weather forecasting."

This was fantastic. I had to control myself – all I wanted to do was jump out of my skin and yell with glee. Roger was a critical member of the team we'd need to cross the Tasman.

He shuffled over to his chart table as we followed him, smiling ear to ear, like he was the Pied Piper. Circling his hand on the map, reminding me of the Karate Kid's "wax on, wax off" movement, he began: "The Tasman Sea encompasses the body of water between Australia and New Zealand, some 2000 kilometres across. It's a southwestern segment of the South Pacific Ocean. She was named after the Dutch explorer Abel Janszoon Tasman, the first recorded European to encounter New Zealand and Tasmania. The British explorer Captain James Cook later extensively navigated the Tasman Sea in the 1770s as part of his first voyage of exploration.

"A number of factors play havoc on seafarers, all contributing to her fierce reputation. Along the coast of Australia there is the EAC ..."

"Roger," I interrupted, "I've heard of EAT – Ear and Throat – but never an EAC. What's that?"

He gave me the "Oh my God, are you serious" look again.

"It's the current that thunders down the coast of Australia, from near Cape York down to Sydney, where it does a right-hand turn and heads off towards New Zealand."

We sat blankly, staring at him.

"Okay," he sighed, "let's take one step back. Have you seen the film *Finding Nemo*?"

"Sure have," we replied in unison.

"Do you remember the part of the movie where Nemo's dad is in a roaring current with turtles surfing all around him? You know that part where the turtles turn to him and say, 'Cowabunga, dude!'"

We finally had something to relate to. "Oh, that one."

"If we can get you guys in that current, it will greatly help your chances of getting across. As you reach the 160 degree latitude, the winds will mainly be coming from the west. The EAC is quite volatile and its position changes constantly depending on the time of year.

"With current speeds of up to 5 knots, the EAC is a major current system, and its source is in the Coral Sea. It takes the form of a surface stream, tens of metres deep, that runs towards Australia along the boundary between the Coral and Tasman seas. The EAC follows contours of sea-surface elevation. The slope created between the different water masses gives strength to the current, meaning that the current is strongest at the edge …"

Roger went on to explain – in *great* detail – about the currents the Tasman experienced and why. We were fascinated and hadn't even grilled him about the winds yet. Eventually, Jonesy asked him if there was a consistent wind across the Tasman.

"I guess there are three distinct systems," he continued enthusiastically. "Generally in summer, the east coast of Australia experiences predominantly northerly to nor'easterly winds, where systems generally form on the hot dry air from inland, flow south over New South Wales, Victoria and Tasmania. These systems generally form on the western side of Tasman Sea highs."

Roger elaborated at length about "Southerly Busters" (extremely strong wind and heavy rain from the south), caused by shallow cold fronts moving up the coast from Victoria and Tasmania, the 11–16-knot winds usually experienced mid-Tasman, and the westerly winds that prevail across New Zealand as a whole, among countless other crucial pieces of information about the climatic conditions we could expect.

Eventually, our eyelids started to droop – this was a heap of information to digest and it was getting late. As we said our goodbyes and thank yous, we got ready for the long drive back to Sydney for work in the morning, now only five hours away.

Life became incredibly busy. We were both working full time, I was trying to get out climbing as much as possible and at night-time conducting research into each of the different topics we'd identified. If we could address each "risk" on paper, technically we should be able to cross the Tasman. The biggest issue we had to deal with was the constant barrage we were receiving from our families and trying to understand how our "careers" fit into life.

My job seemed so unfulfilling, but I continued on with the accounting for two reasons: the first being that I hate not finishing something I've started; the second being the fear of failure. Climbing one weekend up in the Wolgan Valley – on the other side of the Blue Mountains, north of Lithgow – Dunc could see the turmoil bubbling inside and offered some advice: "Sometimes it's better to put a book down halfway through than being stubborn and pursuing it all the way to the end."

How right he was – it was time to commit. The trigger was failing my Chartered Accountancy exam late in 2005. I hadn't deserved to pass – all my energy was being channelled into crossing the Tasman and climbing. That failure was exactly what I needed to show me I was trying to fit too much into my life and that something had to give. If we were going to kayak to New Zealand it needed our full attention.

As I wrote in my diary:

To approach such an expedition part time, as we've been doing, is foolhardy and naïve. This beast must become our lives. To kayak 2200 kilometres across an ocean I have to be prepared to sacrifice everything. To organise the logistics, equipment, training, and

sponsorship, we have to give this dream complete respect. If not,
we fail – we die. Simple.

　　We'll be questioned by everyone we know – and don't know
for that matter – about our reason for pursuing this ideal. But as
Mallory said: 'What you get from adventure is just sheer joy. If
you have to ask the question, you won't understand the answer.'

It was incredibly exhilarating to have finally, genuinely, committed myself. I knew we'd need to take 18 months off work to tackle the expedition properly, which, among other things, would mean a year-and-a-half without some of the creature comforts I'd begun to take for granted as a professional in the "real world". I knew it was a sacrifice worth making:

I woke this morning feeling alive. I'm pleased I've taken the step
to turn off the highway blocked by traffic and I'm about to
embrace a journey that's going to be bumpy, less travelled and
bloody exciting. Over the past three years I've complained about
not having the drive or conviction to get out there and live. Well,
here you go … Buckle up, buddy.

We'd begun strategically telling close friends – those who were sympathetic to our passion – about our plans. It was important to form a core group of supporters around us who believed in what we were doing. Then it was time to tell my employer. In my mind I was committed – if they weren't willing to accommodate me, I'd resign.

　　Fearfully heading into work that Monday morning, I put it all on the line and told Margaret, one of the partners at the firm, about the expedition. As I put it in my diary, I was "nervous as shit", but just explained the truth about how passionate I was about realising this dream. To my amazement, she said that more people at the company should dream big and that I had her full support. Even better, she said she'd hit the big boys at the firm up for sponsorship when we were ready. She said it was an inspiration to see a young man pursuing his dreams and wished she'd had the courage to do the same at my age.

Most people think of multinational companies and employers as being completely unreasonable and only focused on making money and growing the business. But from my experience, when I explained my ambitions to the partners at my accounting firm, they were surprisingly supportive. I guess it might be as simple as the fact that when someone sees someone else going out on a limb, they usually want to be as encouraging as possible.

Having committed everything to the Tasman, I was again starting to put pressure on myself to succeed. But from very early on, my approach was starkly different from Justin's. We'd always approached life with different levels of vigour and commitment and, with so much now at stake, it soon began to strain our relationship.

We'd often talked about it over the years, and we'd reasoned that his attitude stemmed from a combination of his comfortable upbringing and being able to rely on his natural ability, whereas others had to work harder at school and uni. Justin had grown up in what your average Aussie would call a palace. It was far from your quarter-acre block with a Hill's Hoist and barbecue out the back. There were often up to 20 people living there – cooks, gardeners, maids and servants: the lot. He was also the youngest child, so his family always looked after him even more. From an early age, everything had been done for him. What did he need drive for?

One particular Saturday early in our training, as I recorded in my diary, was a good example of the tension developing between us because of our different approaches:

Jonesy really pissed me off. We were meant to meet for our weekly big paddle at 6am. He rocked up two-and-a-half hours late and paddled like an incompetent donkey all day. It turns out he worked at the bar till 1am and then spent a few hours chatting up some chick. Where is his commitment and drive? I don't think he understands the concept of this whole thing. We f*** up, we die.

Normally, in other events in our lives, failure is a great opportunity to learn and move on – not with crossing the ditch.

His continual lack of motivation is also starting to piss me off. I need to always tell him what to do, set deadlines for him, repeatedly follow him up on stuff. I want him to show some drive and go and organise stuff himself – it's up to him to get rid of some of his fat [he was starting to pack on the pounds too] and set himself a ruthless training regime.

That Saturday had been our first kayaking experience out at sea; not a great time for Justin to have stayed up most of the previous night:

We paddled the closest that we have to NZ. We headed directly east from the heads for 45 minutes. Wow. To paddle out to sea, with land nowhere near, humbled us big-time. Definitely outside the comfort zone. On the way back there was 25 knots and quite a bit of swell that made life interesting. I was glad I didn't get seasick.

Jonesy was pathetic. He couldn't keep his kayak up, nor paddle with enough drive to stay safe. He didn't drink any water, he didn't put suncream on. I can't keep forcing him to look after himself. Mountaineering has taught me this stuff – even though you're a team, you need to look after yourself. If you can't look after yourself ... what good are you to the team?

Crossing the ditch is fitting in with the rest of his lifestyle. It needs to be the other way around. The rest of his life needs to fit in with this. I've sacrificed my career, stopped my Chartered Accountancy study, financial goals, going out on weekends etc. When is he going to show equal commitment?

Unfortunately, that day wasn't an isolated incident. Eight weeks after I quit work to commit myself full time to the expedition, I was beginning to get incredibly frustrated and even thought about abandoning the whole thing:

> *Jonesy is showing no commitment/drive and I don't really have anyone to turn to. No-one understands. Jonesy is the only person I can turn to in these situations, but he's the root of the problem! Got this SMS from him on the weekend: 'Hey, mate, just got your missed call. Am in the moshpit of my favourite band. Got a problem. My parents need me to pick up some shit. So kayaking tomorrow would be impossible to make.'*
>
> *This was after he spent the week prior pissing it up and dicking around with the footy heads at uni games in Queensland. There's too much fat in his life taking away from crossing the ditch. If we're to do this properly, that fat needs to melt. If the fat stays – he goes. Simple. I'm not going to compromise.*
>
> *I can't keep nagging him like I am and driving the momentum continually. I'm over feeling angry and disappointed with him. I've lost my trust and faith in him. If his heart isn't in it, it's time to jettison the burden of having Jonesy along. Do I run with this myself or do I lay crossing the ditch to rest? I don't think I'm ready to tackle the Tasman by myself.*

At the height of my frustration, a friend, Gordo, offered some great advice. He said that in life, there are leaders and followers, and that I was a leader and Jonesy was a follower. I needed to accept that. Another interesting point he made was that even if I were to put in 80 per cent of the work and effort to cross the Tasman, without Jonesy's 20 per cent neither of us would get there. His 20 per cent contribution was critical for the expedition to be successful.

Gordo was right, but with the pressures our difference in attitude was causing, I knew we needed to cement our commitment to the expedition. I came up with the idea of a "contract", prioritising crossing the ditch as our absolute focus. For the next three years it would be the first thing we'd look at when we woke and the last thing we saw when we went to bed.

Jonesy was slowly starting to evolve and commit to the Tasman. He began getting stuff done – like contacting prospective sponsors and developing our website – and training harder and more regularly. For me, though, this evolution was never going to be fast enough. Why couldn't he change in a click of the fingers?

By now, our blueprint for the Tasman expedition had been completed. We'd answered all the questions we'd asked ourselves and addressed every issue that needed addressing. It was time for us to get some feedback on our methodology and risk mitigation strategies from professionals.

We sent the document to numerous sailors, our weather forecaster Roger Badham, and to a fellow kayaker, Andrew McAuley. We didn't know Andrew personally, but we looked at him in awe and admiration for his kayaking feats – including the first direct crossing of Bass Strait, as well as the Gulf of Carpentaria. He was the most active kayaker in Australia at the time, setting new benchmarks in sea kayaking. We felt his input would be invaluable.

Within a couple of weeks, though, we received two phone calls from people whose numbers were in the document, alerting us to the fact that someone else was planning to cross the Tasman. It seemed that Andrew, whose own Tasman plans had been on ice for some time, was suddenly putting his own expedition together. And he had eight months' worth of our research to help him on his way.

He'd provided us with advice and support regarding skin issues he'd faced and seating arrangements, yet he hadn't told us of his own ambitions. And while we'd been quite open about our plans with various experts and consultants, he'd told Roger that his expedition was "highly confidential and top secret – no-one must know". I felt disappointed and betrayed. Had we been naïve? Why hadn't Andrew been honest with us?

In late-November 2005, a couple of weeks after we'd found out about Andrew's plans, we met with him for a coffee down at Circular Quay. He seemed stunned that we knew what he'd been doing and was immediately apologetic about having used our risk management document. He added that crossing the ditch had always been a dream of his, as he saw it as the last in a series of three crossings – Bass Strait and the Gulf of Carpentaria being the other two – that he'd be the first to do.

Andrew revealed to us that when he'd found out about our plans to cross the Tasman, he hadn't slept for three nights. Crossing the ditch was something Andrew had always dreamt of doing. We could see in his eyes the turmoil this had caused him. Who were these two young schmucks about to take what was rightfully his? Compared to his achievements we'd done nothing – he was much more qualified. The two advantages we had over him were (a) that there were two of us, and (b) our extensive risk-management work. Andrew had one of these and was putting it to good use, and his experience more than made up for the other one.

*   *   *

Our kayaking skills were progressing well – we were beginning to spend more and more time out at sea and we'd finally learnt to Eskimo roll, although with my gut regularly playing unpleasant games, I'd started to sense that I was in for a long road dealing with the motion of the ocean.

We'd put most of our risk-management work together and we were now in the process of designing a kayak around the vital equipment we'd identified in the research. All we needed was a proper design and cash to fund this little exercise.

Initially, the funding of the kayak didn't seem to worry us – we knew (or we thought we knew) we'd get there somehow. It was this youthful naivety that saw us attempting the crossing in the first place. For some reason, the thought of two mid twenty year olds raising $250–300,000 for a paddling expedition was low on our worry list.

About this time, we became aware of the UK paddler Peter Bray, who in 2001 had successfully kayaked across the North Atlantic unsupported. We bought his book, *Kayak across the Atlantic*, and found the yacht designer/surveyor – Rob Feloy – behind his kayak design. We got in contact with Rob and he was immediately interested in the project. We started tossing ideas back and forth, and before long we had a rough 3D CAD design – sexy software that engineers use to draw things like kayaks in 3D – of what was to become our boat. We designed the boat with the Tasman specifically in mind. Studying the data we'd punched with Roger, we identified that 60–70 per cent of the wind should come from the west, so we built the cabin based on that assumption, and weren't too concerned about its relatively large size (but as we'd discover, assumptions can be dangerous). With projects such as this, it was crucial to form a group of people around us who were excited by the project right from the start. The remuneration was always going to be barely adequate: they had to be doing it for other altruistic reasons.

Further good news came when we received an email from Andrew a couple of weeks after our meeting, saying that he'd been "premature in approaching the Tasman" and that he didn't have time to prepare for the crossing. It definitely wasn't going to happen in 2006, he wrote, and added that April 2007 was a more likely date, although it wasn't definite. The Tasman was all ours!

This news came as a huge relief as we were starting to put our sponsorship proposal together, and obviously the thought of someone else doing the crossing before us would have taken away much of the appeal for prospective investors.

Among the main aspects of our sponsorship strategy was the visual side of things, and a friend of ours, Ben Barin, played a key role for us. One of the first people in the "core" group of supporters we informed about our plans to cross the Tasman, right from the start he was passionate about the idea and threw in his support, designing a website for us, as well as branding and business cards.

From the moment Justin and I took on this project we weren't afraid to come across as professional in everything we did. If we were going to put an expedition of this size and scope together, it was the least we could do for our stakeholders. However, this perturbed a number of people in the outdoor community who said that we were bastardising adventure by having a businesslike approach.

The purist way of crossing the Tasman would have been to do it completely naked, with no provisions or water, in a wooden kayak we'd made ourselves. Each element we added to that detracted from the purity of the adventure, but it also decreased the risks.

Adventure is all about defining a level of risk that you're willing to accept and going from there. In our Tasman blueprint, we identified strategies to combat the dangers, but there were some risks we assumed that others might not have. One of these was not taking a gun or shark shield to fend off predators. The Tasman Sea is notorious for its great white shark and tiger shark populations. We had to balance the threat of an attack against other factors, such as space on board and power drainage.

Having a support boat was an idea we toyed with for a while, but we felt this would detract from what we were trying to achieve in the style that we'd defined. There does come a level of certainty where the activity ceases to be an adventure – where there's no more danger to an expedition than there is to everyday living.

It's up to the individual to define the level of risk they're willing to take and then dealing with the challenges thrown at them. In mountaineering, I'd become quite accepting when it came to absorbing routes with high objective dangers such as avalanches and rock-fall. Climbing without a rope is another one of those grey-area activities where everyone – from experienced mountaineers to people sitting in a pub who've never been anywhere near a cliff face – have their two bobs on, but at the end of the day, who are we to define acceptable levels of risks that other humans should take, given that we all have a different risk profile and understanding of the risks?

One thing I find really frustrating is when people (say ... my parents!) tell you you're going to die etc, with no understanding of how you're planning to combat the risks that you face. Of course, it's understandable from their perspective, but that's why it was so important for us to share that document with Andrew and other seasoned adventurers.

I learnt this valuable lesson when I was in second year uni boxing in the Australian University Games. I was shit scared of the bout I had coming up, and my coach could sense it. He looked like Micky from *Rocky* and he'd spent most of his early life in the ring; then, when he'd got too old to fight, he stepped into the corner to train young fellas like myself. He was missing most of his teeth and had a nose that would make the rugby league legend Laurie Daley look pretty. His back was hunched and under the heavily callused knuckles you could tell each one had been broken a multitude of times. He could see the fear in my eyes.

"What's wrong, fella?" he asked me one day at the boxing gym at Sydney Uni.

"Aw, bit scared of the fight I've got in a few nights," I replied sheepishly, staring at the strapping around my knuckles.

"What is it ya scared of?" he said in his usual gravelly voice.

"Dunno."

"What is it ya scared of?" he growled, ignoring the sound of other boxers sparring in the background.

I was feeling even more sheepish by now. "I suppose … getting knocked out in my first proper bout in front of a crowd of uni mates."

"Then keep your hands up next to your head for the whole night. You won't win … but you won't get knocked out either. What else are you scared of?"

"Not being quick enough to get any jabs in."

"Dance on your feet and jab when you get the chance. You're quicker than the best that I've seen – I reckon there's six fights between you and the Commonwealth Games. You've done the training and spent hours and hours on the speed ball and pads."

He kept on digging and one by one we addressed all the things I was scared of in that first fight. It was an important lesson – breaking fear down into digestible portions and analysing each one. I went on to knock the bloke out and – as I mentioned earlier – win the AUG middleweight crown.

5

STEPPING STONES

"Bloody terrible. Today we began our Coffs Harbour to Sydney paddle at 4am. We got 13km then turned back. My head was weak and I was spewing my guts up for a solid two hours. Seasickness is hideously crippling and makes kayaking extremely difficult. In prior training I've been psyched to conquer this challenge but today I was f***ing over it. Larry Gray, Andrew and Pete Bray would have been able to handle the conditions today. We need to toughen up or move aside. My confidence has been shattered – what have we gotten ourselves into?"

From the inception of the idea of kayaking to NZ, there'd been a lurking fear about how we were going to deal with seasickness. I went through a phase where I thought that if I subjected my body to getting sick, part of its natural response would be to acclimatise to the motion of the sea. Week after week I put myself through this torture and each week I found myself throwing up just as much as the week before. After realising that I was beating my head against a wall, I decided to try some anti-seasickness drugs. I

started with the herbal stuff – wrist bands and ginger tablets –
which I quickly learnt had next to no positive effect in keeping
my breakfast down. I then moved on to consumer drugs that were
readily available at the chemist. Kwells began to work a treat:

*Awesome, awesome, awesome. Went sea kayaking today –
didn't get seasick at all!*

As soon as we found this solution we started doing overnight
paddles up and down the coast. On one occasion, we set out to
paddle from Wollongong to Sydney into a 45-kilometre-per-hour
nor'easterly wind, which made progress painfully slow.

*What a shit of a day. The inherent problem with sea kayaking is
that the probability of having a stunning day seems to be minimal
– eight out of 10 paddles you're constantly battling with shit.
Today we were against the wind and the current and there were
billions of bluebottles everywhere. We both got done so many
times we lost count. One of the f***ers landed on my face and
wrapped its "thin dick" tentacles around my neck.*

*To add more insult to the whole situation, you can't get any
rhythm or momentum as crashing through waves slows you down
as effectively as trying to drive a Toyota Corolla through a brick
fence. The drugs are working great though. Still, I'd much prefer
to be spending my weekends up at the mountains.*

That weekend, the sea had been littered with thousands of
bluebottles. I was stung by 19 of them on the Saturday – the first
day – and on the Sunday I lost count. By the time we'd paddled
into Bondi late that afternoon, the stings on top of stings made us
look like lepers – to the horror of everyone we saw on the beach.

Over the following days, our chests and backs erupted in angry welts and blisters. The adventure taught us some valuable lessons, like: the palms of your hands and the balls of your feet can't get stung; and pissing on a sting helps ease the pain.

Throughout my diaries at the time I constantly made comments about wanting to be up in the mountains, but by the end of the Tasman crossing, our bodies had come to accept the discomfort at sea and we enjoyed paddling more than ever before. Being cold and wet became life and our bodies adjusted to that.

Having said that, mountaineering had a few advantages over kayaking endlessly across an ocean. In some ways, sea kayaking is monotonous in that you're principally concerned with reaching the "summit". The actual activity lacks the *wow* factor. It contrasts with climbing, in which style (whether or not you choose to free-climb or aid-climb (using or not using equipment to help with the ascent)), as well as your actual progress – appreciating the various stages of the climb – is what you enjoy, and getting to the top and back to the hut is only a small part of the experience.

In the midst of these weekly ocean excursions, Justin and I were feverishly working on our sponsorship plans. First stop was my former employer. We'd spent over a month putting together a swish proposal and we truly believed we had something to offer the company I'd left four months before. We assumed that we'd be able to attract them as our major sponsor, but unfortunately when we presented to the Chief Marketing Officer, we were shut down.

It was incredibly frustrating. One of the core messages the company liked to communicate in their marketing was that they were different – they were an *innovator*. That certainly wasn't where the CMO was coming from. He harped on about how partners at the firm wanted risk-free clients, risk-free marketing and the firm wanted risk-free fundraising. In hindsight, I guess kayaking across the Tasman was a little different from the average proposals that flooded through the door each day.

Maybe we didn't sell the message well enough. Anyway, it hurt that we'd spent so much time tailoring a presentation to them when we could have been speaking to companies who actually had a sense of adventure.

The sponsorship road was proving to be much more difficult than we'd originally anticipated. The following week, we met with Air New Zealand and made a mind-blowingly stupid mistake. They were impressed with the proposal, our professionalism etc, but then asked, "We're just not sure how sponsoring you guys is going to result in getting more bums on seats."

Justin and I looked at one another blankly and dopily replied, "Neither do we." That was that.

With all these rejections we were copping, each blow hurt, but we were learning valuable lessons about what these companies wanted. Sponsorship was a two-way relationship which had to be mutually beneficial – we weren't a charity. We honestly felt we had something to offer, but obviously weren't conveying our message clearly enough. We kept telling ourselves that you learn more from rejection and failure than from anything else.

Now began the long road of approaching over 130 different companies from right around the globe. Flicking through a *BRW* magazine I came across an interview with David Spence, the CEO of a company called Unwired. They were in the business of providing wireless internet to consumers in Sydney, and the article delved into David's love of the ocean and his experience in the tragic 1979 Fastnet Race off the English coast that claimed the lives of 15 sailors.

David's approach to management and strategy was inspiring. He was aggressive and always had an eye open for innovative opportunities. We knew we had to get a proposal in front of him, but it proved to be difficult. Because of the company's relatively flat management structure, we finally got a proposal to the brand manager, Olivia Donohoe, who elevated it to the CMO. She then discussed the proposal with David. Her take was that our proposal was the best that she had ever seen. With their marketing team happy with the proposal, and with the CEO's love of the ocean, we felt we had a decent chance of securing our major sponsor for the expedition.

Gear sponsorship was relatively easy, but getting companies to part with cash was much more of a challenge. As a result, we tried to keep our costs to a minimum by sourcing all our products from the suppliers. This was time-intensive but delivered results. We sourced everything from all the kayak materials (fibreglass, resin, epoxy, foam, Kevlar and carbon fibre) to each item of clothing and food. On the low end, this included phoning 10 almond farmers, looking for someone willing to part with 20 kilograms of nuts! We finally found someone in South Australia who shipped us two 10 kilogram boxes.

As the design neared completion, the need to find some funding to build the kayak was becoming more urgent. We had to raise approximately $80,000 for the labour alone with zero dollars in the bank. The issue was that potential investors wanted to see something tangible before they parted ways with their cash, but we needed the funding to build the kayak in order to attract investors. It was a Catch 22 that all small businesses are faced with. We knew that investors would get excited by the unique shape of the kayak, but we needed something to show first.

As we dealt with these sponsorship issues, we were also planning to kayak across Bass Strait. It was a huge milestone to help prepare us for the Tasman. We left Sydney on 21 March to drive down to Port Welshpool, a coastal village in Gippsland in Victoria, where we were to start our 340-kilometre crossing of the strait via the eastern route. (Parts of Wilsons Promontory, the southern tip of the Victorian coast, weren't accessible by car, so Port Welshpool was an ideal starting point.)

There are 28 islands between the Australian mainland and Tasmania and our course linked three of these: Hogan Island, Deal Island – in the Kent Group – and Flinders Island. Pre-trip jitters on our drive to Melbourne were compounded by a look of despair on Jonesy's face: he was losing the battle to a nasty fever.

I chuckled, "Perfect partner to go paddling across Bass Strait!"

Four days later, Justin's fever subsided and we began our journey in a yellow two-man Pittarak kayak – dubbed the *Queen Mary* – with an uneventful five-hour paddle to Refuge Cove on the mainland. The weather had been great and we'd enjoyed very welcome tidal assistance. Camping in the cove that evening, we knew from the forecasts that our first island crossing wouldn't be blessed with the same good conditions.

In the morning, the pristine, isolated landscape – with low cloud hiding the receding peaks – made us feel like we'd entered a Jurassic Park time capsule. There was little chit-chat; full concentration was required for the choppy conditions. No sight of land for almost two hours heightened our sense of isolation. We paddled round the southern tip of Hogan Island to find ourselves hidden from a southerly wind that had caked salt down the left-hand side of our thermals. After we reached the shore and secured the *Queen Mary*, we settled in for the evening. Although there aren't any trees on the island, the birdlife, penguins and the general elation of being on our own out there was magical.

Next morning, our tranquil shelter became a cauldron of froth, thanks to a change in the wind direction. The exit looked dangerous, and the thought of paddling into a 50-kilometre-per-hour wind didn't appeal. Instead, we spent the day exploring, accompanied by a 10-centimetre plastic penguin mascot we'd been given as part of a telco promotion. After 30 hours out of the kayak, it was amazing how rapidly our bodies had adapted to the stresses of expedition paddling. Both of us felt much stronger after our rest day (although that may have had something to do with eating all the chocolate mousse we had on board!).

The paddle from Hogan to Deal was straightforward, until we reached the island and had to battle both into headwinds and against currents – something we'd get very familiar with out on the Tasman – to make landfall. Once ashore, we were immediately struck by the change in landscape from the barren Hogan Island. As a stark contrast, Deal Island is covered in a thick blanket of shrubs and trees.

On our fifth morning we woke feeling a bit anxious. This would be our biggest crossing – 65 kilometres. With a cold front expected the following day, bringing gale-force weather, we were hoping we'd be able to seek refuge at Killiecrankie, a small fishing village with a population of 15 on the northern tip of Flinders Island. A 6am weather forecast we got from our satellite phone made us feel a bit more confident that we had a window to get to safety.

We started paddling on a compass bearing of 124 degrees with no sight of land. As each hour passed, our umbilical cord with Deal Island was slowly severed, leaving us more and more exposed. We were alone. It was a humbling experience sitting in a primitive kayak, surrounded by hundreds of kilometres of ocean, with only a smattering of islands dotted around us. Our minds wandered to eight months ahead: we'd be out on the Tasman then, halfway to NZ! This was why we were crossing Bass Strait: for the physical, mental and psychological preparation.

It was right about now that we were most grateful for our trusty GPS. It didn't allow current drift or tidal influences to manipulate its readings, giving us constant measurement of our actual speed. Without it, our progress could have been cunningly deceptive – the GPS readings kept our compass honest.

Hours passed, and slowly Flinders Island crept over the horizon like Atlantis rising from the sea. A wave of relief washed through us as we reached the shore. We'd paddled about 220 of the total 350 kilometres and now had the biggest stretch of ocean behind us; we could enjoy the company of people – not penguins – and we had the comfort of knowing there was land nearby for the rest of the journey.

"Gale warning for all Bass Strait!" was the Bureau of Meteorology forecast for the following day. Although we'd received an adverse weather report, the weather looked favourable at the time, so we jumped in the boat and set our sights on Trouser Point, on the southern tip of Flinders Island. As we paddled out from Killiecrankie, an old salt clearing his lobster nets casually warned: "Wouldn't go out there today, boys."

Enough said; back to land we went. Better not to disrespect 50-odd years of local knowledge and an unfavourable weather forecast. Nestled in a tiny hut behind sand dunes, we hid from the intensifying storm. While it still raged, we hitched a ride with a local fisherman to Whitemark – the capital of Flinders with a population of 50 – to tuck into a pub meal and down a couple of beers. Later, we discovered our "free ride" had sentenced us to five hours' labour moving the local souvenir shop around the block for the owner!

Shifting display cabinets motivated us to get back on the water pronto! The cold front passed the following morning, and with an okay from our old mate, we were off down the western coast of Flinders Island to set up for the Franklin Sound crossing.

As we progressed further south, the chill penetrated our bones. Throughout the day, there was a constant coolness in the air requiring us to wear Gore-Tex jackets even while paddling. Our fingers felt like wooden roots curled around our paddle shafts. At Trouser Point we lit a fire to provide warmth and to cook; our supply of fuel was diminishing rapidly. The nagging cold didn't allow our bodies to recover efficiently while we slept and we went through a huge amount of wood trying to stay warm during the night.

As we started across Franklin Sound the next day – a stretch of ocean renowned for more vessels lost than anywhere else in the Bass Strait region – we were blessed with lake-like conditions.

"Hey, Jonesy," I yelled. "How'd you like to push to Tassie today?"

This was wildly optimistic compared to our original plans. Was I suffering from summit fever, where mountaineers – forgetting their basic safety buffers – recklessly push on to the summit? Did Jonesy think I'd been out on the water too long? No wonder there was silence …

"Let's see how we feel in a couple of hours," he replied cautiously.

Hours went by and we found ourselves at a crossroads: head for land or go direct to Tassie? As conditions remained idle we called our friend Ben – who'd been giving us our weather forecasts – to make sure the weather bureau didn't expect any adverse weather shifts. Good news – we were given the go-ahead and on we went.

Soon, though, the tide shifted direction and our speed dropped. We considered worst-case scenarios (it's amazing how your head can compute a seemingly infinite number of different speed, distance and time possibilities). The slog continued across Banks Strait – a stretch of ocean renowned for sinking ships and epic misadventures – and as Tassie drew closer, the number of birds and penguins in the water grew. So did our singing, and they were treated to Jonesy and I bashing out "Amazing Grace" and "Waltzing Matilda" – Andre Rieu would have been jealous. Then, 5 kilometres out, we knew our judgement had paid off; the tide swept us towards Tasmania like a landing jet. Touchdown!

After over nine hours on the water we arrived at our destination – well, sort of. We'd found Tasmania, but had *absolutely* no idea where we'd landed! Unfortunately, there were no waving flags or cheering girls in mini-skirts waving pom-poms; just a deep glow of self-satisfaction. We'd paddled 350 kilometres across Bass Strait over nine days: it was a special moment, reflecting on how we'd set a goal we believed in and we'd achieved it. Considering Jonesy's illness prior to the event, and the fact that we'd never attempted anything remotely like this before, crossing Bass Strait was an amazing stepping stone.

6

GETTING UGLY

Although we returned to Sydney full of vigour and enthusiasm, I found readjusting to being around people incredibly difficult – I just wanted to be out there again. It was now early May 2006 and we had six months left – that was when the weather conditions would be optimal – to get all our funding in place and get the kayak built. We were now totally committed to the expedition. We worked part time here and there for cash to get us through the week – Justin doing a bit of bar work, me doing some consulting – but we spent every waking hour thinking, doing, eating or shitting crossing the ditch. Any activity that didn't add value to our crossing was off the agenda – dinners with friends and dates with girls had to wait.

There were so many different facets of the Tasman crossing that we needed to think about and organise – sponsorship, construction, seamanship skills, and, of course, training. At about this time, an army bloke by the name of Patrick Brothers got in contact with us. At first, we didn't know who he was, or where he was coming from. He gave us a brief description of himself over a few emails. It was just your typical resume really – paratrooper, special forces unit (with a multitude of HALO (High Altitude Low Opening) and LALO (Low Altitude Low Opening) jumps), many operations overseas in hostile territories, several Ironmans completed in less than 10 hours: the list went on and on. He sounded more machine than man.

We invited Pat round to Jonesy's place one night and had no idea what to expect. But instead of a six-foot-five, exoskeletal automaton entering the room, a relatively slight, computerish geek opened the door. We carried out a little idle chit-chat for a while; not the normal icebreakers about weather or footy scores, though, but about what it's like jumping out of a plane at night into enemy territory weighed down by 50 kilograms of gunnery. As he sat on the chair, both feet planted flat on the ground, knees forming a perfect right angle, and with an erect back so straight that you could do your ironing on it, I couldn't help but stare at his elegant hands. How many men had those hands killed? Had he ever strangled someone with them?

Pat was one of those people we instantly trusted. He was overzealously focused, but at the end of the day was a bloody good bloke. There were multiple layers to his personality that we'd never see nor understand, but at the core of it he was a straight shooter. Pat was in a transitional period, where he was about to leave the army and embark on the next phase of his civilian life. In his final year of an MBA at the University of New South Wales, he created a "paper business" called Race Recon – a theoretical business as part of his studies. The plan was to set up an international media and technology company focused on supporting world-class expeditions, action sports and environmental research. Pat saw our Tasman bid as a great tool to test out a number of his business ideas. He'd had many years of managing soldiers in extreme operations and brought plenty to the table – planning, authority management, expedition communications etc. Jonesy and I were to be his guinea pigs; taking the business from paper to reality. We soon formed a strong bond with him.

We were training close to 30 hours each week, consisting of a heap of paddling – both inshore and offshore – weights sessions and plenty of cardio. The aim was to make ourselves as indestructible as possible and to bulk up both fat and muscle stores, which we knew would melt off us on the Tasman. We just didn't know how much.

Part of preparing mentally for the challenge was to do a series of "getting ugly" training sessions. One of these was a food and sleep deprivation exercise, designed by Pat and a few of his army mates. It was important to know how our bodies would react to these stresses in a relatively controlled environment. In hindsight, this was some of the best training we did, as we pushed our boundaries to the point of hallucination and reached fatigue levels that prepared us for similar experiences out on the Tasman. It would've been scary to go through it for the first time alone at sea in a kayak.

We arrived at Victoria Barracks in Paddington not quite knowing what to expect. The sun was just beginning to set as Pat and his fellow pain inflictors gave us three unlabelled tins of food, not telling us how long these tins were supposed to last us. The only briefing we had was that they were going to subject us to extreme sleep deprivation and make it their mission to break us. At the time, this phrase seemed somewhat ambiguous, but we were to learn quickly that the whole exercise wouldn't stop until we were squirming like a newborn child, crying, "We give up!"

We started with some physical training (army blokes called it PT), night running and paddling. Believe it or not, Justin and I were actually enjoying ourselves. At the end of each exercise, we'd thank Pat and his colleagues, then eagerly want to dive into the next challenge. In the past, we'd be out bush and do this to ourselves; now we had a team of army blokes pushing right through the night – it was awesome fun!

As dawn broke they continued pushing us, yelling from time to time "boot-camp" style (it was starting to be slightly less fun by now), eventually allowing us a 10-minute break to smash the first tin of food – coconut milk. They pushed us through the day; then on our second night, after 35 hours of activity, we opened our second tin – peaches. This fuel would have to last us through our second night.

As the exercise wore on, they constantly evaluated our mental awareness by getting us to learn Morse Code. On the first night, we'd been able to memorise up to five codes in five minutes, but over the following days recalling even one became difficult.

On the second night, Pat barked at me, "What's the letter 'l', Cas?"

"Er … dash, dash, dot, dot?"

"Get down and give me 10 push-ups – it's dot, dash, dot, dot."

After my push-ups, I stood up and he asked again, "What's 'l', Cas?"

"Um … dot, dash, dash, dot?" (D'oh.)

"No! Another 10."

This went on six times. I just couldn't remember – the fatigue was finally starting to get to me.

"Right. If you can't remember now, Jonesy's going to have to do the push-ups for you until you get it."

After Justin took 40 push-ups for me, I finally got it right! To this day, he reckons the last couple I "forgot" on purpose – sorry, mate.

Then the hallucinations started. I saw a seven-foot-two baby in nappies sucking its thumb and Jonesy saw equally surreal objects. The imagery was so vivid, yet there was still some reason within me saying it was an illusion. They continued to punish us, often trying to break the bond that Justin and I had with one another – pitting us against each other and trying to cause tension between us. In this, at least, they failed miserably.

We were a united unit throughout the exercise, which played a huge role in us getting through the regime. We constantly encouraged each other, took push-ups for the other one when one of us was going through a rough patch, and we kept close. This was to be one of the key factors that got us across the Tasman. Together, we were a team 10 times harder to break than if there'd only been one of us.

We made it through to 70 hours, then the trainers pulled the plug. "You bastards are ready for the Tasman – you're as tough as nails," Pat told us as we sat at Coogee Beach, eating fish and chips that he'd shouted us. It was the first sign of affection any of them had shown us in three days. As the first greasy chip (with chicken salt) touched my tongue, it seemed to wake me up from a trance. For the first time in days, I looked around at the "civilians" playing and sunbaking on the beach; at 3am, we'd been doing sprints and push-ups, about to puke where they now lay. Unfortunately, I'll never quite be able to look at Coogee the same way again. Still, we were deeply satisfied that we'd got through the training, as we hadn't had any idea how we were going to react.

After a few days R&R, we returned to reality – construction delays and financial pressures. In October 2006, we learnt that Andrew McAuley had been putting together a bid to get across the Tasman before us. It wasn't the fact that he was attempting to cross the Tasman that we found disappointing and frustrating, it was how he'd gone about it so secretively. We'd been to a lecture of his in August on a recent Antarctic paddle he'd done and he'd mentioned that his next expedition was to be a kite-sled trip to the South Pole (a kite-sled being exactly that – a kite-powered sled that would be able to charge across Antarctica at speeds up to 150 kilometres per hour). Imagine our surprise, then, when we were told by the Australian Maritime Safety Authority and a couple of other people that he was planning to "beat them [i.e. us] across the Tasman".

We were confused. Why hadn't he told us of his plans? There was plenty of scope for us to still work together and showcase the differences between our expeditions – he'd be paddling solo in a stock-standard kayak, and he'd be leaving from Tasmania.

When we heard this news, we once again confronted him to ask what the story was. He responded: "I'll update my website when I get around to it – should answer your other questions." This was when things started getting really messy. Both Justin and I had stopped trying to make excuses on his behalf and started deeply resenting him. There's nothing worse than feeling misled by someone you look up to and respect. After all, he was Australian Geographic Adventurer of the Year and we just couldn't make sense of this behaviour. We weren't Scott and Amundsen fighting to be the first to the South Pole; nor were we Edward Whymper and Jean-Antoine Carrel fighting for the crown of the Matterhorn.

While both Andrew and ourselves were setting out with the same destination in mind, right from the beginning we had incredibly different approaches to the expedition. After assessing the risks, Justin and I decided – for a few reasons – that there was no way we were going to leave from Tasmania.

First was the water temperature. On the route we took across the Tasman, the average water temperature was 17–22 degrees Celsius. Leaving from Tasmania bound for southern New Zealand, according to CSIRO data the maximum water temperature would have been 12 degrees. Away from the coast, the air temperature in a kayak is a reflection of the water temperature, and the cooler water down south would have meant we'd have had to consume more calories, as our bodies would've had to work harder to stay warm. And if we'd had an abandon-ship scenario, it would have meant decreased survival times in the water. Andrew accepted these risks because the distance from Tassie to NZ is 600 kilometres shorter than the route we were aiming for.

But although the route further south is significantly shorter, the storms you encounter are much more intense. Being below the 40th parallel – a circle of latitude 40 degrees south of the earth's equatorial plane – low-pressure systems come out of the Southern Ocean with ruthless ferocity. One storm we experienced out on the Tasman maxed out at 90 kilometres per hour (with gusts every now and then far exceeding that). A thousand kilometres further south, that same low-pressure system was blowing above 150 kilometres per hour!

Another, more subjective goal was that Justin and I felt we had to paddle from mainland Australia rather than an "island". We both love Tasmania, but this was one of the goals we set ourselves. Also, we didn't want to use a sail. Originating from our discussion with the kayaking legend Larry about what constitutes a kayak, we passionately believed that by adding a sail, it became a sail boat. These were self-imposed rules and in no way were they meant to detract from what we thought of Andrew's expedition.

Falling back on the risk-management work that we'd done, there was also no way we were heading out onto the Tasman without being prepared in a similar fashion to a yacht making the same journey. There are stringent safety guidelines for yachts and fellow ocean rowers, and this ruled out us taking a stock-standard kayak, as we simply couldn't fit the gear in it that we'd need.

Andrew advertised on his website that his approach was to "reach for big, bold goals on a shoestring budget". Our approach was different, in that right from the start, budget constraints were never even a factor we considered. During climbing trips I've slept in parks and inner-city gardens, and scavenged for food from bins to let me extend my budget for a few more weeks on the rock. To us, though, there was a time and a place for shoestring-budget adventures – the Tasman wasn't one of them.

Around this time, I was also surprised and disappointed to hear that Andrew had phoned several of our stakeholders, apparently trying to gather information about our expedition. He'd called my accounting firm to find out what my exact work situation was (I'd taken extended leave of absence from there, but they were still technically my employer), our major sponsor Unwired, attempting to discover what our sponsorship agreement included, and finally the Australian National Maritime Museum to ask why they were allowing us to launch from their docks.

We were finding ourselves in the middle of this "race to cross the Tasman"; only, we didn't see it as a race. There was no room on the Tasman for ego and we were only going to leave if we were 100 per cent ready.

As we struggled to understand how Andrew could get himself ready in time, Justin and I had the difficult task of informing our sponsors of his bid. At this stage we had close to 30 sponsors investing in a project that they believed would be the first successful kayak crossing of the Tasman. Obviously, that's how we sold it to them. But as Andrew started attracting some media attention, our stakeholders were getting increasingly concerned that we hadn't been up front with them.

This left us in a difficult situation. We felt the most proactive way to deal with this pressure was to send Andrew a final plea, so we wrote him a letter, essentially asking him to delay his departure. We explained that we'd attracted sponsorship based largely on our expedition being the first crossing of the Tasman. And from what Andrew had told us of his plans, we'd been happy to sell our expedition to investors along these lines. Now all this was potentially in jeopardy. As well as sending the letter to Andrew, we forwarded a copy to all our sponsors, showing them that we were indeed looking out for their interests.

However, Andrew didn't want a compromise, he didn't want to meet up and discuss our dilemma – he was going and that was that. He left from the east coast of Tasmania on his first attempt to cross the Tasman on 2 December 2006.

I felt sick. I wrote in my diary that day: "I've got a deep hollow sensation within – it's a gut-churning reaction right under the ribs. My legs feel weak. I can't believe he's actually left. The wheels are set in motion – all we can do is sit back and watch."

Regardless of everything else, we thought Andrew had done incredibly well to mobilise his expedition so quickly. It wasn't long, though, before his first setback. Within two days, he was back in Tasmania. It had been too cold for him and he hadn't been able to sleep. I was surprised to hear that he'd paddled for 20 hours straight on his first day. I thought he should have followed the example of people like Jim Shekkadar and John Muir. Shekkadar, who rowed across the Pacific, and Muir, an incredible Aussie adventurer who'd hauled sleds to both poles, walked across Australia and climbed Everest, had averaged three hours per day in the first week of their expeditions to allow their bodies to adapt to the stress of expedition life.

It must have been tough for Andrew to turn back once he'd made the decision to head out to sea, especially as he'd obviously been racing the clock to get out there before us. We heard that he'd only done one overnight sea trial off the coast of Terrigal, on the New South Wales Central Coast, hundreds of kilometres from his trans-Tasman route; if he'd done more offshore trials and more trials in the Southern Ocean, he could have rectified issues such as the cold and not being able to sleep. As I've mentioned, the average water temperature was one of the main reasons we weren't leaving from that far down south. Andrew had seen our risk-management document, so he would have known this.

We thought that was Andrew done for the summer, as the weather window is quite narrow. Ideally, any trans-Tasman voyage is best attempted between November and March, as this is when the water temperature is warmest and gales and storms are least common. Later in the kayaking-to-New-Zealand season, there's a higher risk in the north Tasman of tropical cyclones making their way down into NZ waters.

Apart from this initial "trial" having probably freaked him out, we were sure he had too many issues to rectify and not enough time to properly address them before the weather window closed. How wrong we were ...

Andrew worked tirelessly through the festive season in equipping his kayak for the crossing. He added insulation, rigged a hammock kind of set-up to sleep on and took warmer clothing. Before we knew it, he was off on his second attempt.

We fought just as hard to get ourselves ready for the crossing before the weather window drew to a close, as we were still hoping to get away before the end of January. That was the deadline "Clouds" had set for our departure.

By now, we'd begun the construction process, with the same crew who'd made the Pittarak kayak. They were based in a small factory near Newcastle where the owner, Graham Chapman, had been making boats for over 20 years. He had a wealth of knowledge, but more importantly, a passion for unique projects.

As funding still hadn't come through, we had to throw all our own money at the project to get it off the ground. Within a month of construction starting, our $40,000 worth of life savings had been invested in the project and we saw our credit cards being used more and more. We were sinking and needed some external assistance ... quickly. A few small financial backers jumped on, and Justin's mother – who was still pretty sceptical about the whole thing – provided us with a loan so that we could "just get on with the rest of our lives". (Thanks, Mrs Jones!)

Our construction timeline had blown out from a projected eight weeks to over 20 – one-off designs always seem to take much longer than anticipated and our kayak was no exception. We ended up going to Newcastle just before Christmas and staying with the boat builder for two weeks to help get her ready. Each night we lay awake, as shards of fibreglass had splintered themselves all through our bodies from the sanding. This gave us extra time to reflect on the fact that we were slowly falling way behind schedule.

The day before the shed closed for the festive season, we drove back down to Sydney with resin drying on the hull of the kayak, knowing that we had to get the fit-out completed in a week. Craig Thomsen, our electrical engineer, told us we were dreaming, but we didn't let this get us down; we "knew" we'd get ready in time.

Working on the fit-out 16 to 18 hours each day, with help from an army of mates coming round to my parents' suburban garage –

which we'd transformed into a boat-building factory! – was stressful, but fun at the same time. We were drinking way too much coffee, eating fatty greasy food as part of our "bulking up", only getting six hours a night of interrupted sleep and not getting any decent training in. It wasn't the best preparation for the Tasman.

On Christmas Eve 2006, we were ready to put her on the water for the first time. It was a day we'd been waiting for for years – five, to be exact. The night before the first dip, we were up till after midnight working on the wiring inside the cabin. It was important for us to install most of the electrics prior to that first dip, so we could see how the weight of the equipment affected her water line and stability.

We woke early and drove her down to Bobbin Head, accompanied by a few close mates and family. We were all excited, and to be honest we were expecting to see her blissfully glide through the water. As we reversed her down the ramp and her smooth, shiny hull slid in for the first time, a few bystanders gave a cheer. But when the kayak plunged into the cloudy water, the first thing we noticed was that she was sitting significantly higher than her DWL (Designed Water Line). We were horrified.

And then it got worse. She toppled onto her side and sat there listing on a 40-degree angle – that was her neutral position. Everyone there to witness the launch was silent, jaws dropped in disbelief. A million thoughts and emotions flooded through me – the most vivid being fear. We'd spent the last two years of our lives on the project (six months of that full-time) and put our life savings into it; we'd attracted a string of sponsors and talked up the expedition with the media and everyone else we knew. And now we had a kayak that didn't even float properly.

What was wrong? We took her out for a paddle and each painful stroke hurt us emotionally more than anything else. After getting a feeling for what was going on, we pulled her out and sat down, devastated. Everyone, including Jonesy, turned to me and asked, "So what now?"

I was in the driver's seat, but what we'd seen had got me so down I wanted someone else to absorb the responsibility and provide direction. Why couldn't Jonesy take the proactive step to rectify the situation? All I wanted to do was crawl under a rock and hide – let someone else deal with it.

Of course, as much as I felt pressured by people looking to me for answers, I knew I enjoyed taking responsibility for things, even though this hadn't exactly been one of our happiest moments. When we returned home, there was so much doubt running through my mind about what had gone wrong. Was it a design or a construction fault? We uploaded a couple of videos that we'd taken of her performance onto the internet to allow Rob Feloy, over in the UK, Larry Gray and Graham, the boat builder, to see what the problems had been.

It was Christmas time and understandably it was hard to get hold of these guys. But eventually we tossed some ideas back and forth as to what might be causing the problems, and right from the start opinions differed. It was difficult to manage the conflicting advice coming in from various parties. From Justin's and my perspective, we weren't experienced seamen, and we had to rely on logic and reason. The fact that the boat was sitting 8 centimetres above her DWL, fully laden, indicated that we needed to get her lower in the water.

We took the approach a yachtsman would take (thoroughly sanctioned by the builder) – we began to add ballast. We started lining sheet lead and lead bricks through the hull of the kayak, which helped, but wasn't enough. Fortunately, there were no occupational health and safety officers around as the backyard lead-smelting production line we had going would have horrified them!

Taking the boat down to the water, we realised this wasn't sufficient, so we decided to add a weighted centreboard with a lead bulb down the bottom of it. This finally resulted in her sitting beautifully upright, but she had become hideously heavy: she'd put on 180 kilograms over the festive season. We all seem to gain a little over this time of year – our kayak was no exception.

Rob maintained right from the start that the stability of a vessel should come from the hull shape. She was now sitting properly in the water, which was a good thing, but we were to find that this led to a whole wad of issues we weren't expecting; the most noticeable being that she was horribly heavy to paddle through the water. Fully laden we were weighing in at just over 1.2 tonnes, and we had to work hard each stroke to keep her moving.

Late one evening, I sat in the cabin with tangled red and black wires everywhere. I was blankly staring at the electrical diagram as I tried to make sense of which wire to connect to the PV discharge box (that was the name we gave it, anyway). Justin, myself and a few mates were working on the electrical system a couple of days after Christmas, and we were exhausted. As we hadn't yet named our trans-Tasman baby, and to take our minds off our fatigue, we started joking about the possibilities:

"Screamin' Seaman," I blurted.

The boys laughed, and said that our sponsors wouldn't be too happy with that one. We threw up a few others that seemed to get more and more absurd, before my brother Clary walked into the garage and, half grinning, cockily said, "Call it *Lot 41*."

We stopped working for a second and stared at one another.

What the hell was he talking about? Sensing our confusion, he continued.

"Well ..." he started. Moving onto the bow of the kayak he paused, crossed his legs like a doctor and leant slightly forward. "*Lot 41* was the lot number of a racehorse over in New Zealand back in the 1920s. A Sydney trainer, Harry Telford, was a bit of a battler, and he knew his thoroughbred bloodlines. He saw *Lot 41* was up for sale and immediately wanted to get his hands on him to train.

"He contacted an American businessman, Mr Davis, who agreed to buy him. However, after Harry shipped him across to Australia, Davis was disgusted to find that the horse moved awkwardly and had a face covered in warts, and he refused to pay for the costs of training him.

"Harry took on all the risk and made an arrangement that he'd receive two-thirds of the takings ... that was if there *were* any. He started training the horse hard, but he lost his first four races. Stable hands laughed at the horse, calling him a donkey. Anyway, he was named Phar Lap and became one of the greatest racehorses of all time.

"This was around the time of the Great Depression, when unemployment was up around the 30 per cent mark, and Phar Lap's success was a massive inspiration to people all over Australia. It gave them hope that things would eventually get better."

We sat in silence.

"Ah, you boys like it ... don't you?" Clary smiled.

It was perfect – we had a name for our kayak. *Lot 41* represented so many of the qualities we were trying to promote ... and it also had the Australia/New Zealand link. Phar Lap was known to have had a heart two-and-a-half times the size of his peers – that was exactly what we'd need to cross the Tasman.

Now that we'd named our baby, we could move on to more urgent practical matters. We'd struggled with *Lot 41*'s newfound weight when we'd paddled inshore, and taking her for a gallop offshore was even worse. The smallest of waves would wash over the pits, which made for uncomfortably wet paddling.

Both the central point of windage and centre of lateral resistance had been altered by the lead, which saw the nose of our kayak always blowing up into the wind. (The central point of windage (CLW) is that point on a craft where an equal level of surface area is exposed to the wind on either side of that point, when the wind is blowing from the side. The central point of lateral resistance (CLR) is a similar point, but below the water's surface, taking into account the surface area below.) Offshore, with the CLW being behind the CLR, this meant our nose kept blowing up into the wind, and with the extra lead, New Zealand seemed a long way off.

On 6 January, we had our official launch down at the Australian National Maritime Museum at Darling Harbour, where 400 spectators showed and all the TV stations had crews present. This was committing ourselves – we were due to leave within a few weeks. Because the actual centreboard which would address the stability issue wasn't ready yet, we craftily engineered a marine ply centreboard with 40 kilograms of weights from the local gym attached to the bottom. We hoped this would prevent *Lot 41* embarrassing herself – and us – by flopping on her side once she hit the water. We had our fingers crossed all day that this would keep us upright: we were terrified that the ply would break. Fortunately, it held firm.

After the launch we had some serious offshore testing to do, and our weather window was running out. Months earlier, we'd plotted an extensive list of offshore trials that we'd need to complete in order to prove both to ourselves and all our stakeholders that we were ready. But with time against us, we compromised and decided that one sea trial from Sydney to Newcastle would suffice.

We headed out to sea on our big offshore trial, which we expected to take three days, knowing that this was an essential box to tick before we headed east to NZ. If we couldn't paddle to Newcastle, how could we attempt to cross the Tasman? There was no chance.

On the big day, Terry Wise helped us crane *Lot 41* into the water at the Cruising Yacht Club at Rushcutters Bay. (We'd met Terry a few months earlier, when we'd been trying to find a sailing school to sponsor our Sea Safety Survival training, Marine Radio Course and the like. After beating our head against a brick wall with five other schools, we spoke to Terry, who, without hesitation, said, "Yep, sure – how else can I help?") The crane enabled us to attach the lead bulb on dry land, which was heaps easier than what we'd been doing – holding our breath and trying to do it under water! Terry then followed us out of the harbour on a yacht – *Brindabella* – with a crew of students he was teaching.

The previous couple of days had been quite frantic, doing last-minute prep for offshore. We'd been working long hours, but the quiet optimism the lead bulb had injected was more than enough for us to plough on. Finally, when *Lot 41* was in the water and our paddling clothes were on, we were ready to depart.

We weren't exactly psyched, though – this sea trial felt like a formality and something we *had* to do. We still had a million and one things to finish off and spending three days out at sea didn't feel like it was going to add much value.

As we set out, we could feel proud that, only a month before, we'd put *Lot 41* on the water and she'd flopped on her side – now we were heading out of the harbour on a three-day offshore voyage.

But from the start, it didn't feel right. The pressure knotted our stomachs as we made painfully slow progress out of Sydney Harbour into a 20-knot northeaster. We both had a bad feeling about this.

After paddling for six hours, we reached the heads just after midnight and found ourselves fighting a wind that was threatening to smash us onto the southern headland. At first it didn't seem to pose too much danger, but as we continued into the darkness we realised that the wind was having more of an effect on our progress than our paddles were.

To make matters worse, the sciatic nerve in my bum was pulsing pain through my leg and lower back. From all the paddling we'd been doing over the previous couple of months, my pelvis had rotated and had begun to crush a nerve the size of a thin sausage that runs all the way down the back to the feet. My whole left leg went numb – it was frightening not being able to wiggle my toes.

As we fought to avoid the headland and the surrounding reef, we couldn't stop and refuel as we needed to keep fighting against being forced onto the rocks. Our bodies began to cramp; we were growing weaker. First, we could hear the waves crashing on the headland and, as we were forced closer to them, the moonlight started dancing with the whitewash of waves. We were within 80 metres of the rocks and were paddling with every desperate ounce of energy we had left. It had seemed an unlikely threat, but it was now much too close.

I was more worried about losing *Lot 41* than I was about drowning. Somehow we managed to turn the bow into the wind, and began to edge away from the rocks at barely a kilometre per hour. By 2am we were finally creating distance between the headland and us. As we escaped land and headed seaward, we were swept south by the strong wind and current. Our plans immediately had to change from paddling north to Newcastle to paddling down to Wollongong. We crawled into the cabin (which, for some reason, had water sloshing around it) to get a couple of hours' sleep before hitting the sticks again. We were totally exhausted, dehydrated and constantly cramping.

Ten kilometres off Bondi Beach, throughout the next day the sea built and constantly buffeted us. We realised we were taking on water in nearly all bulkheads (the partitions inside the hull which, in theory, were meant to limit water leakage) – bad news. With the lead that we'd added, she was no longer positively buoyant; that is, if we took on enough water, she was going to sink.

We pumped and pumped, but it was a losing battle – the deckline had become our new water line, when it should have been 15 centimetres lower. As we pumped water out of the pits, it poured back in through the pits into the bow, as well as the cabin. We fought hard to get her back towards shore, but we were moving painfully slowly in a sinking kayak, 5 kilometres off the coast of Coogee. My mind drifted to those lucky people sunbaking on the beach, blissfully unaware of us out there, about to sink.

Justin was intent on getting Lot 41 back to land by our own means, but when a game-fishing vessel came by and asked if we needed a hand, we couldn't say no. He towed us back into the harbour, and when we finally moored up, the kayak was a sorry sight. She lumbered on her side from the volume of water she had filling her belly – about a foot sloshed above the cabin floor. Both the pits were full of water, as was the bow. We sat in a park, looking at Lot 41, feeling completely shattered. We'd survived, but our hearts had taken another beating.

After that disastrous offshore trial, on Australia Day 2007 we made the heart-wrenching decision to delay our bid till the following summer. We'd set ourselves a goal, we'd sold our expedition to the world, and then we'd had to delay: we'd failed. At this stage, Andrew was two weeks into his crossing and we assumed that he'd make it to New Zealand.

7

WET, COLD, SCARED ... ALONE

With our dream to kayak from Australia to New Zealand lying in tatters, never did we think our lives were about to become a whole lot more complicated.

After we informed our stakeholders, we decided to take a month off the project and re-evaluate our position on our return. We were over kayaking, over the project, but worst of all we were over each other. We'd spent so much time working and training with one another – we just needed some space.

Justin dealt with the disappointment of the horrendous sea trial by getting blotto in Sydney for a few days, then heading back to Indonesia, thoroughly depressed: less about the kayak not working than about what seemed to be the end of our friendship.

I took off down the coast to the Croajingalong National Park, on the border between New South Wales and Victoria, for some deep R&R. For the first week, I slept between 14 and 18 hours a day. I started taking small walks along the beach, often finding myself breathless and exhausted after a mere 10 minutes. Initially, I was also utterly depressed. If I ever thought about the project, my stomach would gurgle and I'd feel like puking. Slowly, though, I realised my body – and my mind – was doing what it needed to do to rejuvenate and re-energise itself.

On the morning of the fifth day, I was sitting in my van eating oats as rain spat on the roof. It seemed as if something was calling me down to the sea. As I made my way to the beach, completely naked, I looked out to the turbulent ocean and thought of Andrew. I'd been feeling deeply resentful about how he'd treated us, but suddenly I felt something completely different.

I stood, arms by my side, water beading on my nose and fingertips as I stared out to sea. I found myself whispering under my breath, "Go for it, mate, best of luck …" I repeated similar things for a few minutes. As my passion built, I found myself yelling out to sea, arms waving above my head, and – from out of nowhere – for the first time since my dog had died when I was 14, I began to cry. The tears turned to weeping and became lost in the rainwater trickling down my face. I had let go – let go of my feelings of anger, of wanting to prove something to the world. I was beginning to accept myself.

It must have been quite a sight, with storm clouds frothing the ocean and this loony standing there completely naked, yelling at the ocean and crying! I dropped to my knees and picked up a couple of handfuls of sand, clenching them tight. As other thoughts came flooding through, I realised that over the previous 12 months I'd abandoned the most important reason for being (and I know this might sound clichéd) – love. I'd distanced myself from my family and friends to achieve my goal, forgetting that, as the saying goes, happiness is meant to be shared. I'd found myself alienated with no-one to turn to – I imagined it might have been the same for Andrew. I could picture him having a similar epiphany out there on the Tasman, and it was thinking about this shared isolation that drew me towards him.

In an instant, I'd gone from hating him to accepting the situation and wanting to bury the hatchet. I looked down at the sand falling between my fingers and – with Andrew due to arrive in New Zealand during the next few days – I knew I had to fly there to congratulate him on a job well done. I hoped we'd be able to move on with our lives with minimal bad blood between us.

On returning to Sydney, I booked a flight to New Zealand and left two days later. It was a torturous 14-hour bus ride then from Christchurch to Te Anu, where Andrew planned to arrive, and after getting off the bus, I was surprised to get a phone call from his wife, Vicki.

"I understand that you've flown across to New Zealand," she said.

"Yep, that's right," I told her. "It's been a phenomenal voyage for Andrew and I want to shake his hand when he gets out of the kayak."

"That's very nice of you, but I don't want you there," Vicki replied in a deadpan voice. "This has been the worst six months of my life and you and Justin have contributed to that. I just want this whole thing to be over."

Stunned, all I could say was, "I'm sure this has been an emotional time for you ..."

"You have no idea."

"But all I want to do is shake his hand and then disappear ..."

"Please don't make this any more traumatic for me than it already is," she concluded. "Andrew's been through a terrible ordeal and we just want family and a few close friends there."

I was gutted. I'd flown to New Zealand and spent 14 hours in a bus in an effort to remedy the bad blood between us. I didn't know what else I could have done. I received a text from Vicki an hour later, reiterating that she didn't want me to show. I went to the backpackers and mulled over my options.

Obviously, I didn't want to be there when Andrew arrived if I wasn't welcome, so I ended up meeting a German backpacker and going trekking with her on nearby Stuart Island for four days. Returning from our circuit, we got a boat across to Ulva Island, where I remember lying on the ground staring up through the temperate rainforest trees and visualising the scenes at Te Anu. I imagined Andrew paddling through the calm fjords, with a couple of kayaks and a few larger vessels bringing him in. As he got out of the boat, he'd collapse and be helped to shore before being embraced by his family and whispering, "Never again. Never again."

The imagery was so vivid, I believed it. There didn't seem any doubt now that Andrew was going to make it to NZ – I was able to accept that. My compulsion to be the first across the Tasman had vanished and I realised I still had the motivation inside me to finish what I'd started and what Jonesy and I had been preparing ourselves for all these years. A chapter in my life was closed and I was ready to move on.

Andrew's expedition, though, had taken a tragic turn for the worse and unfortunately I couldn't have been more wrong about the arrival scene. When we got back to our B&B later that afternoon, a New Zealand couple who'd done the trek on Ulva with me came running out and screamed, "They found his kayak yesterday – he's not in it."

"What?" I replied, perplexed. Surely they'd been misinformed.

I ran to the computer in the mess hall of the B&B, logged on to the internet and saw that it was true – Andrew had disappeared. I quickly rang Pat to see what else he knew and he told me the facts. Unspoken, we knew Andrew was in trouble: because his kayak was so small, it would have made it incredibly difficult to get into his survival suit in an emergency, and the chances of finding someone in the water were remote. As each minute passed, the odds of finding him alive were growing ever longer.

"What can we do to help?" I asked.

Pat's response was blunt but realistic. "Not much."

"How many planes have they got out looking for him?"

"Two."

"That's not enough," I replied, feeling exasperated. "Do you think we can get AMSA [Australian Maritime Safety Authority] involved and send some search and rescue planes across tonight from Australia?"

"Who's going to pay for it?" said Pat, practical as ever.

"No idea. I don't care. We need to find him before tomorrow evening."

"I know, mate."

We both knew he was unlikely to survive that first night. He would have been so exhausted and so worn down, he would have resembled a chemo patient rather than a valiant explorer.

Talking to Larry – who experienced so much in his years of kayaking – he was upset but said, "I knew it was only a matter of time. I warned him that once he ate through his supplies, which provided a substantial part of his ballast, the kayak would become tippy. If he went over in the paddling position, Casper [the lid that he pulled over the cockpit] would fill with water and act like a keel. In his wasted state, he wouldn't be able to right the kayak in that situation. I suggested to him having an inflatable bag to put in Casper, but he wouldn't listen."

Many people, including Justin and me, have mourned how unfortunate Andrew was to be lost at sea so close to land – 65 kilometres off the coast of New Zealand. However, Larry brought up a point that hadn't occurred to us – that he was quite lucky to get as far as he did with such a basic design.

The last 30 days, he would have been mind-numbingly wet, cold, scared ... alone. Fatigue could have led to a series of misjudgements and bad decisions, and I can't help but imagine his final hours, floating in the freezing water without a survival suit, thinking of his wife and son and knowing he was about to die. In fact, I had the recurring, nightmare image – it came to me every day for weeks after Andrew's disappearance – of a tear running down his face as he gave a last thought to his family.

Forty-eight hours later, the New Zealand authorities called off the search. The emotional rollercoaster I went on during that time shocked me. Initially, I found it difficult to accept the news; and once I did, I had unrealistic hopes that he'd be found washed up alive on some beach. Later, the overpowering emotion I couldn't wash away was the dirty feeling of guilt. It was pretty hard to come to terms with the thought that if it hadn't been for me and Jonesy, this guy might still be alive.

We were adventurers, and as adventurers you have to ultimately accept responsibility for your actions. At the end of the day, there's no-one and nothing to blame, natural forces or anything else, for the outcome of an adventure. It is solely up to the individuals to achieve their objectives and come back alive. But no matter how many close friends told us we shouldn't feel guilty, I couldn't let it rest – it wouldn't sink in. The words Vicki had said constantly reverberated through my mind and I believed that Andrew would never have pushed so hard, and arguably gone out without sufficient testing, if it hadn't been for Justin and myself planning on crossing the Tasman.

During this period, I spent a lot of time reflecting on how much I was willing to sacrifice to achieve this target: what it was worth. Through these difficulties, the most pertinent lesson I learnt was that life is an experience to be shared, especially with the people closest to you. It's a lonely – and in Andrew's case, a tragic – passage if you do it entirely by yourself. It was this juxtaposition that confused me – I wanted to take people close to me along for the ride, and enjoy the experience with them, but because they loved me and wanted me to be safe, they didn't want the ride to happen. Where is the balance?

After I got back from NZ, I knew I needed to move away from home. I wasn't making any contribution to the family, and I felt that if I did find my own place, I wouldn't be inflicting my all-consuming Tasman obsession on them. Through visiting them once a week, we'd be able to amicably talk about things, with none of us having to constantly deal with the differences between us. I also wanted to reconnect with the friends I'd forgotten about, and God, who I hadn't really given much thought to for a good six years. The irony was that, to do this, I had to distance myself from them first.

Everyone dealt with Andrew's death differently. Unfortunately, many people close to him started numerous outlandish rumours about us. They needed an outlet to help grieve his loss and we bore the brunt of it, which, untypically, angered Justin more than me.

One rumour was that Jonesy and I had conducted a media conference when Andrew disappeared – although it wasn't subsequently mentioned anywhere in the media – to say that he wasn't the first across the Tasman and that he'd actually sailed across anyway. In other words, that Andrew clearly hadn't made it to shore so he couldn't claim that title; also, that his kayak had a sail on, which he'd used from time to time, so his expedition hadn't even really been by kayak. Another rumour was that when Andrew's SOS had come over the VHF, it was me making a hoax call – because I was over in NZ at the time.

I'd always believed that the adventure community was different from the world of office politics. However, as rumours became "fact" among some outdoor enthusiasts, I realised this wasn't the case. Baffled by the situation, I'd spoken to Larry, who described a history of disputes between adventurers, more or less confirming my thoughts. Justin and I had naively imagined that because we were all connecting with the natural world – our office being the great outdoors – we'd somehow transcend these undesirable human traits. Sadly, though, like all humans, we couldn't help polluting the landscape.

In the same way, we'd always thought of adventurers as living the ultimate life – freedom, purity, happiness. But our experiences were showing us that they (and I could probably include us too) were as flawed as anyone else. Because we're always striving to be stronger, fitter or faster – searching for a bigger mountain, larger ocean, reaching goals with less equipment or higher exposure to danger – our restlessness means that we're always searching for that elusive "summit".

At the time, I was confused about whether or not losing your life doing what Andrew did is, in fact, tragic. Putting aside his shortcomings – and we've all got those – here was a bloke who clearly had an intense flame burning inside him, and died doing something he was passionate about. There are other people who spend their whole lives in fear – fear of standing out, fear of failure, fear of success. To me, this seems much more tragic, but in many cases, society looks at this as being "responsible". Andrew hadn't let fear hold him back and neither would Justin and I.

Committing my thoughts to paper helped to cement my motivations for wanting to cross the Tasman and, as our preparations continued, life began to feel more fulfilling. Instead of being driven by anger – the "f*** you, f*** the world" kind of mentality – I started motivating myself by the love of what I was doing, positive thoughts of family and friends and enjoying not beating my body into submission. Interestingly, with this different motivation I began to train harder than ever before – I especially loved the freedom of the pre-dawn training sessions down on the water.

And for those first few months of 2007, every paddle I did, I couldn't escape thinking about what had happened to Andrew.

8

THE JOYS OF SEASICKNESS

Jonesy and I had to work on our relationship – we were close to wanting a divorce and there was no way we were going to be able to cross the Tasman if the resentment continued. Things had been strained more than ever due to the amount of time we'd spent together towards the end of 2006, the kayak not working and because of what seemed to me to be Justin's lack of initiative and drive. The main aspect of the project that I was still enjoying was the training – it provided my escape.

However, 2007 was a new year, and we had to approach the project with a slightly different tack. We went for an approach where Justin's responsibility was to co-ordinate the reconstruction of the kayak, and mine was to find another $50,000 of sponsorship. Jonesy really enjoyed immersing himself in the more detailed work, while I seemed to be better at the big picture, conceptual stuff – it was a good combination. We'd spend most of the time apart – including training – and report back at the end of the week on what we'd identified as our weekly targets. This distance revitalised our relationship – it was the only way we could deal with each other.

Part of the *Lot 41* reconstruction process was to fly our designer Rob Feloy across from the UK to spend some time seeing the kayak on the water and help devise a strategy to fix the problems we'd been having. So far, Rob thought it was a construction issue, Graham said it was a design problem, our electrician Craig blamed them both, while they both blamed him – no-one wanted to accept responsibility.

We didn't quite know who to trust, so we asked close to 10 different professionals in the marine design world for their advice. Their suggestions ranged from "The design is a dog – start again" to "Put a keel in the bottom and widen her beam". We weren't designers and found it difficult to say that one person's advice was more appropriate than anyone else's. Drawing up a matrix with all the different ideas, we began a process of eliminating each potential solution based on intuition and common sense.

There seemed to be three plausible options. For those nautically minded, they were to: add a long keel line through the whole kayak; add a lead bulb; or, finally, widen its beam – that is, make *Lot 41* wider. (Generally, the wider a craft, the more stable it will be.) Rob was keen on the latter. We ordered some foam and when he arrived in Australia we began to widen *Lot 41*. Starting stupidly wide, we began the process of cutting her down to a manageable width – surprisingly, this had a profound impact on her initial stability. It was a time-consuming process – adding foam, then heading down to the water to test it out – but we were finally starting to make some positive steps towards getting *Lot 41* seaworthy.

In May 2007, I organised to crew for a yacht being delivered from Brisbane to the Philippines. We figured it was a great opportunity to gain valuable sea miles and test my seasickness on a lengthy passage. Justin didn't get round to it, so he found himself short of yet another experience – we'd agreed at the start of the year that he'd have to organise things off his own bat, and if he didn't he missed out. To be honest, I was more disappointed in not being able to share an amazing journey with him than in his lack of initiative.

Our departure from the Royal Brisbane Yacht Squadron was delayed by the yacht not being ready – something I was beginning to get used to! Chris, the Kiwi skipper, was meticulous and wouldn't leave until the yacht was 100 per cent ready – a great lesson in passage planning. He carefully scrutinised the boat and her safety equipment, and spent the nights before we set sail examining the marine charts through these vibrant black-and-white-striped spectacle frames that would have been invisible on a baby zebra.

Eventually setting sail, we found ourselves bashing into a 40–45-kilometre-per-hour northeast wind all the way up the coast. We were sailing outside the reef and as soon as I went below deck, my face went green and my stomach churned. The other crew member woke me at 1am for the graveyard shift, and from the moment I sat up in my bunk, I knew I was about to spew. I quickly chucked my harness on and made my way on deck. I held it in for about 10 minutes, but then found myself leaning over the stern, violently spewing every few minutes. Looking up to a blanket of stars, I pleaded to feel better, even just to let me enjoy their beauty. The drugs weren't working – I began to suffer. I somehow lasted through my three-hour shift, then hit the bunk again.

Preparing for my next stint on watch I shoved a Stemetil suppository up my bum, which had next to no effect either. In the first 24 hours, I thought I was going to die. Then after 40 hellish hours, I was scared that I wouldn't:

From my first night watch I booted and booted and booted. Initially my food, then my liquid, then fluorescent bile. I couldn't hold down any food, water or tablets. If I moved position off my back I booted. I was unable to do my night watch on the second night and felt terrible – I was letting the others down and was pathetically immobile. I've eaten half a bowl of rice and three Vitabrits in four days. So weak – can hardly move. Urine is almost green. Do you call this living the dream?

With none of the medication working, I had now become well accustomed to the steps of getting sick. First, my whole body would go cold, leaving my hands and feet clammy and sweaty. Then, the extremities would get pins and needles, leading to coughing and burping. When my stomach dropped like an elevator, I knew it was time to find a bucket, because the vomit wasn't far behind. Uncomfortably – to say the least – I'd find myself shitting my pants as I spewed – part and parcel of being seasick. The pain and discomfort continued for the next week and I prayed for it to be over. I couldn't eat, I was horribly dehydrated and every time I lifted my head from the horizontal, I wanted to puke.

Eight days after leaving Brisbane, miraculously we reached the calmer waters closer to Papua New Guinea. I began to return to normal and found the sailing around the north coast of PNG stunning, as the water was as calm as a millpond. But although it was such a relief, it didn't mask the bigger issue. I was starting to think that the chances of me crossing the Tasman were becoming slim to nil. I was getting over putting myself through such brutal punishment: "I think this is going to be my last sea adventure for a very long time," I wrote.

Motoring along the north coast of PNG, we had our first glimpse of the unreliability of the engine – the trouble we had starting it and our failure to get the boat to reverse were early hints. At this time, we received news that a couple of typhoons had ripped through the area in which we were meant to sail between there and the Philippines and that the Australian embassy had issued a travel warning because of political unrest – basically, "Do not travel into the southern Philippines". Combined with what I'd learnt about my seasickness – not to mention the fact that neither the other crewmate nor myself was getting paid for all this – continuing the delivery didn't seem all that appealing. I felt horrible telling Chris, but hoped he'd respect my decision. No such luck – he was pissed. Unfortunately, he felt stranded in PNG and cornered.

"I'll stay with you for a few days and help get the yacht properly provisioned," I told him. "After that, I plan on getting off."

"No, you won't," he replied bluntly.

"What do you mean?" I asked, taken aback.

"You said you'd crew all the way to the Philippines – you can't leave me. Besides, I've got your passport."

I couldn't quite believe what I was hearing. "What are you saying, Chris?"

"I'm saying that I have your passport and I'm not giving it back till we get to the Philippines."

We argued for a few more minutes, but there was no middle ground. Although I could understand his predicament, I wasn't willing to sacrifice my safety to keep him happy. But as the standoff continued for a few more days, it seemed that he wasn't going to hand my passport over. I was going to have to get it myself.

The other crewmate was keen to leave the boat as well, and I volunteered to grab her passport too. So that evening, I stealthily crept into Chris's cabin while he was asleep. His earplugs were in and he was snoring as loudly as a freight train. I was petrified that he was going to wake up as I was reaching over him – he always slept half awake. It never ceased to amaze me how, if the sails were flapping or the sea was hitting the hull from a different angle, he'd suddenly be wide awake and up on deck to see what was going on. As I leant over to get the passports my heart throbbed. I was sure he could hear my heart beating as its bellowing seemed to fill the cabin. I snatched the bag, took it into another room, searched through it there, grabbed the passports, and then took the bag back to Chris's room without him noticing. I made it back to bed: but with my heart racing, it took me ages to get back to sleep.

The following morning I told Chris I was leaving the day after next. He said, "But I still have your passport."

"Not any more – I'm out of here."

It was a shame to leave on such bad terms. I really respected Chris and understood why he was acting the way he was. It's that pigheaded stubbornness that keeps you alive when you're an adventurer – you have to listen to your gut, whether you're up just below the summit or out at sea.

Choosing to fly, rather than sail, back to Sydney, I struggled with motivation for the Tasman project, as the seasickness cloud seemed to darken my entire outlook. Justin and I started having serious chats about me not going; something Jonesy didn't even think was an option. For the first time, he was showing determination and drive. He believed in us as a team. The problem for me was: was it too late? I'd almost convinced myself that the expedition was over for me. "Can I satisfy myself by saying I gave it my best shot – gave it everything?" I wrote. "Or will it gnaw at me forever?"

To my complete bewilderment, a few weeks after I got back to Australia, Pat received an interesting email from my crewmate, describing my condition on the trip to the Philippines. She wrote about how I hadn't even made it 24 hours before coming down with severe seasickness and for 10 days she'd nursed me with hydration fluid packs. Apparently, I was the worst she'd seen in 20 years at sea. She finished by scoffing at my ability to cross the ditch in a kayak when I couldn't handle the going on a 40-foot yacht.

While I felt betrayed by her email, it only motivated me all the more to win the battle with seasickness. This wasn't the only hurdle at the time, though – I was hugely disappointed with the work Jonesy had done while I was at sea. Without holding him accountable each week, nothing seemed to have got done: no training, and no work on the kayak. As I wrote in my diary, getting stuck into my best mate (just for a change):

> This past month he was meant to finish the steering, footwells and bow bulkhead – but the pits have been cut and that's it. He's been for one paddle, doing weights a couple of times each week, and weighs 98kg ...

I was now on a desperate quest to find an anti-nausea medication that worked on me. Deep down, I thought I'd tried everything, but we kept on trucking along with the sponsorship and reconstruction assuming we'd find a solution. In mid-June, two weeks after returning from PNG, I had an appointment with two professionals in the one day – a navy doctor and a traditional Chinese medicine (TCM) practitioner. Classic East versus West mentality.

The navy doctor took the hardline approach with drugs they give chemotherapy patients. When I went to the pharmacy to get my prescription, they said it'd take a few days as I'd need "drug committee approval". These were pretty hardcore, something that didn't worry me in the slightest – as long as they worked.

Approaching the TCM practitioner, she examined my issue from a more holistic approach and immediately started me boiling a concoction of herbs – cicada shells and a whole lot of other stuff – and acupuncture twice a week. It seemed a little "hocus pocus" compared to what I was used to, but who was I to disrespect 3000 years of accumulated knowledge?

Within a few weeks, sciatic problems I'd been having had disappeared and I was starting to feel my overall health becoming much more robust. There had to be something to this TCM stuff that I had no idea about. The combination of drugs from Western culture – "drug committee approval" had taken three days – and the acupuncture seemed to be working, but I needed to trial them inside the cabin tossing round at sea.

It was my responsibility to conjure $50,000 out of nowhere. I thought long and hard about how to go about doing this. We had to offer something different – something unique. Our 2006 sponsorship proposal had followed quite a traditional model, and while Olivia Donohue, the brand manager at Unwired, had been highly impressed by it, it wasn't delivering the money we needed. We had to show that if someone sponsored our expedition, we could provide "products" that would directly increase revenue. Whacking a sticker on the side of the kayak and wearing a T-shirt with a sponsor's logo just didn't cut it.

We developed a number of advertising campaigns for both our current sponsors (to encourage them to beef up their investment) and potential sponsors. Justin and I basically devised several ads for our investors – including organising our own photo shoots and graphic design and coming up with campaign slogans. As a result, we had advertising material that was pretty much ready to slap into a newspaper or web page. After over a hundred rejections from companies we'd approached, this slight change of tack helped deliver the funding we were after.

Around that time, Brad Gordon – the owner of one of our sponsors, Activate Outdoors in Sydney – started calling us the Tasman Rats. Slightly confused, we asked him one day why he was referring to us as a rodent that's pretty low on the whole animal social hierarchy.

"Simple. Given how tough you guys are, it'll be even more difficult to drown you than to drown a rat. Have you ever tried drowning a rat?"

Justin and I looked blankly at each other. "Can't say we have, Brad."

"Well, they're bloody impossible."

Of course, we still had plenty of actual training to do. That August, we headed down to Melbourne to deliver a Bavaria 32 yacht up to Sydney for a stockbroker who'd just bought it. This would be a great test of how my concoction of anti-nausea remedies was coming along. The result was – not good.

Back on land. The last day got pretty rough – 5m seas and 35 knots of wind. Got hammered by rain/hail etc. Jonesy did great. I booted again and felt like shit. Being up at the helm was alright, but as soon as I went below deck I got belted. The sea is brutal, man, so unforgiving – relentless. Gym work, interval sessions, training ... all seem pathetically inadequate for preparing us for the Tasman. All strength is completely sapped when crippled by seasickness – all you have left is your mind. That's the question – is my mind strong enough? I'm afraid. No, I'm shit scared.

Back on land, another doctor suggested I try hypnotherapy. Why not? This began a series of sessions for the next four months that I prayed would work. As the hypnotherapist I was referred to pointed out, the drugs I was now taking were some of the most hardcore on earth for anti-nausea. They cost $40 per tablet: for them not to be working, my mind must have been getting in the way. Her reasoning made sense. During the months of therapy we reprogrammed my mind in the "anchors" that I had around being at sea.

She provided me with meditation tapes which I began to religiously listen to each day leading up to and out on the Tasman. It became routine at sea that as soon as I jumped in the cabin, I'd put my earphones on and listen to half an hour of hypnotherapy. It sounds a bit hippyish, but with soft music in the background – similar to what I imagine you'd hear in a Buddhist temple (not that I've been to one) – a voice talks you through some breathing exercises, then paints a picture in words of pleasant surroundings. On a number of different levels this helped me deal with the motion. It trained me to enjoy getting into the cabin instead of dreading it, relaxed both my mind and body after a tough day's paddle and provided a much-needed escape from the ocean.

While I was trying to find a remedy for my seasickness, Justin had his own silent battle raging. From when he was a little boy, he struggled immensely with confined spaces and was badly claustrophobic, to the point where he had uncontrollable panic attacks – he used to hate playing hide and seek and dreaded his older brother locking him in a cupboard.

In between puffs of cigarette smoke, Ben, our website expert and philosophical consultant, gave him a number of breathing exercises and logic to channel his nervous energy: "The situation is not good, it's not bad – it just is." And another, as he swigged down a beer: "It's much worse out of the cabin than it is in here."

During our expedition, I'd often look down the tight end of our cocoon and see Justin's lips repeating this logic over and over.

This mantra allowed him to rationalise his suffocating fear and desire to throw himself out the cabin door. There was no room to panic out there, and he did a great job of containing himself.

But on the day before our first proper overnight sea trial, we weren't focusing on seasickness or claustrophobia: we were thinking about pigs. Up at the local hospital, we were schooled by our expedition doctor Glenn Singleman in how to suture and put IV drips into our veins. The former on pigs' feet, the latter we practised on each other.

On the first couple of sea trials we learnt heaps. Our first overnighter we paddled 20 kilometres seaward and cast the para-anchor – a parachute that secured us to the current, rather than to the ocean floor – then paddled back the next day. (This anchor kept the kayak perpendicular to the prevailing conditions and stopped us from tumbling sideways down the face of large waves. As a result, the cabin door was also sheltered.) During this trial, we identified some critical issues that needed remedying: the rudderstock – a rod attached to the rudder – was leaking 10 litres of water into the cabin per hour; the need for a new rudder; and the tangling of our sea anchor lines, both on deployment and retrieval. More importantly, the anti-nausea remedies still weren't working.

By the time we drove three hours north to Port Stephens in early September for a three-day offshore trial down to Sydney, we were feeling anxious but ready. Mum and Dad took us up – it was great for them to be part of our "mini-ex", as they could get more of a hands-on appreciation for the amount of work that went into preparing *Lot 41* for offshore.

Preparing to leave the boat ramp, we slipped the kayak into the water, put the rudder on, got into our paddling gear – all seemed great until we fired up our electrics. The power went on, but our

Comar Unit (a thingy that allowed big ships to see us on their radar and us to see them on our Toughbook laptop) wouldn't transmit or receive. After fumbling with it for a few hours, there was no getting it ready. There was no way we were going to paddle past all the container ships at Port Newcastle if they couldn't see us. Frustrated, we packed up and headed down to Sydney.

Two days later, with the transponder fixed, we did the 180-kilometre paddle from Port Stephens to Sydney. We were out for three days and two nights. This was the first time I'd been out at sea overnight and not spewed – you beauty! A "simple" (why hadn't I thought of it before?!) combination of the acupuncture, 80 bucks a day of chemo drugs, and hypnotherapy was the key. I've often wondered which one had the most impact. I'd have to say I was dependent on all three. We were incredibly relieved to have made this little discovery. On the final day, we rendezvoused with the NSW Water Police some 15 kilometres northeast of Pittwater, for some practice drills and to instil confidence in the authorities that we were covering all bases.

Working through the safety exercises, they received news over the VHF that there was a strong front expected to hit from the south. Immediately, they cut the tow lines away and said they had to get back to the harbour to rescue some much larger vessels that were already in trouble. "You boys will be right – you're obviously well prepared" were their parting words as a dark, heavy cloud bank began to roll in from the south.

We tried to leg it as fast as possible to get into protected waters before the front hit. As we paddled towards Barrenjoey Headland a fleet of yachts zoomed past our bow, rounded Lion Island and began to head back down south. Within half an hour, we could hear the wind approaching, foam and white horses formed everywhere – then *bam*. Forty-five knots from the south … and we were still 4 kilometres out to sea. The entire fleet turned round and limped into the leeward side of the Barrenjoey Headland.

In these kinds of conditions on the Tasman we would have chucked out the drogue (similar to a para-anchor, but designed for heavier weather) and bunked down. Being so close to the shore, we couldn't do that, as we would have been beached on the coast. Flashbacks of our ill-fated sea trial eight months earlier floated through my mind. We finally got into the calm waters protected by the headland, and the yachties looked on in disbelief. Some shook their heads, while others muttered, "You crazy bastards."

In the longer trials to come, we actually learnt less, as we'd refined our systems on board by that stage. Rectifying the big issues was obviously imperative, but learning how to manage the simple things made life much more comfortable: things like hanging our toothbrushes from the ceiling, which encouraged us to brush our teeth – without them there, we might have conveniently forgotten about it. We learnt the best way to clean our bodies with 200 millilitres of freshwater each day and how best to arrange our beanbag seats to prevent chafing. Padding was added to all parts of our body that came in contact with the kayak. Any hot spots during these sea trials would saw right through us by the end of the crossing.

Lot 41 had performed beautifully, but more importantly, my seasickness was under control. Our caution with the transponder had been a clear sign to our parents and all our stakeholders that we weren't going to get out on the ditch if everything wasn't 100 per cent right to go. It seemed to instil a lot of confidence in them. We were now ready for the Tasman.

In the days before we set off on the expedition, my diary showed how many different thoughts were racing around my head:

It's real. We're about to cross the Tasman. How do you prepare yourself for such a long, arduous, hazardous journey? Do you constantly think and analyse the emotions that your body is churning through or do you just do it? The systems are set up, Lot 41 is ready – we just need to do it now.

The meditation and positive visualisation has been amazingly powerful. Now meditating an hour each day. Two weeks to go. I'm so proud of who we've become and what we've achieved.

I was restless last night. Why … I keep asking myself. I'm confident in our training, our systems and our risk management. I know we're not going to get killed, so what am I scared of? Once we're out there doing it, we'll have fun most of the time – we'll be in a groove. What else? Seasickness? Nah … I've dealt with that. Sciatic? The Unknown? That's it. What does a 15m breaking swell actually look like? How will it feel? How bad are salt sores? How much weight will we lose? What will be the physical toll?" "I cried and cried and cried this morning – was it fear or was it a culmination of this dream finally being realised? I think both.

9

SEE YA, AUSTRALIA!

Staring up at me was a maimed chicken carcass, drowning in a hollandaise sauce – our last proper meal on land. The nervous chatter from our family and friends didn't really register as I held my knife and fork, looking down and reflecting. I was getting pretty edgy by now: I wished I had the paddle shaft – instead of cutlery – between my fingers.

There were a dozen people at the table in a restaurant in Forster, on the mid north coast of NSW, where we'd begin the expedition in the morning. Justin's and my parents were there – they'd been so anxious (and initially hostile) about our plans, but here they were, showing their support when it mattered. A few mates had come too. Tom, a good friend from school, had jumped into playing a lead support role in the previous week or so. Almost unintentionally, he'd become our manager of sorts. He knew how emotionally charged up we were, so he took all the "other-stuff" pressure off us, leaving Justin and me to prepare *Lot 41*.

While it was fantastic that everyone was there, to be honest the whole scene felt a bit claustrophobic, and the conversations around me were slightly overwhelming. I knew, though, that with 15 hours till our departure they were all feeling the way I was. The chatter was just their way of trying to soothe the atmosphere and swallow up a bit of time.

Surprising myself, I stood up and blurted out, "I need some space ... I need to go for a walk."

Everyone looked shocked – they'd travelled all this way to see us off, and now I was telling them I wanted to be alone. I guess we all deal with stress in different ways. Some people eat, others smoke and drink – I just needed a bit of solitude.

As I turned my back to walk away, air exploded into my lungs. I scampered to the water's edge to see, feel and touch the spray off the breakwall. The ocean was getting under my skin – it felt like I was entering expedition mode.

I had the iPod going and horribly clichéd music (but I loved it!) blared through my earphones. The theme song from *Legends of the Fall*, Enya and "Blowin' in the Wind" by Bob Dylan were on repeat. As I stood by the water, the power of the ocean surged and crashed against the rocks, blasting spray all over me. It was weird – it was like the courting stage, when you know nothing about each other, and the spray from the breakwall almost seemed like that first kiss.

As I gazed at the dark ocean, suddenly I felt quite lonely. I wanted some wise mentor to rationally talk me through the feelings that were welling up inside; someone else who'd been there, experienced the same anticipation, to take me through the rest of the countdown.

I was so focused on what lay ahead – and so oblivious to the outside world – that it didn't even occur to me to wonder how the dinner had ended up. But with Justin at the table, I knew my main course had found a good home. I strolled to the dock where Craig was doing some last-minute rewiring of the bilge. Realising I had nothing much to offer, I headed back to the cabin I was staying at in the local caravan park to try to snatch a few hours' nervous kip.

That last night, I actually slept pretty well. Waking just before dawn, I went for a walk, and as I did, I noticed my hands wanting to touch everything around me – from the smooth leaves of gumtrees to the coarse texture of sand on the beach. I took my shoes off so I could feel the ground. The gravel, the dirt, the sand – I wanted to absorb it all; brand my memory with the sensation.

When I got back to the cabin, Jonesy and Tom were beginning to stir.

"Morning, J."

"Morning, Cas."

"Hey, Jonesy, how would you like to go for a paddle?"

"Aw yeah … where to?"

"Dunno, mate … How 'bout New Zealand?"

"Sounds good to me. *Wee bang!*"

The day was finally upon us. We were there.

After a pretty relaxed breakfast, we made our way down to the jetty near the town centre, where *Lot 41* was waiting. She looked ready, although the question we'd asked ourselves for years resurfaced: were *we* really ready? We'd always told ourselves that on the day of our departure we wanted to look at our kayak and set-up and know that the weakest link in the operation was us. Box ticked: *Lot 41* was ready to go for a trot. That final morning was filled with checking, rechecking and triple checking our critical gear and ensuring we had everything on board and ready to go.

Once the boat was prepared, we got swept up in a whirlpool of media interviews and meeting the local people of Forster. Almost three years earlier, Clouds had described to us in great detail the strong, warm current that roars down Australia's east coast, the EAC (East Australian Current). He'd been watching its position closely over the previous month, wanting to find the optimal location to leave from. As it was the closest point on the coast to give us access to the current, Forster was the obvious place – although we'd only reached that conclusion three days before the launch.

It was critical that we caught the ebb tide out of the harbour, as the water flows at an exceptionally fast rate. Our departure time of 1pm was dictated by the tide tables. Unfortunately, because of the huge volume of water flowing out of nearby Myall Lakes via a very small opening, the tide tables were incorrect, and we found ourselves nervously waiting for an extra hour. We were to learn right the way across our passage that the power of the sea would dictate our every move. We couldn't fight the ocean: it was up to the Tasman to allow us a passage across.

Some other kayakers had come to paddle us out of the heads and were able to test the tidal strength for us. We got the green light – the tide was ready. We jumped into the cabin of a moored vessel and got dressed in our battle fatigues: one pair of merino wool thermals each. These would be the only set of clothes we'd have until we reached the shores of New Zealand. Then we vigorously rubbed Sudocrem – which had the consistency of thick, thick zinc cream – on our backsides, underarms and anywhere we expected to get chafed.

How we both longed to just be out there. Separating us from the ocean were the formalities prior to departure, and once our passports were checked off by Customs, it was time to farewell our families and friends.

The disappearance of Andrew McAuley heavily clouded the atmosphere on that wharf. You could see on the faces of everyone there a look of "Are we ever going to see you again?" Mates who'd always taken the piss were soberly quiet with tears welling up. There were no jokes, only silent embraces. As I held my baby sister Lil, I began to sob – I could feel her pain and suddenly wanted nothing more than to go on a holiday just as we had as kids and be surrounded by my family. Then there was Mum: she held me just so tight. How do you let your son go on a journey you're afraid will be his last? Dad had left early that morning. He couldn't deal with the intensity of that final farewell.

Before stepping into the kayak, Jonesy and I embraced each other powerfully. It was time to rock.

Justin popped his head into the cabin to switch on the power for the bilges and tracking beacon. Silence. There was nothing – no power.

"Shit," came Jonesy's reply. Then he continued, "Quick, call Craig – we're going to have to delay departure."

With our goodbyes said, cameras rolling, and the crowd cheering, postponing the launch would have been slightly embarrassing.

I calmly asked, "Hey, Jonesy, mate – are you sure the main power's on?"

Wiping the sweat from his face, Justin muttered, "Whoops!" Crisis averted.

The moment we sat in *Lot 41* we'd succeeded in our mission. Just to be there, we'd fought countless setbacks and inner demons. Never could another naysayer give us grief about being talkers ... not walkers.

As we paddled out of the marina, a local began to chant: "Aussie, Aussie, Aussie."

Most of the crowd of 400 responded: "Oi, Oi, Oi."

It continued. "Aussie," "Oi," "Aussie," "Oi."

"Aussie, Aussie, Aussie."

You probably know the rest!

Making our way to the edge of the breakwall, we were engulfed by a flotilla of kayaks. Being among our fellow paddlers helped soothe the nerves. On our right-hand side was Bruce Richards, one of the owners of Pittarak kayaks, who'd been with us right from the start. We'd discussed the idea of paddling across the Tasman with him four years ago when the idea was a mere foetus. Back then, Justin and I had never been to sea in a kayak. He saw two hopelessly naïve kids who had a long way to go. As we paddled out, I remember turning to Bruce for comfort and saying, "How does she look?"

"Bloody fantastic," Bruce replied. "I'm just so proud of you both."

That was about the most pertinent reassurance we could've got at that moment.

"Thanks, Bruce ... thanks for everything."

The kayaks dropped off one by one, as did the larger vessels. Bruce was determined to be the last man standing; to be out at sea with *Lot 41*. Then he'd get to paddle back to land in isolation. He'd probably be reflecting on his first contact with us four years earlier, when we were two kids with an idea much bigger than he thought we could digest.

We paddled through for six hours, breaking every hour for five minutes to chew on a bar or some nuts. This would become our routine on the Tasman. It was important that we kept our glycogen levels up so we could paddle for hours on end without fatiguing too quickly. (The energy we used while paddling was similar to trekking. Our heart rates were usually around 105–130 bpm.)

Lights began to flicker up and down the New South Wales coast as dusk approached. We were 20 kilometres out to sea, knowing that tomorrow we'd leave the sight of land. Tomorrow we'd be well and truly alone.

With land still not far away, that first night was reminiscent of another sea trial as we drifted 16 kilometres south-southeast with our sea anchor deployed. We nervously went to sleep half expecting to have to get up in the middle of the night to paddle our way off the coast. Waking every couple of hours, we had to keep an eye on our drift. At 2am we'd moved 10 kilometres east of Sugarloaf Point – 30 kilometres south of Forster – and out of immediate danger of being washed back onto the shore. The speed we were travelling at indicated that we were on the edge of the thunderous East Australia Current that Clouds had warned us about.

DAY 2

We woke at 5.30am and were in the pits paddling by 6.30. Jonesy was feeling a little seedy after spending some time on the laptop looking at the ocean current maps, so he took a Phenergan, one of my hardcore seasickness tablets. But he felt it weighing down his eyelids and struggled to fight off sleep all morning. Just before midday, he sucked on some ginseng bark, which did a decent job of keeping him awake.

"Mate, I've got no idea how you take these things twice a day without falling asleep!" he called out from the rear pit.

"Anything's better than feeling seedy out here, bud," I replied.

The weather was stable, progress was exceptional and spirits on board *Lot 41* were high. After a mere 24 hours, we'd travelled 78 kilometres southeast from Forster and we started playing the "When will we arrive in New Zealand?" game. My first guess was 16 December, while Justin, who's always been the one to err on the side of caution, guessed 18 December. A dose of optimistic naivety is often a critical personality trait of anyone setting out to achieve an unlikely objective – we were no exception.

It was on day 2 that we invented the simple, but riveting (to us) "24-hour stat game". It beat "I Spy" hands down. Religiously, each day at 1.15pm – the time we'd left Forster – we'd guess how far we'd travelled in the previous 24 hours. The person whose guess was closer won an extra bite of chocolate or a jelly bean. Okay, it wasn't exactly *Mastermind*, but it was this kind of game that kept us amused out at sea.

Flying along in the EAC, we were greeted by our first albatross. We weren't expecting to see these majestic birds until we were at least a week out to sea. With their monstrous wingspan, improbable aerodynamics and delicate gliding, they really are the Airbus 380 of the natural world. They have an intangible, regal presence, quite similar to the lion back on land. They reign supreme.

As we deployed the sea anchor at the end of the day, we felt quite chuffed with our progress. Although we were well out of the sight of land, surprisingly we weren't too fussed. In fact, we were loving it.

Pat – who'd steered us through the food and sleep deprivation exercise with his army mates a few months earlier – had agreed to be our eyes and ears on land. Every night at 8pm, we'd have our daily schedule, in which we discussed a pre-determined 10-point checklist – weather, physical health etc – and agree on a suggested bearing for the next day's paddle. Unfortunately, our sked that evening wasn't what we wanted to hear. We'd apparently travelled too far south during the day and risked being swept up in an eddy back to Australia – right back to Sydney, to be precise. Pat wanted us to get out and hit the sticks all night, but after 12 hours in the pits we were shattered.

We discussed our options and agreed to get four hours' kip and then start paddling again at 3am. The elation of our fast start hadn't lasted long. Mother Tasman was about to put us through the first of a series of obstacles. She was beginning to test our resolve – snapping like a scorpion at the slightest complacency or disrespect.

Nevertheless, we were still feeling pretty good as we settled into our sleeping bags.

"Goodnight, Cas," Jonesy called out. "See ya in a coupla hours."

"Night, mate ... See ya, Australia!"

Justin and myself as young kids. As Craig – the *Lot 41* electrical engineer – used to say: "That's cute."

The two of us as teenagers. No wonder girls didn't talk to us.

Above left: Justin and myself wearing skirts together. Cadets at school gave us our first taste of the outdoors.

Above right: One of our early bushwalks together. Ninety kilometres in 50 hours and no sleep. Fun!

Right: Celebrating our successful 2560-kilometre paddle down the Murray River in 2001–02. Note the huge crowd there to greet us.

Below: Midway across Bass Strait, during our 350-kilometre paddle in 2006 between Wilsons Prom and Tasmania.

Above: A model student at the University of New South Wales. Justin (on the left) studying hard for his end-of-semester exams.

Right: Here I am mountaineering in NZ with Mount Aspiring in the background, two weeks after the fall that nearly killed me.

Below: Rock climbing at Mount Arapiles in Victoria on the iconic Kachoong in 2004.

Above: In the early stages of construction of *Lot 41*. Our overgrown baby dwarfs the red double kayak in the background.

Right: The insides of *Lot 41* before the top half was put on. You can see the "waterproof" bulkheads that failed on our disastrous sea trial in January 2007.

Bottom left and right: Justin and I worked for thousands of hours on *Lot 41*.

Above: An ad we designed for our major sponsor. We went to some pretty extreme measures trying to obtain funding for the reconstruction of *Lot 41*.

Left: It's January 2007, we're 10 kilometres off the coast of Sydney on our first sea trial, and we're about to sink.

Below: Lot 41 on her side and full of water after that dismal sea trial.

Some of the team who made it all possible. *Top, left to right:* Terry Wise, Craig Thomsen, Rob Feloy. *Middle, left to right:* Tom Mitchell, Pat Brothers, Roger Badham. *Bottom, left to right:* Ben Barin, Larry Gray, David Spence.

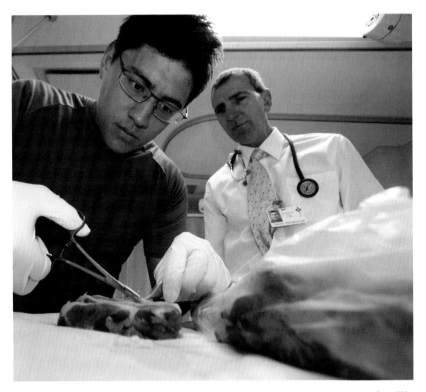

Dr Glenn Singleman teaching us how to suture and apply IV drips to one another. We practised on pigs' hoofs, hoping that we'd never have to use our training on the Tasman.

Battling seasickness sailing from Brisbane to Papua New Guinea, May 2007. At first you think you're going to die. Then you're afraid you won't.

The last time we saw Andrew McAuley (left) alive. We thought of him constantly when we were out on the Tasman.

Departure from Forster, on the New South Wales north coast, at the beginning of the Tasman expedition, 13 November 2007. Okay, it's time to rock!

Saying goodbye to Mum was one of the hardest things I've ever had to do.

Justin reminding his mum to eat her vegetables while he's away.

Paddling out past the breakwall at Forster: 2200 kilometres to go.

10

NUDE MANOEUVRES ON THE
HIPPY TRAIL

DAY 3

Aagh! Unfortunately, the four hours' sleep we'd allowed ourselves
on that second night was rudely interrupted every half an hour by
a mouthful of cold Tasman sea splashing over my face. The cabin
of *Lot 41* was no bigger than two coffins stacked on top of one
another, and when both of us were inside, with hatches battened
down, the stuffiness and condensation were almost unbearable.
Moisture would drip from the roof and our skin would stay damp
and clammy. At every available opportunity we'd leave the cabin
door or portholes open to allow some fresh air to waft in.

The stern of *Lot 41* faced up into the wind, so we were safe
from the majority of waves, but the occasional rogue would surge
from the bow and soak me, as my head was at the door. This was
part of our initiation at sea and a step towards understanding the
different sea states. By the end of the expedition, we intuitively
knew how far we could leave the door open or which porthole not
to close. This game we played each night had big stakes: the more

the door was open, the more fresh air penetrated the cabin and the better we slept. But if we got too adventurous, we'd cop a mouthful of water.

At 3am, fighting the sleep monster who was dragging our eyelids shut, we got up, knowing we had to get a good 15 hours' hard yakka in to escape the "Sydney eddy". Paddling in the dark for the first time on the expedition, we nervously made our way into the pits, swamped by the rich blackness of the Tasman – it looked like an endless void of crude oil. Putting my wet thermals on, a rogue wave crashed over the top of me, threatening to tear me out of the kayak. I was scared. As I scurried like a rat into the front pit, I began to dry retch. I'd been here before – I was about to vomit. Sickening memories from the delivery to PNG six months before and countless uncomfortable days off Sydney's northern beaches began to consume me. Then a lava flow of breakfast and the previous night's dinner erupted uncontrollably out of my mouth.

My immediate reaction was anger: we didn't have the rations to waste. I knew how quickly my strength would melt away if I couldn't hold my food down – the expedition could be over before we'd really begun. A cloud of semi-digested food permeated the surrounding water and I recognised chunks of food I'd eaten before we left Forster. It made me weirdly homesick. I'd never been one to chew my food properly – as a kid, I'd always got into trouble with Mum for scoffing down my meals.

As I sat in my pit and secured the spray skirt (a neoprene cover worn around our waists that sealed the cockpit lip to stop water from coming in), I began to feel more comfortable, with the oil-slick sea temporarily kept at bay. Justin slid over to his pit and we began paddling in a half-dazed state into the darkness. Today would be a defining day – if we rested too long, we'd find ourselves back in Sydney Harbour …

The monotonous black hours rolled by and we found ourselves constantly nodding off, our chins smashing against our chests. I've never been one for No-Doz, but that morning I became a convert. Our adage throughout the rest of the voyage became "Why suffer when you don't have to?" Some people might extend that question to: why were we out there then? At the time, we were asking ourselves the same thing.

Engulfed in complete darkness we paddled in silence. Night paddling is quite pleasant when you can steer off the stars, rather than focus on the compass. We were greeted by a dreary dawn, with the jet-black night giving way to an overcast sky that radiated a spectrum of dirty greys across the landscape.

Endurance events in the past have always taught us that with the coming of the light on a new day, morale is automatically charged up. After a couple of hours in the pits, the motion sickness started to abate and I found myself able to hold down food again. To our relief, the seas began to subside and by 9am we were faced with a stunning morning. Throughout the journey, it never ceased to amaze us how quickly the sea state could turn nasty and just as easily switch the other way.

We were able to rip off our waterproof jackets (kayakers called them "cags") and enjoy the tranquillity of a 10-knot northerly. Looking at our marine charts, we'd exited the Australian shelf and now had 4 kilometres of ocean beneath. The water had also changed colour – it was now a deep azure. Bubbles danced off the paddle blades on entry and swam in the clearest water we'd ever experienced.

Apart from the expected blisters on our paws, the biggest discomfort was an outbreak of pimply-looking lumps that formed on my entire back. We didn't know whether it was an allergic reaction, nutrition related or something else. Fortunately, we were able to paddle with our shirts off that afternoon, which gave it a bit of a chance to air out, and the lumps cleared up a few days later.

After 15 hours of paddling, we'd fought our way out of our first test – the Sydney eddy. The Tasman rewarded our efforts with a stunning dolphin performance, as a school of 30 of them gracefully danced by our starboard bow. Back on our target course, we looked forward to a good night's sleep.

"I wonder what the people looking at the tracking are saying," Jonesy commented as he prepared the evening meals. "'They're going to make New Zealand in 10 days ... good on 'em!'"

Although we'd had a couple of tough days, we soon settled into our daily routine. Our morning ritual consisted of Justin turning on the satphone (short for satellite phone) and me looking at the GPS to see where we'd drifted through the night. Then we'd send Pat a message via the phone, communicating how the night had gone.

As Jonesy packed up the sleeping gear, I'd tie a rope round my tummy and make my way into the rear pit, naked, to empty the bowels. Pooing in public was remarkably easy – and surprisingly good fun. I squatted at the edge of the boat, with my perfectly pristine bum still a few days away from an explosion of chafing, salt sores and blistering (sorry for the imagery there). When I was finished, I used the salt water to clean up; we didn't have the luxury of nice soft dunny paper on board. I then lathered a thick layer of Sudocrem between my butt cheeks and under my armpits.

Next it was time to get dressed, as I donned a wet, chilly pair of thermals which had been sloshing around in the bottom of the cockpit all night. In order to prepare for this torturous process, we'd had cold showers all through the previous winter to prepare us for the inevitable discomfort.

Once I was dressed and ready to paddle, Jonesy would come out and repeat the same process. While he was getting ready, I'd bring in the para-anchor via the retrieval line. This floating line was attached to the apex of the parachute, so, as you began to retrieve it, the parachute would collapse, allowing you to pull it towards the kayak.

Jonesy was on the helm as such, and I was the navigator looking at the GPS to make sure we were on course. Both of us had a deck-mounted compass to keep a check on our relative bearing but this was often slightly deceptive. It was quite difficult for Justin to maintain a consistent reading as the waves would continually buck us off course. If we were greater than 20 degrees out, I'd often say "direction" and he'd respond on the rudder. On windy, cloudy days, poor Jonesy had to stare at his compass for hours on end, cautiously fiddling with the rudder. He'd get irritated if I mentioned the "D" word when he was drifting off for more than 30 seconds, but why paddle further than we had to? The pull of the ocean dictated our direction over ground much more than we could. In that first week especially, we could be paddling due east, and find ourselves drifting just as quickly to the south, due to the strength of the EAC.

One thing that had already amazed us about the expedition was how many people seemed to be taking an interest in our progress. Pat had mentioned in the sked that first night that the media had jumped on our departure from Australia – all the major domestic TV networks had run stories about the expedition, while CNN and BBC World had also picked it up. Jonesy seemed to get more excited than I did about this exposure, but it was still quite motivating.

Then there was the website we'd set up to allow people to follow our journey – www.crossingtheditch.com.au. We'd expected maybe 500 people to log on to the site each day, but from day one, 5000 people logged on, and that number built throughout the expedition.

DAY 4

We woke in the morning to an alarming SMS – there was a serious risk of getting swept up in another adverse current. This one was twice as strong and would tear us north towards Lord Howe Island. We hit the sticks at 6.30am on a bearing of 170 to 180 degrees. Paddling hard all day, we fought to get further south. We were at 34.639 degrees south and had to get to 35 degrees to avoid being swept up in the current we dubbed the "hippy trail" (because it'd take us on a meandering detour via Lord Howe Island). As we packed up shop that evening, our GPS was showing that we were drifting north. We were heading for Lord Howe and we were buggered.

Just making our 8pm sked, as we'd tried to paddle for as long as possible, we found ourselves at a crossroads. We either had to hit the pits all night or the whole expedition would be over. We decided to paddle two hours on, two hours off – with one of us resting and the other paddling – at least until 6am. The current was sucking us up north, and while we didn't know whether paddling all night would be enough to get us out of this current, we weren't going to go down without giving it everything.

At that low point, you seem to always be able to take one more stroke. Trying to fathom 1.7 million strokes is on a scale the body can't digest; however, it can take just that one more. That night, we kept telling ourselves it was those single strokes that would get us to NZ.

But I was beginning to feel beaten. I was tired, and hadn't been able to fuel sufficiently from the previous morning's vomiting. All

I wanted was rest. Suddenly, Jonesy stepped up to the plate. "I'll do the first shift," he said enthusiastically.

I was taken aback. When we were bushwalking, I'd always shoulder the heavier pack or fetch drinking water from the nearest creek: I was the stronger one. And now here was Justin taking the lead. I was too exhausted to argue with him, and he crawled over me, performing the first of many "nude manoeuvres" to come. I drifted asleep immediately, knowing I'd have to get up in a couple of hours for my shift at midnight.

Seconds later, the cabin door creaked open.

"Cas, it's time for your shift, mate," came a garbled, but chirpy voice.

I thought it was part of a dream. Two hours couldn't have flown that quickly.

"Cas, get up, mate, it's 0300," Jonesy repeated.

As I woke, I realised that he'd paddled three hours more than he was meant to. The next morning he explained that he'd found nirvana for the first time in his life – although he'd been past the point of sheer exhaustion, he'd never been happier. Despite the negative situation he'd felt an absolute certainty that we were doing what we were put on the planet to do. Kicking myself into gear, I knew I had to get out and paddle for my mate. He'd just done an awesome job and I wasn't going to let him down. Exiting the cabin, looking like someone who'd had four hours' sleep in the previous 48, I heard Jonesy say, "This is why I'm out here with you … you're bloody tough and as mad as a chimp."

A blanket of stars beamed above. The sky was like a black canvas wrapped round a light globe, poked with little holes releasing shafts of light in all directions. And with the sparkling reflections of the stars in the waves, you could almost pretend you were floating … until a rogue wave would bring you crashing back to reality. As I struggled to paddle east, the sleep monster kept tapping on my shoulder: I had to get through the night. After downing a couple of No-Doz tablets and listening to a "Love Songs" playlist, the energy around started to change. The stars began to fade as the glow from the east warmed – I was surprised how light it became before the sun peered over the horizon.

That last hour was hard. Every few minutes my head would drop, and I'd feel my hands let go of the paddle. I'd pull my eyelids open and continue for a couple more minutes before the cycle repeated itself. For the first time, I almost found the barrier where I literally couldn't take that one more stroke. But that was why we were out here: to test ourselves. The only thing that kept me going that last hour was the all-consuming determination not to let my best mate down. Sure, we'd had our differences before we'd left, but the truth was I loved Jonesy like a brother.

It was only later we learnt that more than 500 of our family, friends, and people we'd never met were up with us that night, watching our progress and sending us all the positive energy they could muster. I'm certain that energy had an impact on our attempts to escape the hippy trail. I paddled through to 6.30am, and as I looked down at the GPS, hands white and wrinkled, I noticed we'd begun to drift east-southeast. We'd got out.

DAY 5

A rogue wave leapt stealthily into the cabin at 11am, drenching us completely. It was the Tasman's idea of a quiet wake-up call.

Bleary-eyed, we rose feeling exhausted, but chuffed. We were back on track. The focus over the next few days would be to try to reduce our fatigue levels and establish some sort of sustainable routine. We couldn't keep these all-night pushes up for the entire passage: our bodies wouldn't handle the punishment.

We paddled a few leisurely hours in the afternoon, then entered the cabin nice and early. Before falling asleep, Justin called his parents for the first time on the passage. After some idle chit-chat, he told his dad he'd had the most amazing moment of joy and clarity the previous night, and that he'd never been this happy in his life.

Unfortunately, from my perspective, I hadn't come anywhere near reaching nirvana. In fact, at times I'd felt almost the complete opposite – out of my element and scared. Speaking of nirvana, though, that night, for the first time on the voyage, we were able to get a decent sleep – about eight glorious hours.

DAY 6

As we stuck our heads out of the cabin the next morning, we realised day 6 was going to be wet. When it was a wet day's paddle, we had our spray skirts done up and Gore-Tex cags over the top. Although this kept us relatively warm, the barrier didn't give our skin a chance to breathe. We soon discovered that this resulted in both of us getting violent outbursts of prickly heat when we entered the cabin in the evening (prickly heat being a skin irritation that attacks in waves, feeling like thousands of needles jabbing into you – it's kind of unpleasant).

Lying side by side, Justin's head was crammed up the far end near the rudder and mine was next to the cabin door, so I could spew easily if I had to.

Jonesy kept me awake for about two hours that night as his body spasmed – with his hands involuntarily slapping and punching his naked torso. Sleeping in the womb of *Lot 41* was cramped to say the least, and whenever Justin uncontrollably spasmed, I'd be woken up. It wasn't his fault, though, and I couldn't get angry at him.

That day we'd had our first decent "deep and meaningful" chat. Adventures have always given us the time out to think and talk about all the important stuff in life – back home in Sydney, we were often too busy to reflect on the past and dream about the future. We mulled over the universal topic – girls and love – for hours. Our conversations out in the wild have always seemed to gravitate towards this supernova. We've spent hours – no, days – in these kinds of discussions while kayaking and bushwalking. On this particular day, I found myself talking about my high-school sweetheart Jen, who I never properly dated (she was the girl I'd invited to the tragic school formal), while Justin was reminiscing about a girl he'd gone out with a couple of years earlier (his only "real" relationship).

Another game we played that day was to paint a picture of our lives in a year's time. One of us would prod the other in growing the vision. We then did the same for two years' time, five years', 10, 20 etc. The rule was that you had to spit out exactly what you were thinking – you weren't allowed to let your mind get in the way of what you said. As a result, the words came out so quickly they were almost incomprehensible. Which made the game more entertaining, for some reason. After listening to my premonition, Justin concluded with absolute certainty that I was destined to be a madman.

Our conversations were interrupted only by the occasional wave crashing over us, and the Squealing Game. Each time we were splashed by a wave, we'd see who could make the most girly *sqweal* – a hardcore game for two courageous young adventurers, I know. Somehow, Jonesy always seemed to one-up me on the *sqweal* pitch.

Getting ready for cabin mode at the end of day 6, we did a stocktake of our bodies. We were both alarmed by the chafing between our arse cheeks, the angry-red skin reminding us of the bubbling surface of a lava flow. My right shoulder felt as though I was back in Year 5, with the school bully giving me dead arms all day for eating olives in the playground. The final point of note was the large blisters that had formed on our thumbs. We'd been training close to 30 hours a week in the build-up to the crossing and before we'd left we had significant calluses. Unfortunately, because we were so wet the calluses disintegrated and fell off, leaving soft, tender skin underneath which took a beating.

As we did our 8pm sked, Pat told us that we'd paddled 70 hours out of the last 130 – no wonder it was like experiencing the world's worst hangover. We'd never imagined that our hangover expertise from all those parties at uni would actually prepare us for dealing with the Tasman!

DAY 7

We began the day with a contentious question, destined to fire the debate and scorn between us for hours: who's the most gorgeous woman in the world?

"I can't remember her name, Jonesy," I said, because I couldn't remember her name, "but she's short, blonde, in a modern, olden-day movie …"

"You're going to have to give me more than that, Cas."

"Okay, in the movie she has really red lips and small feet."

"Oh, *that's* a giveaway," said Jonesy, possibly with a hint of sarcasm.

We went on for an hour, with my clues becoming more and more hopeless. Eventually, Justin asked exasperatedly, "Is it Elisha Cuthbert?"

I still wasn't sure, but the name kind of rang a bell. "Yeah, that's it – she's beautiful."

Two weeks later, Jonesy was talking about a movie with Scarlett Johansson, and I realised it wasn't Elisha I'd been thinking about at all, it was her. It's probably pretty obvious I don't subscribe to *Who* magazine.

These conversations were a great distraction from the niggling physical problems we were experiencing. For instance, the chafe on the bum was getting bad: we'd quickly learnt that as soon as you planted yourself on the beanbag any wiggling would agitate the raw chafe and pain would dart right up your back. The pain was so bad, in fact, that every hour I found myself having to lather Sudocrem all over my backside.

As I was in the front pit, poor Jonesy was subjected to the hideous sight of me dacking myself, bending slightly forward like a lawn bowler and rubbing this cream into my bum crack. Prior to the ditch, Justin (like most people) had associated zinc cream with beach family holidays and summertime. Sadly, he now sees it in a completely different light – it'll never be the same!

It came out of nowhere. The monotony of life in a stark landscape tends to bring out your inquisitive nature, and we were no exception. Paddling along in silence that afternoon, Justin blurted out, "I think there's something in the water 100 metres up ahead."

I muttered the first thought that occurred to me. "Great, our first shark ..."

"No, mate," Jonesy replied. "It's yellow."

I stupidly tried to picture a funny looking yellow shark. Even more stupidly, I pictured it out loud.

"No, you idiot, I think it's a buoy or something."

We eagerly paddled towards it, welcoming anything at all to break the monotony. Bobbing up and down, we were only able to get a fix on it when both the mystery object and *Lot 41* were on the crest of a wave. As we pulled up, we realised it was a yellow fishing buoy – about the size of a soccer ball. We glided next to it, stared at it excitedly, poked it … then lifted it out of the water. To our astonishment, the underbelly was littered with barnacles and algae. An ecosystem had formed underneath with countless slimy mackerel: little did we know that *Lot 41* would nurture a similar ecosystem in the not-too-distant future.

It was a fantastic discovery. Our faces beamed with childlike excitement and we laughed and yelled as if the Wallabies had won the World Cup in the 80th minute. This simple encounter kept us talking and happy for hours. Where had it come from? Had it fallen off a fishing vessel in a storm or drifted from a distant land? How long had it been at sea for? The questions allowed our minds to roam and drift for the rest of the afternoon.

As we paddled eastward late in the day, with the conversation having finally petered out, an ominous-looking storm cloud hovered in front of *Lot 41*. Would it engulf us?

"Hey, Jonesy, do you reckon we can try and steer around this thing?" I asked optimistically. With a cruising speed of less than 4 kilometres per hour, we hardly had a chance of manoeuvring around the front like a bigger vessel might.

Out at sea, you can clearly see the boundary where rain ends. It was a concept I'd never thought about back on land – with buildings, trees, hills, etc obscuring the view – but there has to be a line where sun starts and rain stops. Because you're free from obstructions out on the ocean, the line is quite distinguishable.

Unfortunately, we didn't miss the squall. Strong winds hit us, then rain, but before long we popped out the other side to a beautiful afternoon.

We'd seen the beauty of the ocean but I hadn't felt it. Well, not till the twilight hours of day 7. The last hour of paddling –

between 6.30 and 7.30pm – quickly became my favourite time of day. It was when the sun had just disappeared behind us, leaving the water a rich black and the sky a soft array of pastel colours. Through most of the journey, to our left the sky was baby blue, violet and purple, with the occasional burning orange cloud providing a contrast to the backdrop. On the right, the sky was a little angrier, with fiery oranges, reds, and yellows.

We often talked about the different landscapes on either side of the kayak personifying two females. On the left was the quiet, elegant lady wearing either a long night gown or dinner dress; on the right the much more fiery woman, with bright red lips and fingernails – great dancer and super sexy. It wasn't hard for us to see how natives around the world created folklore around "the heavens" and nature, when here we were, doing the same thing ourselves.

Typically, though, at this time of day I'd prefer not to talk, but listen. Some days I'd focus on the waves, the wind and the paddle blades dipping into the Tasman; other days I'd put on my favourite iPod playlists, featuring kd lang, James Taylor and Cat Stevens.

My ultimate songs to finish off a day's paddle were hidden in my "Tasman Top" playlist. This included the likes of "My Heart Will Go On", the theme song from *Titanic*, "Then I Kissed Her" by the Beach Boys, Billy Joel's "Uptown Girl", "Heaven" by DJ Sammy, "Desperado" by The Eagles, a bit of the old Frank Sinatra, the theme song from *Legends of the Fall* and "The Gambler" by Kenny Rogers. Never let it be said that I'm not at the cutting edge of popular music.

When camping, I've often got agitated at the time it takes Jonesy to pack his gear up. At the end of the day on the Tasman, I'd patiently wait in my pit while J washed and got into the cabin. This ritual became part of "Cas's special time" and I'd enjoy these moments immensely. Most nights, I'd use this time to do a video

diary, concluding that evening matter-of-factly: "All going well …
we should get to NZ in less than a month now."

While I was talking to the camera, we'd do a five-minute drift
test, where we'd let the kayak drift with the wind and waves to see
which way she naturally wanted to go. There were two things we
were trying to establish: the first was whether we could suck any
additional mileage out of the wind without the para-anchor
deployed; the second was to see if we could get away with not
deploying the anchor. As we then wouldn't have to spend time
retrieving it, this would generally mean a smoother night's sleep
and give us an extra 15 minutes' paddling in the morning.

Although this seems insignificant, we quickly learnt that it was
the little things that made all the difference. An extra 15 minutes
paddling each day – if extrapolated out to 62 days – would save us
15 hours over the entirety of the expedition: the equivalent to
two days. Similarly, we identified the importance of one person
paddling during the five-minute break we'd take every hour. This
would reduce our time at sea by a whopping 60 hours (five days)
over the entire trip!

After I'd done the usual daily video diary, Jonesy would make
his way into the cabin and begin preparing the dehydrated
evening meals, while I moved the dry bags – waterproof bags that
contained our first-aid kit, flameless ration heaters, repair kits and
extra food – from the cabin into each pit, strapping them down,
then putting a cockpit cover over the top.

Meanwhile, Justin would reach down the sides of the cabin,
where we'd stored most of our food, and pull out a cryo-vacked
meal pack. Before leaving Forster, we'd painstakingly removed
every meal from its original packaging and sealed them in airtight
plastic bags. This reduced the size and weight of the rations and
stopped cross-contamination of foods.

It was a complete lucky dip what he'd grab. There was no double dipping allowed; what was plucked was what we had to eat.

Day 7 ended on a high note. That evening Pat revealed that we'd had over 50,000 unique visitors to our website and that both the *Sydney Morning Herald* and the Melbourne *Age* online had us as their feature story for the day.

DAY 8

Lot 41 was designed to have two independent electrical systems. If one went down, we had the other as back-up. As part of our routine, we'd rotate the use of the batteries each day so as not to bleed one system down in its entirety. We quickly realised on day 8 that no power was being distributed from the "aft battery".

"Shit," Jonesy mumbled.

We knew it had to be a loose connection – but where? There were over 5 kilometres of wiring through *Lot 41*. Prior to us leaving we'd done a series of troubleshooting days with our electrical engineer Craig Thomsen. He'd dive inside the cabin and break something on purpose. Our mission was to identify the problem and fix it with the tools we'd have out on the Tasman. Using the problem-solving methodology Craig had instilled into us during these exercises, we quickly got to work.

We needed to sort the problem out quickly, because our tracking was down and Pat would be getting anxious. Pulling out the multimeter, we started testing the power distribution box and feverishly worked backwards to the battery. Bingo! One of the battery terminals had corroded – despite our having lined the terminal with Vaseline, the salt water had penetrated it.

The weather forecast we'd received the previous night appeared nasty. Nevertheless, after we fixed the battery into the pits, we got out and did some paddling, as it didn't look too bad outside. Although we'd pushed ourselves quite hard the past week, this was the first time on the expedition that we had an adverse wind and current – a ꜰꜱꜱte of things to come. We fought into a brisk easterly for six hours, making a mere 13 kilometres.

We'd now been out for over a week and felt like we were flogging a dead horse. A five-minute drift test quickly revealed that we were gliding northwest at 4 kilometres per hour. We'd decided prior to leaving that, in these situations, we'd chuck out the para-anchor and get some rest. So we did. We spent the afternoon dozing and watching *Transformers* on the Toughbook computer.

We quickly learnt *Lot 41* would drift with the current, regardless of what the wind was doing. It was blowing from the northeast quadrant at 20 knots, with an underlying current pulling in the opposite direction. The result: an obnoxiously violent sea state. Steep sharp waves were created by this wind-against-current scenario. The one saving grace was that we were still moving towards NZ. Sleep was non-existent that night – between us we managed to capture about 40 minutes. Waves constantly buffeted the kayak, causing the cabin to be pulled through the face of the larger ones. Adding to our woes, Justin's prickly heat was close to unbearable as he slapped his body through the night; although rubbing water bladders (we had 50 litres of reserve fresh water on board, stored in 8-litre bags) over his body seemed to provide temporary relief.

DAY 9

The condensation in the cabin made us incredibly uncomfortable, and our Tasman tormentor relished the opportunity to play the "How far open do you leave the door" game. Every minute it was ajar was a short-lived victory to J & J – we revelled in the fresh air flow. But just as I'd be drifting off to sleep, a wave would either crash over the top or a rogue would jump through from the opposite direction, soaking my whole side of the cabin.

We named the different types of waves that entered the cabin of *Lot 41*. First there was the "freak of nature". This was a wave that came from 180 degrees from the prevailing conditions. How, you may ask. Funny you should say that – it's the same question that had us baffled the entire voyage! Next up was the "little bastard". These guys stealthily crept up on us from an angle closer to 90 degrees. They were quite clever, really – they often had the uncanny ability to leap through any open porthole or tiniest opening of the cabin door completely silently. Finally there was the "bombora". These were the waves that engulfed the whole kayak and if there was any ventilation hole, cabin door or porthole open, water would rush in.

Lot 41 was designed to be watertight (with a couple of vents built in under the solar panels) but not a submarine. Obviously, we needed to leave something open to allow fresh air into the cabin: there was a very real risk that if we'd had everything closed we could suffocate, much the same as people in snow caves without ventilation. The carbon monoxide and dioxide can build up and the victims can drift off to sleep forever without being aware of what's happening.

The first thing these waves would hit when they entered the cabin was my face, followed closely by the "pillow" I had my head on. This was a washing bag filled with polystyrene beans. Its primary purpose was to be a spare beanbag seat which we sat on while paddling, but it also provided a wonderful pillow to rest our noggins on.

Unfortunately, the bags were also used to kneel on when we had to hang a pee out of the cabin – a mixture of urine and saliva was splattered on them throughout the trip. That smell infuriated me at times but, oddly, also transported me to the big walls of Yosemite Valley, where the ever-pungent urine aroma floods the bivies on the walls.

We'd now been out for over a week, and although we'd had some massive days, our progress had been phenomenal and we'd already started playing the dangerous game – what day would we arrive in New Zealand?

11

DEREK THE DESAL IS SICK

Apart from crossing the Tasman safely, one of our other major goals was to share this adventure with as many people as possible. Technology made this possible. When we'd first left school and gone for bushwalks with a Kodak instant camera, we'd try to capture what it was like out in the bush or in the water, but the photos never did the scenery or the experience justice. Podcasts and the ability to send photos back from the ditch worked so much better, as anyone could live our highs and our lows in real time.

On the Tasman, a community formed in which people adopted me and Justin almost as their own children, many seeming to log on religiously to check our progress. Some stayed up all night staring at their computer screens when we were doing it tough, others posted encouragement multiple times per day.

They could hear the fear in our voices when we were scared, when we tried to sound upbeat, when we really wanted to be anywhere else on earth apart from that kayak – the truth pierced through our voices. On our return, we learnt that a lot of people took more from our tone than our actual words.

Podcasts were incredibly effective in communicating our message and bloody simple to set up. From our end, all it required was for us to call on the satellite phone to a number that went through to a voicemail. Pat would then upload this straight to the website. The online forum allowed people to communicate both with us and other forumites. The constant encouragement and positive energy sent through to Justin and me was fantastic. We'd never met Ol Oiler, PhDuck, Bern and CathyM – these were their forum names – but the stories they posted gave us glimpses of their lives. Through our podcasts and actions, these people were able to develop a connection with us, and us with them.

DAY 10

Waking on the morning of day 10, I felt sick. Out on the Tasman, however, "seasick" was a word we were forbidden from using – it carried too much baggage. We'd been held captive in the cabin for the previous 42 hours. The sea was angry and we just couldn't get out and paddle. The lack of sleep, insufficient hydration and not being able to stand up had resulted in us both having throbbing headaches. We referred to it as "cabin-skull-crushing syndrome", caused by lying down for extended periods of time.

Above my head, I had my favourite photos of family and friends and my eyes focused on a small image, no bigger than a beer coaster, of me and Dunc, high up El Capitan in Yosemite Valley. It removed me for a brief moment in between squalls that continued to batter us all morning. We were both beginning to feel weak.

Finally, on day 10, the Tasman gave us a break: a chance to get out paddling again. Justin, *Lot 41* and I were a three-man team out there, but while Jonesy was doing great and *Lot 41* was dancing along, I was struggling. My constant cabin sickness was beginning to play games with my head. A spiral was forming: first came the feeling of queasiness, which, combined with a couple of spoonfuls of fatigue and being on half rations in the cabin when we weren't paddling, resulted in my mind constantly generating negative thoughts. That would ensure that I arrived back at my starting point of feeling seedy.

As I've mentioned, I'd equipped myself with a number of weapons to combat the seasickness. Through the mentoring of a hypnotherapist and listening to meditation tapes, I'd slowly begun to learn how to allow my mind to drift to another state. The first thing I'd do each night when I returned to the cabin was put on a half-hour tape. This ritual trained my mind to see the cabin as a happy place rather than a den of torture. I eagerly looked forward to that 30 minutes of escapism. My favourite tape was the special Wolgan Valley one my hypnotherapist had constructed for me, followed closely by "Soar Like an Eagle". In this one, I glided effortlessly through the sky like an eagle. Way cool.

The Wolgan tape started with some breathing excercises, then painted a canvas of vivid images from the most special place on the planet, where I'd spent those fantastic weekends climbing with Dunc – from the vibrant orange sandstone cliffs to the fire trail meandering its way through the valley floor. These tapes extracted me from the harsh realities on board *Lot 41*, and let the pleasure of being in the Australian bush flow through my body. There were times I reached a level of clarity where all my senses had left the boat and drifted into the Wolgan. I could smell the gumtrees and hear the bellbirds sing above the fresh flowing water of the creek: it became real. Often I felt like an astronaut re-entering the earth's atmosphere as I came out of the trance. Adjusting to the reality of being on board a kayak was a shock, like waking up from a dream. However, I'd always "reboard" *Lot 41* calmer than when I'd left.

This half-hour quiet time reminded me of when I used to get home from "proper" work. When I worked as an accountant, I'd crash on the couch for half an hour, hypnotically staring at the TV until I mustered sufficient energy to go and make dinner or get my gym clothes on.

It wasn't the only reminder of the good old days at the office. We now thought of ourselves as mavericks and adventurers, but funnily enough, here we were with a uniform, regimented hours and an unpredictable, temperamental boss – except this one would kill us if we didn't follow instructions.

There was no work/life balance, we could only dream about sick pay and RDOs, and we were on call 24 hours a day, seven days a week: public holidays no exception. I'm sure the ACTU would have taken some class action on our behalf if they'd been in contact!

DAY 11

For the first 10 days of our voyage, our water maker – we named it Derek the Desal – had been working tirelessly, delivering 10 litres of desalinated fresh water each day. With only 50 litres of emergency water stored on board *Lot 41*, we needed to produce fresh water daily for drinking, rehydrating our Back Country dehydrated meals and for washing.

Prior to leaving, we'd never paid too much attention to the amount of water we actually use in day-to-day life in the city, but stats tell us the daily average is approximately 340 litres per person! In order to consume a measly 5 litres per person each day we had to take stringent measures to make sure we didn't dip into our emergency supply. We often chuckled at the humour of having a stingy 200 millilitres of water to bathe each night. "That's not a bath, it's a mouthful" was our running gag.

The most vital piece of equipment on *Lot 41* was therefore the water maker. It was by far the most energy-sucking gizmo we had on board: solar panels on the back of the cabin fed energy down to three 70-amp-hour car batteries in the bottom of the kayak, primarily to fuel Derek, who normally produced a nice murmur while he pumped. All of a sudden, he stuttered a little and started drawing more milliamps. Justin looked in the cabin, but couldn't see anything unusual. It appeared Derek was sick.

Merrily cruising along on day 11, we began chatting about bushwalks we'd done together. The fun came in scratching our heads to remember the intricate details – the best food on a particular walk, the name of that ridge or spur.

The details we extracted from the recesses of our minds amazed us, and we laughed about the 50-kilogram packs we'd shouldered as we walked around Fraser Island when we'd just turned 18. On that walk, we had all our fishing gear (including 3 kilograms of lead sinkers!), a grill to cook sausages and fish, jaffle iron … the list went on. For some reason we had a full roll of cling-wrap with us. To this day, we haven't been able to figure out why!

As we mulled over the cling-wrap issue, Jonesy accidentally knocked his hat off his spray skirt as he was putting suncream on his face, and sent it flying into the sea. Sure, we had a spare one on board, but hats seem to be one of those possessions you grow really fond of. We quickly back-paddled and found it floating on the water's surface like a jellyfish or plastic bag. Scooping it up, we continued to paddle and chat. (Hats aside, we'd gone to great lengths to make sure all items on board were either tethered to the kayak or us. That included all the cameras, GPS, notebooks, sunnies … and of course ourselves.)

Any change we could muster in our daily routine – any change *at all* – had us giggling with glee. Food was one aspect of the journey that we'd carefully planned and considered. On the one hand, it was intricately scientific, ensuring we'd be consuming an adequate number of calories and micro and macro-nutrients; on the other, food in any extreme environment plays a significant role in terms of morale. Therefore we wanted food that not only served the dietary requirements we'd carefully laid out, but also tasted great.

Our 100 food packets were carefully cryo-vacked and stored throughout *Lot 41*. Each day's rations weighed 1.5 kilograms and included 6000 calories – approximately the same caloric intake as 15 Big Macs. We had a vast number of different dehydrated meals, and quickly established that our favourites were roast chicken, spaghetti bolognese and chicken babotjie.

A whole week had drifted by with no roast chicken and we were beginning to get worried. Finally, on day 11, a roast chicken was discovered, accompanied by our arch-nemesis – Thai green curry. But as we cooked the meals up on our dwindling supply of fresh water, there was something amiss with the chicken.

We cooked it up regardless. There were no flames on board *Lot 41* – the risks were too great. "Cooking" involved dumping a flameless heating pad into a small bucket, then adding 100 millilitres of salt water. We'd place our meals in a foil bag then allow them to heat up in the bucket. When the salt water infused with the pad, it created an exothermic reaction – providing the same amount of heat as if we'd put the meal in a microwave for 40 seconds.

Justin prepared the meals, and I was responsible for the "cooking". He did all the work – fishing out a cryo-vacked meal, emptying the contents into a foil bag, adding water and a sachet of olive oil (and for the first 10 days we had a small supply of fresh garlic and lemon), then passing it out to me, to add the salt water into the bucket. We often joked that he was the slave-driven housewife meticulously preparing the entire meal and I was the beer-swilling husband lazily turning the steaks over on the barbie and claiming the credit for a culinary masterpiece.

As I stirred the meals occasionally in the rear pit, I caught glimpses of a gorgeous white fish with longitudinal black stripes. Each time I called Jonesy to come and have a look, the fish would dart deep into the water and disappear into the darkness. This happened four or five times; by the final time, Justin thought I'd gone mad and gave me plenty of grief about the imaginary "tiger fish".

That night, tragically, our most prized meal was rancid, and a small negative voice surfaced for the second time that day: "Boys, it's only day 11, your water maker is playing up, now some of your meals are going off," it quietly whispered. The voices were hastily squashed – we weren't too concerned. Our progress appeared to be great and we thought we were going to arrive in New Zealand with plenty of rations to spare.

Most nights, we'd either deploy the sea anchor or drift without it. On this particular evening we found that we were drifting southwest with it deployed, and north with it not deployed. As a result we had it out for half the night, then at 12.30am I got up to bring it in. This resulted in a neutral drift through the night. I yawned, in a half-dazed state, my fingers running over the retrieval line as I coiled it in the bottom of a dry bag. It felt like I was back climbing again – pulling a rope down after the final abseil, ending a big day's climb. I said to myself in the brisk night air: "I can't wait to be back climbing again … it's just so good for the soul."

DAY 12

Bumbling along at 6.30am our paddles seemed to be getting stuck in mud. I peered down, and realised we were paddling through seaweed. This change in texture was almost as exciting as seeing the yellow buoy a couple of days earlier! We were now 700 kilometres away from Forster, causing us to mull over where on earth the seaweed could have come from. As we pondered, I thought I saw something on the horizon off our starboard beam.

"Jonesy, there's a sail over there," I casually blurted out as if we were on a day's paddle along Sydney's Northern Beaches.

"Are you sure it's not a tiger fish?" he replied, feeling pretty pleased with himself.

"No seriously, there's a yacht over there." My tone was beginning to crescendo as the sail got closer.

"Shit, there is too!" Jonesy yelled, finally seeing the boat in the middle distance. "Let's try and raise them on the radio."

I leant forward and pulled out the handheld VHF. "What should I say?" I asked uncertainly. (We'd both obtained our marine radio operator licences prior to departing and we'd been trained in how to communicate on the radio. Although the shock of stumbling onto another boat out here on the Tasman had thrown me a bit.)

"Unknown vessel, Unknown vessel, Unknown vessel," I began. "This is *Lot 41*, *Lot 41*, *Lot 41*, do you read me … over." I sheepishly turned to Jonesy, seeking assurance that what I'd said made sense.

He nodded in encouragement and we silently waited for a reply. There was nothing for a while, then suddenly the silence was broken by a short-wave crackle. "*Lot 41*, *Lot 41*, *Lot 41*, this is yacht *Aquarelle*, *Aquarelle*, *Aquarelle*, reading you loud and clear."

This was fantastic. "*Aquarelle*, this is *Lot 41*, *Lot 41*, *Lot 41*. We're currently en route to NZ in a kayak."

"*Lot 41*, this is *Aquarelle*," the voice replied. "We heard about you two crazy bastards the day you left Forster – it was all over the news in New Zealand. How are you doing?"

"Brilliantly."

He told us they'd like to come and say hello, so they changed course and made their way towards us. Over the radio we helped guide them: "20 degrees to port", "too much – 30 degrees to starboard" etc. Soberingly, they'd only spotted us when they were a mere 30 metres away. For some reason, the Comar Unit (the same one that wouldn't turn on during our Port Stephens sea trial) had begun pulsing our position rather irregularly. We'd heard horror stories of other vessels being run over at sea, and it isn't surprising that ships like the Danish *Emma Mærsk*, weighing in at just over 150,000 tonnes, don't even feel the bump when they hit sailing vessels, let alone a 1-tonne kayak!

At night-time, we displayed Max the tri-colour nav light, but our experience with *Aquarelle* indicated how useless this weak navigation aid was so close to the water – it was only a metre above the surface and waves would often cover the line of sight. If a seaman on another vessel saw Max while on watch, we'd be crushed before they had any chance to avoid us. Nevertheless, we religiously left Max on each night; more to comfort us than to avert oncoming traffic. It was just one of the risks we had to absorb while on the Tasman.

It was a stunningly glassy day and the bow of the *Aquarelle* sliced through the water like a fighter plane through clouds. We couldn't stop giggling and staring in utter bewilderment at the immaculate detail of this dazzling yacht, as sunlight beamed off the stainless steel stanchions and winches, creating reflections dancing on the sails.

Aquarelle approached with two sailors on board. They came upwind of us and a powerful, pleasant aroma engulfed *Lot 41*, diesel fumes giving way to the smell of bacon cooking. "How are you guys?" they asked.

"Absolutely fantastic," we said again. We weren't sure if they were expecting a different response from when they'd asked us over the radio.

"Can we offer you anything? Do you need some fresh water? Bacon and egg roll or a beer?" they asked, possibly examining us for signs of madness.

Each query hit home like a dagger. *Yes, we'd like all of the above*, we thought instantly. Unfortunately, the "rules" of doing an unsupported journey don't allow any provisions to be taken on board. If we'd taken as little as a piece of fresh bread, our crossing wouldn't have been classified as "unsupported". (Back in 1996, a 17 year old named David Dicks set out on an unassisted, solo circumnavigation of the world and broke a rigging bolt in the mast near Cape Horn. A replacement bolt was flown out to him and there went his voyage's "unsupported" status.)

From our point of view, we were in the middle of nowhere, and applying these harsh regulations just seemed so completely out of place. Who were the people who made these rules?

As the skipper, Graeme Templeton, prepared to sail off, we took a few photos of each other. I'm not sure who was more taken aback – him or us. When we got back to Australia, we saw a photo on the front page of a local newspaper and we looked like two stunned, zinc-creamed mullets!

Then, as quickly as they'd entered our little Tasman bubble, they were gone and we were alone. With the sun setting and the memory of our encounter with *Aquarelle* slowly beginning to fade, I reflected on the absurdity of our situation. *Aquarelle* and *Lot 41* shared cutting-edge composites, technologies etc, but although in recent centuries the wheel had been invented, then cars, then planes, for our own obscure reasons we'd saddled ourselves with the ancient technology of the kayak and a simple paddle, rather than harnessing the power of the wind with a sail – talk about a backwards step in evolution!

The ocean had become almost eerily calm as we paddled on in deafening silence. Justin had never experienced silence like this before; my mind drifted to the last time I had. It had been on a mountaineering trip in the New Zealand Alps, high up on the west ridge of Malte Brun – with a Snickers in my hand. There were no birds, no wind: just snow, ice and rock. The silence begins to pulsate in your mind. I can now see how people go mad at sea when a boat is becalmed. The mind begins to crave a sound – any sound – to tickle the eardrum and ignite a nerve impulse to the brain.

I wasn't going mad (at least I didn't think I was) but I did have something on my mind. Breaking the silence, I said to Justin in one big breath: "Mate, I feel so retarded having to rely on you so heavily in the cabin … it's doing my head in." I breathed in deeply, as though it was alleviating a weight I'd been carrying for the whole journey.

"Don't feel bad about it at all," Jonesy replied. "I can see how much it pisses you off. But if it wasn't for the huge amount of work you did for both of us when we were getting ready, we'd never be out here. I'm going to do all I can to give something back to the team."

"Thanks, Jonesy … that means a lot."

There was a pause, then Justin was quick to change the topic and we talked about how amazingly silent the ocean was. "It's almost oppressive," he said. "You could easily feel the world has forgotten about us and that time has stopped. The water looks like velvet … like silk."

I continued our rambling out loud. "It doesn't feel like we saw two other people earlier today, does it? It feels surreal – did we actually see another boat?"

Back in Australia, it was the day of the Federal election. We'd lodged absentee votes (in case anyone from the Electoral Commission is reading this). It was bizarre to think that ballots were being counted, and our mates would be at election parties and probably watching the cricket. We seemed just so far away from all that.

As Jonesy passed me my dehydrated mush that night, I couldn't help jealously reflecting on seeing Graeme Templeton sipping from a ceramic mug, and eating a slice of toast off a plate. All of a sudden, our meals took on the appearance of fuel for a car, rather than a delicious motivational tool.

To take advantage of the great conditions, we decided to paddle through the night. I was rostered to the 7–11pm shift, and Jonesy to the 11pm–3am. That resulted in me paddling 17 hours straight, which took its toll on us the following morning. At 1am, I had a hallucination, convinced I saw a UFO – so much so that I woke Justin up to see it (I didn't want him to miss out!). After staring blankly at the sky for a few minutes, clearly unimpressed, he said, "Can I go back to bed now?"

Pleasant paddling that evening took us further away from the Australian coastline. The cabin door creaked open and I broke the evening's silence to wake Jonesy for his shift. "Hey, Jonesy."

"Yeah, man."

"Time for you to go for a paddle … How you feeling?"

"Mmmm … sleeeeeepppppppyyyyyy."

"Did you get any sleep?"

"'Bout half an hour."

"Time to get up, mate. The current still seems to be against us … little bastard."

12

ROCK AND A HARD PLACE

DAY 13

VIDEO DIARY, DAY 13 – JAMES

"I'm feeling completely haggard. That 17-hour paddle
yesterday really took it out of me."

We woke up feeling absolutely shattered. Jonesy was as stiff as a
board, and for him to sit upright in the morning, he had to crane
his neck awkwardly to one side to avoid hitting his head on the
cabin, a mere 150 millimetres above him, as his body contorted
the other way. It reminded me of a move that belonged as a
Houdini act in Cirque du Soleil, rather than someone carrying out
a menial task like sitting up.

Sure, we'd put on a few kilometres during the night, but now
we felt like we'd been mowed down by a bus. Was it worth it? A
dilemma we were to struggle with the entire way across the
Tasman was whether to use calm conditions to eat up some
kilometres or get some decent, uninterrupted sleep.

I got angry about us each having paddled 17 hours the previous day, because we'd identified fatigue as one of the major threats that could stop us from reaching New Zealand alive. We mulled over the 19 hours Andrew McAuley had paddled straight on his first attempt to cross the Tasman. Honourably, he'd retreated, unassisted, on the second day of his paddle after identifying that he was too cold and not able to sleep at night. Andrew had taken a vastly different approach to the expedition to us. We identified sleep as a critical factor in our risk management work and, as such, designed the cabin of *Lot 41* to ensure we could get maximum rest.

Fatigue leads to bad judgement, and out at sea bad judgement has caused numerous deaths. Here we were, drifting away from the strategy that would keep us alive on the Tasman. Mother Tasman, or for that matter Mother Nature, would slam down on any complacency.

Climbing had taught me these lessons. A famous quote by the American mountaineering legend Ed Viesturs, "Mountains don't kill people, they just sit there," has always wafted in the back of my mind when pushing boundaries in the outdoors. Simple lessons, like sticking to your turnaround time, not being bullied into doing things beyond your abilities, and not placing the importance of the summit above the objective dangers you're willing to assume, can often be clouded when you're out there. From an armchair, it's always easier to say what people should have done.

Although Jonesy and I had made some great progress overnight, throughout the day every little thing he did annoyed me, and me him. Fatigue was malignantly growing within us, impairing our judgement and darkening our outlook. That afternoon, after another chat, we sternly agreed that the previous night was the last time on the expedition we'd prioritise mileage over managing fatigue. And as I wrote in my diary, that night we got a "wonderful nine hours' sleep – the most on the expedition so far".

In the late afternoon, a nasty squall blew through, ruining the tranquillity, but it soon passed by, leaving us paddling for a few hours towards a vibrant rainbow.

DAY 14

VIDEO DIARY, DAY 14 – JUSTIN

"Sleep is the key to the Tasman. It keeps us from making irrational decisions, keeps us from getting angry with the situation ... everything seems so much smoother. Even the protein bars and nuts tasted good today."

Waking to calm conditions, we jovially paddled due east, naked. To a passing albatross, our white, wrinkled skin might have reminded it of plucked chickens. Feeling well rested, our morale had picked up, our speed was 6–7 kilometres per hour and we chattered like cockatoos on coke. Life on the Tasman couldn't have been better.

DAY 15

The Tasman had spoilt us during the previous few days, and we woke to a stiff 35-kilometre-per-hour southeasterly headwind. We just couldn't make any progress. The para-anchor was chucked out and we bunkered down in the cabin for a bumpy ride.

Lying there, we began discussing the direction our friendship had taken. "Why have we drifted apart the last years, Cas?" Jonesy asked.

It was a good question. We spoke about the fact that we've got different values and different approaches to tackling life, and that our friendship was strongest out in the bush, where the differences between us didn't seem important. We'd sometimes find it difficult to see eye to eye in the city, but often, as soon as we slip on the paddling thermals, or bushwalking boots and guitars, we instantly began to resonate on the same frequency.

I'd also always thought that Justin had a vastly different personality in the big smoke. He loves going out, enjoying the nightlife, picking up girls, and I guess ... being somewhat smug ... we also have a vastly different work ethic. At times I'm psychotically driven and motivated, while Justin is often the complete opposite. This difference was one of the most challenging hurdles we had to overcome in preparing for the Tasman.

We both knew that when we were out there on the expedition, it'd be difficult for us not to arrive better mates than when we left – we'd already seen each other at our deepest, darkest moments, our highest points of elation and everything in between. It was in the three-year preparation phase, when *Lot 41* wasn't performing, we were struggling to raise finances and our families were telling us to give it away, that we sometimes found it difficult to maintain our respect for one another.

"It's not like we're on the Murray," I remember saying, "where we talked with each other – now we talk at each other. There was a three-year gap in our thinking. We don't seem to have the same innocence – we seem to bombard each other with our own values and opinions rather than work through together." It was obvious that as we'd got older, we'd both become more opinionated, so our views clashed more.

Then there was the fact that we were business partners as well as friends, which only added to the confusion and occasional tension.

Justin was also frustrated by me not cutting him enough slack, given that we're best mates, while I suggested that seeing as we're best mates, surely he'd want to go the extra mile. He agreed, adding that that was why he didn't mind taking the extra burden in the cabin.

Later, as I lay reflecting on our conversation, I stared at the A3 photo collage stuck to the cabin roof above my head. I chuckled quietly as I realised the stark contrast in my photos with those above Justin, who had a similar collage.

Mine were a compilation of mates from climbing, canyoning and bushwalking. The only ones from "city life" were those of my family and our dog, Max. Jonesy had a handful of photos from sailing, a few walks and a couple of paddles, but the majority were of big nights out on the town.

It summed up our personalities and what turned our dial. With such contrasting images playing a role in motivating us, it's a wonder we could remain best mates. It was definitely the time we spent "out there" that really brought our friendship together.

DAY 16

The wind had begun to abate and we were keen to get some paddling in, but crawling out of the cabin that morning, I noticed the retrieval line for the para-anchor had fouled around the rudder tiller bar in the previous day's bad weather. In much the same way as a stockman cracks his leather whip, we made a string of futile attempts to untangle the knot from the rear pit. It was soon pretty clear, though: one of us was going to have to go in and sort it out.

We played Scissor, Paper, Rock and unfortunately I lost (damn Rock). It was cold, windy and my turn to go for a dip. It's funny how our relationship has developed. In situations like this one, although I'd "lost" I much preferred going in, rather than see my best mate back there. We discussed this later in the journey and realised we both felt much the same way.

Donning my PFD (personal flotation device) and clipping into the safety line, I slithered into the water like a seal. I gasped as my torso entered the freezing ocean. I knew I didn't have long to untangle the mess before my hands and mind went numb and I began to suffer from hypothermia: I had to work quickly.

There was less than a metre between *Lot 41* and me, but it suddenly hit home how safe I'd felt cradled on board the kayak and how dependent on her I'd become. I felt so exposed now, suspended in kilometres of nothingness and weeks away from land.

As I approached the rudder, I tried to assess the situation, with waves continually swamping me. Like a guillotine, the rear of the kayak chopped up and down through the swell, as I bear-hugged the rudder and started my work. I fumbled uselessly with my ever-numbing hands, not making any progress on the knot, feeling more exposed by the minute.

I pulled out my knife and placed the blade between my teeth – there was no time to waste; I had to find the line that needed to be chopped. Holding onto the kayak with one hand, knife in the other, I looked like a rodeo rider fighting to stay on a bucking bull.

Hacking the serrated edge of the knife against the retrieval line, I broke through after a couple of attempts. Our retrieval line was now cut. I began to shiver from the cold. Tearing at the remaining knot, I managed to free the rudder. I just had to make sure I brought the cut line back to the kayak so we could bring in the para-anchor.

Lurching into my pit like a drowning rat, I curled into a ball, shivering violently, and began dry-retching. My lungs were full of water. Jonesy took charge and immediately issued directions like a drill sergeant.

"Here's your cag – put it on," he blasted, knowing that I was close to becoming hypothermic.

Painfully slowly, my mind tried to process what he was telling me as I gazed at him blankly.

"Put it on *now*, Cas," he said urgently. I responded.

"Now put on your spray skirt," he barked.

Desperately trying to stand to put the skirt on, my legs buckled and I collapsed into my pit. Wiggling like a Bollywood belly dancer, I somehow managed to get the skirt over my head, then fumbled a few times fighting to latch it over the cockpit rim. Despite my vagueness, I knew that once I secured the skirt to the deck, the air trapped inside would instantly begin to warm me.

Jonesy quickly retrieved the anchor and passed me a warmed-up dehydrated meal – chicken babotjie. Unco-ordinatedly, I stuffed my face with the food. In between bouts of violent shivering, I found it hard to land the spoon in my mouth, let alone chew. By the end of the meal, I had food smeared all over my face but began to feel the warmth radiating inside me from the meal. Once I'd finished, we immediately started to paddle, knowing that I needed to get the blood pumping. Within half an hour, feeling had returned to my fingers and toes.

Another lesson was learnt: under no circumstances were either of us to be outside the cabin without being attached to the kayak. Our chances of surviving in the water if we were swept away from the kayak were extremely slim. In fact, in a water temperature of 18 degrees – about what it was that day – without a survival suit, you've got about 10 hours.

A survival suit tends to double that time. Spare a thought for Andrew, whose average water temperature was 12 degrees. That would have given him four hours' total survival time, even with a suit on. We only paddled on for 90 minutes, as the sea was too turbulent for us to make any decent progress.

DAY 17

We slept restlessly as we were tossed around through the night. In the morning we did a multimeter check on all our batteries to ensure the readings on the display were accurate. Next to the charge box we'd written a warning: *Do not allow batteries to get below 12V.* Fore battery, 12.4V – check; aft battery, 12.2V – check; spare battery, 11.37V – oh shit! We spoke to our electrical engineer Craig on the satphone and decided the best course of action to get the spare battery back up was to rewire the aft battery to it in order to get more power from the solar panels. Problem solved.

Craig had drummed into us prior to departure that crossing the Tasman was all about *maintenance, maintenance, maintenance.* He hated exercise, and couldn't understand why you'd want to paddle to NZ, but loved the project. He insisted that if we looked after *Lot 41*, ourselves and our systems on board – and did a little paddling on the side – we'd make it to New Zealand. This theory would have been great if the prevailing conditions (wind coming from behind) had, in fact, prevailed! Instead, it meant more time paddling than originally planned for.

As with climbers at altitude, it's so easy to get lazy and delay maintenance tasks, convincing yourself that "She'll be right" or "Conditions will be better tomorrow". Craig's discipline rubbed off on us a little and we forced ourselves to address each obstacle before it became an issue. One of the many advantages of having the two of us on board was that there was always someone there to say, "C'mon, mate, let's do this thing now." (Which usually came from me asking Jonesy to do the work, as the seasickness was still playing games. I felt terrible about it – *honest.*)

Doing these running repairs and maintenance at sea took five times as long as on land. At the best of times, Jonesy is painfully slow

– but always methodical – doing even the smallest tasks, and the
constant rolling swell and pitching kayak made it difficult to rewire
the batteries. Initially, watching him fumble around with the wires
began to get under my skin, but then I began to admire the precision
he was showing in this intricate, electronic, open-heart surgery.

I'd get annoyed with myself for not being able to help out and
take more of a lead role, but often, within minutes of starting a
task, I'd find myself needing to lie on my back as vomit would rise
and tickle my throat. I mastered the art of knowing exactly when I
needed to lie down and push the vomit back before it entered my
mouth – the point of no return.

Deprivation ... it's a funny thing. By stripping life's luxuries away
and pitting myself against nature, my raw needs as a human
started to surface. I began to realise how amazing even my most
annoying family and friends are (yes, you, Ben!), and how good
we've got it in Australia. Since our return I can guarantee I've
never looked at a glass of fresh water the same. That glass of water
on the Tasman would take over 10 minutes to pump.

Out at sea, I started to absorb things that I'd always taken for
granted, taking the time to stare into that glass of water – analyse
its crystal-clear nature, tap the glass and taste the purity of it.
Deprivation had sharpened my awareness of life.

We had a late start paddling at 10am and soon realised that no
salt water was spitting out the reject valve on the side of the
cabin. Jonesy instantly stopped paddling and opened up the cabin
door in time to witness Derek struggling feebly to stay alive. It
coughed, spluttered, then conked out. We were left in silence.

"Now what?" Jonesy remarked.

"Aw, maybe she just needs a rest – we've been running her hard
every day," I replied optimistically.

"Let me jump back in the cabin and have a look at it."

"Alright, mate, I'll just keep paddling."

Justin gazed blankly at the desal. There was a centimetre of water sloshing round the bottom of the compartment, which he mopped up. Surely that wasn't enough to get inside the motor and render it useless?

Jonesy's quick inspection of the unit didn't show any signs of the seals having broken and he began to examine the manufacturers' "trouble-shooting flow chart". After having his head shoved in the desal compartment for over half an hour, he slithered out of the cabin looking slightly seedy. Derek was out of action for the foreseeable future. We began paddling in silence, feeling angry and frustrated. We'd heard of countless ocean rowing teams who'd had problems with their water makers and we'd been pleading with the desal gods to spare us the same fate. If it wasn't working the next day we'd be forced to pull out the back-up unit – a hand pump: something we'd hoped was going to stay buried for the entire voyage.

To help break the gloom, we started joking about the unit: "This desal is as reliable as the New Zealand rugby team in the World Cup."

We began to smile as the jokes kept coming. They began to get ruder … and much cruder. They were all completely inappropriate! (So I'll leave it right there.)

These jokes cheered us up enormously, and with the energy-sapping desal out of action, we found extra comfort in the fact that we could now charge our iPods without having to worry about draining our batteries.

At 11.15am we passed the halfway mark – *wahoo*! Sure, the Tasman had slapped us around a little and *Lot 41* had stumbled a few times, but progress had been amazing. We were going to be in New Zealand well before Christmas at this rate.

"Hey, Jonesy."

"Yeah, mate."

"Can we not arrive on the 24, 25 or 26 December? Can we arrive just before then – I don't want to uproot the family for Christmas Day."

"It's still a long way off, Cas, we'll see how we go."

"Okay, but let's try."

Looking back, I can't believe we had this conversation. We had no idea what the Tasman would have in store for us in the second half of our journey.

"Hey, Jonesy."

"Yeah, mate."

"You realise that this is New Zealand water? NZ clouds! The water now tastes more like Mount Cook than Mount Kosciuszko! This is doable, mate … it's ditchable!"

"You're an idiot."

"Thanks, mate – bang! Mate, now that we're not in a bad mood," I added, "what is it that you get most frustrated at with me?"

Without hesitating, he spat out, "Three things. The first – my opinion has less weight than yours. Even though your instincts seem to be better than mine, it really pisses me off. The second is when I'm trying to steer and you say 'direction' every five minutes. The third is when you get frustrated at me. That's about it, really."

I was expecting something much more damning than that, but I was still surprised at how quickly he'd replied. "Wow … you must have given that little speech a fair bit of thought."

"Not really."

"Thanks for telling me, though, J."

DAY 18

For the first time on the journey, a brisk westerly wind had picked up the previous night to 25 kilometres per hour. Prior to departure, we'd planned that once we left the Australian coast (and the EAC), we could expect close to 70 per cent of the wind to come from the west – were we at that boundary already?

We brought in the para-anchor, which helped suck us 21 precious kilometres closer to NZ overnight (sometimes we could paddle for hours without making that kind of progress, so we almost felt a bit guilty about being handed these kilometres on a plate!). Unfortunately – or fortunately, depending on which way you looked at it – at 3am the wind strengthened, agitating the sea into an obnoxiously bumpy state. We tossed and turned, but just couldn't grab any decent kip.

Rising just before 5am, I put my wet weather gear on and, in completely miserable conditions, started paddling. May as well make the most of this wind, I thought to myself. The only respite from the ever-worsening weather was listening to my "golden oldies" playlist: good old Billy Joel, Bob Seger and Cold Chisel were always going to lift my spirits. Meanwhile, Jonesy had stayed in the cabin to do a satphone link-up with the Channel Seven *Sunrise* program and a little "maintenance".

After our ill-fated sea trial eight months earlier, we'd installed both electric and manual bilge pumps (to expel any unwanted water) in all compartments of the kayak – up in the bow, both the pits and in the cabin. The electric bilge in the cabin had stopped operating, and after realising the motor had seized, we decided to bin it – why carry extra weight when it's not providing any use? We knew we could rely on the manual back-up, so overboard she went.

Our Tasman mistress was beginning to become very adept at stealing what we thought was rightfully ours. The weather was one thing, but after giving it a bit of thought on board, we realised uncomfortably that she was beginning to suck our precious equipment away, item by item. Of course, it isn't just the ocean that has this effect: sand drifts on deserts and snow drifts in Antarctica inflict the same fate. Nature has a way of crushing our efforts and eventually restoring the landscape to a state that seems as if man has never been there.

Ploughing along in favourable conditions (albeit rainy) was a welcome change from paddling into headwinds. We began to have a classic chatting session. First, we started on the old days of playing cricket and footy – scratching our heads, trying to remember who was in our teams back to when we were 15 years old. Then it was who was in the school senior footy team, who was in our maths class, etc. These games would go on for hours. As our brains grew tired, we shifted our talk to big nights we'd had out on the town, and then eventually girls.

In the end, the brain-leeching reflection was too much. Jonesy continued with banter about girls that could have been, but I'd had enough. I stealthily slipped my earphones on and listened to music for the rest of the afternoon, as Justin kept on talking and laughing to himself. Although we were confined to such a small space on board *Lot 41*, paddling in the front pit with the iPod on, it was easy to convince myself that I was out there alone. It was a feeling of solitude that I needed every now and then.

13

HEADWINDS – JUST DEAL WITH IT

DAY 19

As we crawled, sodden, into the cabin that evening, we received the weather forecast for the next couple of days. Frustratingly, it had shifted from three days of westerlies to southeasterlies. All I said in my diary was: "Bugger – really annoying."

We had a late start the following morning, due to the ugly conditions battering us from the southeast. All our months of planning had told us that once we passed the 160 degree longitude we should expect most of the winds from the westerly quadrant. This was based on the last 75 years of historical data and many sessions with Clouds. As the easterly bombardment continued and we started to progress ever more slowly towards NZ, it became routine to plead with Pat to give us some westerlies in his forecast.

Doubt is a powerful seed. Once planted, the mind can make it explode into a towering forest incredibly quickly. For the first time on the expedition, we questioned the data we'd used in our risk management and the rigorousness of our preparation. And although we knew Pat and Clouds were relaying the best possible info on to us, we started getting angry with them, because they'd begun to change the weather forecasts and waypoints (the points we hoped to reach at different stages of the expedition) we were aiming for. We even questioned why Colin Quincey – the first person to cross the Tasman in a Dory (a small, shallow-drafted type of fishing boat that's been used for centuries) back in 1978 – had left from NZ, rather than Australia. Did he know something we didn't?

Although we knew the forecasts weren't their fault – Roger was analysing models and giving us the best information available, while Pat was merely a messenger passing on Roger's analysis – we took our frustration about the weather out on them.

Didn't they realise our goal setting was based on how far it was to our next waypoint? Changing our waypoints made it difficult to know how effective our relative progress was. It felt like being a goal-kicker in a game of rugby and having someone moving the goals around on a remote control, as you're about to kick the ball.

In desolate landscapes, morale relies on achieving imaginary landmarks. Each day, we paddled towards a waypoint, a longitude, a date. There were different milestones we set and looked forward to; they made us feel we were making a dent on the total distance. To an outsider these lat and longs we set ourselves were meaningless, but to us they were critical. No way could we have set out counting down the 1.7 million-odd strokes it took to paddle the Tasman, nor could we have said, "Great day today, only 2034 kilometres to go" – it would have been incomprehensible. We had to break it down into segments we could digest. Waypoints were our "short-term goals" that fed to our medium-term goals of "getting halfway across", "1000 kilometres to go", "500 kilometres to go", "200 kilometres to go" … Interestingly, we'd tell ourselves the whole way across that "the next 500 kilometres is the key". I'm not quite sure what it was about that number, but it always seemed to bring us comfort.

We made it routine to allow ourselves a treat for reaching these targets. The short-term goals were rewarded with a home-made Anzac biscuit or our favourite dehyd meal like roast chicken (temporarily abandoning our usual "lucky-dip" selections); the longer-term goals with a call to a mutual friend for a chat. The first of these was Ben, the genius behind our initial website and branding (and he was still swigging the beers and hacking away at the cigarettes).

We joked on the Tasman about the time Ben was our contact to the outside world when we kayaked across Bass Strait. On what was meant to be the penultimate day of our paddle we were graced with glorious conditions. We'd given Ben a call at 9am after being on the water four hours: we couldn't see land.

"Morning, Ben, how's things?" Jonesy asked through the CDMA phone.

"Yeah, alright," came a muffled grunt. After a short pause he blurted out, "Do you know what time it is? Why are you calling me so bloody early?"

"We need to get a weather forecast. We're thinking of pushing all the way to Tassie today."

Again, another pause.

"Argghhhh … you guys are *so* annoying, call me back in five minutes … I need to hang a shit first."

We reminded ourselves of this story out on the Tasman and couldn't stop laughing. The look on our faces as we sat, dumbfounded (trying to understand his priorities), in the middle of Bass Strait waiting for Ben's weather forecast to come through must have been comical.

The call to Ben that day on the Tasman at the 500-kilometre mark was the first time we'd *ever* heard excitement in his voice. (He was a pretty deadpan guy when he wasn't harassing people about waking him up.) It played a huge role in picking up our spirits on board.

Progress on day 19 was abysmal – at one stage, we paddled 6 kilometres in 4 hours. Considering a normal kayak cruises along at 8 kilometres per hour, adjusting to the speeds of our Tasman turtle was difficult at times. This day, in particular, Justin was frustrated on the rudder. Due to the conditions, paddling and maintaining our easterly bearing was almost impossible. Every time a wave knocked *Lot 41*, we seemed to career off track, pointing us back towards Australia. Whenever I'd yell "direction" (which was a lot), Jonesy would fume and swear under his breath. Aggravating our frustration was the bitter cold southerly wind spitting from deep in the Southern Ocean. Our hands initially turned red; then, after a few hours, they'd gone white and numb.

When there isn't too much of a wind-chill factor the air temperature out at sea is essentially the same as the water temperature. But because of the speed of the wind, and it being less than 12 degrees Celsius in the Southern Ocean (where the wind had come from), it wasn't able to absorb the relative warmth of the surrounding water, and as a result the wind felt like a supercharged air conditioner on rocket fuel.

On tough days like this, our thoughts constantly turned to Andrew and how he'd managed these conditions – by himself – in a kayak much more primitively set up than *Lot 41*. It was in these brief moments of reflection that we snuck a glimpse of how he must have suffered on that voyage. I'll always have an incredible level of respect for his strength of mind to have fought so bravely for as long as he did.

Day 9: Paddling along with the sun belting down on us. The face masks were to stop the inside of our nostrils from getting sunburnt.

Mmm … so that's how it was done.

Day 12: It wasn't all bad. Some days were so calm, we couldn't tell where the sea ended and the sky began.

Life inside *Lot 41* was *very* cosy.

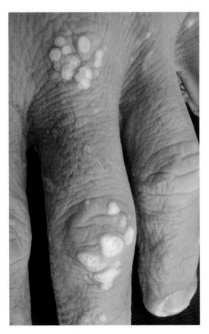

All sorts of blisters, ulcers and salt sores formed in the most unusual places.

Late on the afternoon of day 34, pumping the manual desal, which provided us with enough fresh water to keep us going.

Day 36 and a huge wall of water crashes over the bow. At times, we felt more like a submarine than a kayak.

Absolutely buggered. Around day 55 and still a long way from land …

Taranaki Daily News

"I dare you to pat him." When your kayak is being attacked by a couple of sharks, fear can make you say the strangest things.

Lot 41 from the eyes of a chopper on a calm, clear day – just the way we liked it.

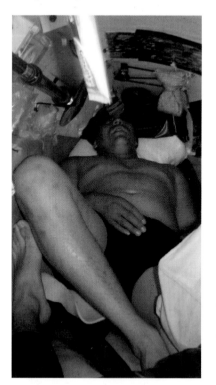

Sleeping arrangements in the cabin. Note the photos from home above Justin's head.

One more stroke. Some days, you just had to keep repeating the mantra over and over again.

The deceptively tranquil morning of day 62. Mount Taranaki is in sight, and the biggest celebration of our lives is drawing near.

Sixty-two days and 3318 kilometres behind us. Land ahoy – you beauty!

An indescribable experience. Being carried up Ngamotu Beach in New Plymouth and greeted by 25,000 well-wishers.

You've got to be kidding! Where did all these people come from?

Taranaki Daily News

Above left: "Pieguts" enjoying his first meal back on land. Amazingly, after demolishing that mountain of meat, Justin went on to devour his mum's and sister's meals too.

Above right: After arriving in NZ, it was strange having people look up to us as role models.

Left: Adventure isn't all about getting ugly. Life after the Tasman would never be the same – not that it's been like this ever since!

Below: Sydney International Boat Show 2008. Sharing our story with people all around the world has been a real privilege.

One of the lessons that crossing the ditch kept driving home was not to take life too seriously. This is Justin and me putting in the hard yards on Sydney Harbour prior to our departure.

At 12.20pm on Sunday 13 January 2008
Australian kayakers
James Castrission and Justin Jones
landed at Ngamotu Beach.

The journey from
Forster in New South Wales to New Plymouth
took 62 days, covering 3,325 kilometers,
resulting in world records for the longest ocean crossing
by a two-man kayak and the first kayak voyage
across the Tasman Sea.

We were incredibly honoured to have our expedition recognised by commemorative plaques at Forster and New Plymouth. Here's the one in NZ.

Life is all about relationships: Mia and me in January 2009. I've never been happier.

Paddling in these less than perfect conditions was particularly hard. During our skeds, we'd tell Pat how we were coping with the expedition by delivering a mark out of 10 in three categories: physical, fatigue and mental state. At the moment, all were terrible. As I mulled over the situation feeling utterly frustrated, my paddle blade whipped up a long stringy thread that wrapped round my face and hand. Aagh! I instantly dropped the paddle and started tearing at my face to pull the bluebottle off. After what felt like an eternity, I managed to rip away the stinging tentacles.

The bluebottle welts on my face were painful, but at least during that evening's sked, there was better news on the forecast front. It revealed that we'd receive some westerly winds in the next couple of days. It was time. We needed a break.

DAY 20

Stirring at 5am, it was hard to get motivated to face similar conditions to the day before: battling into cold headwinds wasn't an appealing prospect. Crawling out of the warm and homely cabin, rain spat on my soon-to-be-frigid, naked torso, causing goose bumps to sprout. "Who needs a cafe latte and a slice of raisin toast first thing in the morning when you can have this?" I thought to myself.

As I started to wring my soaking thermals, I saw a flash dance through the water. Then the rough surface erupted in a cauldron of froth. What was it? Initially, I thought it was tuna, but quickly realised it was a school of Mahimahi, also known as dolphin fish. There was a flurry of energy as these meaty, one-and-a-half-metre aggressive carnivores began attacking the small baitfish that had been nibbling on the ever-growing barnacles under the hull.

The water's surface bubbled and splashed as the Mahimahi took this opportunity to devour a hearty breakfast. We hadn't paid much attention to the baitfish, but watching them fight for their lives in the clear water reminded me of the scene we'd witnessed under the yellow buoy a week earlier. Actually, it was pretty inspiring. This intimate early-morning encounter cleansed us of some of our anxiety, fear and fatigue – it was infinitely more captivating than eating cornflakes in front of the telly.

As we prepared for the day's paddle, *Lot 41* sat sublimely on the fizzing cauldron. Suddenly, some of our friends launched spectacularly into the air with amazing agility, and then there was silence. The sea was calm and all the fish had disappeared.

We scanned the surface of the ocean for the only thing we imagined could have stirred such a rapid response: a shark. Then, sitting in the pits, we began to paddle in silence, staring deep into the turquoise water, expecting any minute to see the shadow of a graceful predator lurking below.

Often you want to just see something to allay your fears, even if it turns out to be bad news. (Not that we were at all like the Aussie soldiers in Vietnam, but we got a glimpse of how it must have felt not being able to see the well-camouflaged Viet Cong troops.) Nothing appeared, though – Lady Tasman refused us that comfort.

At the end of a pretty average day's paddle, we were relieved, but still partly terrified. Jumping into the cabin, we wondered what had caused the mass evacuation of the Mahimahi that morning. I sat staring at Jonesy's fingers scribbling down the weather forecast as he spoke to Pat for our evening sked. His blistered hands were starting to take on the appearance of a gnarled old man's. Darkly tanned, they were wrinkling from the constant exposure to the sun. With tape protecting several blisters, the pencil sat awkwardly between his fingers.

As Justin scribbled down the forecast for the next few days, I sat breathless, hoping that for tomorrow, or the next day, or the next, he'd write "w-e-s-t-e-r-l-y". It didn't happen. For the next week, it was all coming from the east – bloody headwinds. I wrote in my diary, "Huge hit to morale – very quiet, sombre atmosphere on *Lot 41* at present."

We lay in the cabin digesting our meal and chewing over the implications of these headwinds, independently doing the mental calculations – the old "if we only average 20 kilometres a day till the end, it'll take us another 50 days"; "if we cut back our rations, we can last another 75 days" etc. With different assumptions and parameters, this could go on for hours.

DAY 21

> VIDEO DIARY, DAY 21 – JAMES
> "The fatigue is definitely starting to take its toll on us.
> It's alright when you're clocking up the kilometres
> and making good distance, but with these bastard
> headwinds, we're really struggling ... it's hard, hard
> work on the body. We've gotta get some westerlies ...
> or else, we're going to be out here for a really
> long time."

Through the night, like a chunk of steel to an overpowering magnet, we were pulled back towards Australia. Our southwest drift was a telltale sign that we weren't going to make much progress paddling today. In the morning we battled, painfully slowly, towards the east and chucked it in at 1pm. It just wasn't worth it. We threw out the para-anchor and jumped into the cabin, eager to get on the satellite phone and find out from the horse's mouth – Roger Badham – what the hell was going on with the weather. Utter frustration was boiling through our veins – we were hungry to know what was going on up above.

"G'day, Roger," Jonesy made the call. "Justin here from out on the Tasman – how are ya?"

"Probably a lot better than you guys, methinks," he replied as Jonesy imagined the wry smirk covering Clouds' face.

Deciding not to waste time on small talk, Justin launched in: "Roger, what's going on with the weather? When do you think these westerlies are going to arrive?"

"Well … er …there's a tropical cyclone north of Fiji which is generating these nor'easterly winds. The models say that it's going to stick around for the next week or so."

"Great. Is there any risk of it coming towards us?"

"There is a small risk."

This was bad – very bad, in fact. Just when we thought morale couldn't sink much lower, another seed of doubt had been planted. Falling back on the planning work we'd done, Justin said, "We thought the risk of cyclones out here was next to nil at our current longitude and not much higher as we approached the eastern Tasman.

"'Cyclones require hot, humid air to form,'" he continued to recite a passage from our risk-management document. "'Generally, the air temperature in the Tasman is too mild for these cyclones to grow.' Isn't it?"

"That's right," Roger conceded. "But already this summer's weather is proving to be quite abnormal. We're seeing systems passing through the Tasman that I haven't seen in the past 30 years."

We lay in the cabin all afternoon. With not much else to do, we used the opportunity to pump the desal for four hours to build up a reservoir-breaking 12 litres of fresh water. The highlight of a quiet day was a choc-chip cookie each, and some chocolate-flavoured Sustagen. Nibbling away on a biscuit, we were lucky enough to absorb the rays of the fading sun filtering through the cabin door. Sure, it was beautiful, but we couldn't help but reflect on how nice it would be if we were seeing them at sunrise rather than sunset. That would mean that the wind was finally coming from the west …

DAY 22

VIDEO DIARY, DAY 22 – JUSTIN

"The game plan was to use the currents for the first half of the passage, and the second half use the westerly winds. Now … a massive spanner has been thrown into the pot. It's now a patience game. We can't get angry with the ocean, we can't get angry at each other nor with the situation. We just need to deal with it."

Because *Lot 41* hadn't been designed to paddle gracefully into head winds, the easterlies beating on her nose were depressing. Now that the solar panels didn't need to feed the ever-hungry water maker, we had surplus power: there always seems to be a positive in any situation if you look hard enough! And we needed all the positives we could get, after we'd woken to 45-kilometre-per-hour easterly winds battering the cabin. Fortunately, the para-anchor was anchored in a current that the previous night was dragging us south-southeast and was now shifting to the east. Stuck in the cabin all day, we both started to suffer from cabin fever again. We spent the day watching videos on our iPods. *Blades of Glory* and a documentary on chicken farms (which would have been lucky to screen at 3am on SBS, but which was inexplicably riveting) were favourites for the day.

The frustration of not being able to actively do things in the cabin, like ongoing repairs, pumping the desal indoors and night-time skeds, was driving me mad. I felt like a burden, not contributing to half the work there. Jonesy didn't complain once – he could see both the pain the seasickness was bringing me and my deep-rooted turmoil at not being able to lead from the front.

All afternoon we were nervous about what news the sked was going to bring. It couldn't get much worse. Surely?

"Evening, boys."

"Hi, Pat, should we run though it?" Justin said as usual.

"Go ahead."

"Scores. Physical: Cas 7, Jonesy 8. Mental: Cas 4, Jonesy 5. Fatigue: Cas 4, Jonesy 4. *Lot 41*, Health. Batteries, fore, 11.8V; aft, 12.4V. Other: cabin bilge not working, had to rewire battery terminals because of corrosion."

With both of us begging for westerlies, Pat paused for a moment, then went through an unwelcome forecast: "Tomorrow wind east-northeast 15 knots, increasing later in the afternoon swell southeast. Wednesday: wind east decreasing through the day."

Obviously, we were disappointed, but we had a job to do: Justin responded with the weather experienced during the day and compared the actual to the forecast.

He then continued: "Activity: stuck in the cabin all day." (Normally, it would be something like: paddled 0600 to 1900 on 105 degrees. Cas sat on the desal for 1.5 hours and Jonesy 1 hour. Made good progress in the morning, but the wind picked up in the arvo and made conditions difficult to maintain course.)

"RFIs [requests for information]. Can you give Katadyn a call and see if there's anything we can do with the water maker?"

As he often did, Pat then sent through a small 42-kilobyte file that showed our position in relation to the currents toying with us. In the cabin, we connected our Toughbook to a satellite phone, which gave us similar download speeds to extremely slow dial-up connection. As the kayak pitched and rolled, the connection would regularly drop out, but it provided us with critical information to set our strategy and course for the following day.

Then Pat gave us the information we'd been dreading. "Roger said that you boys should get used to the idea that the prevailing conditions are going to be flowing from the east for the rest of the passage."

It was like a punch in the guts. My diary entry that night said it all: "What the …?"

My mood picked up a little after the sked when I called home for my weekly phone call. It was quite funny – all I wanted to hear was what each and every person we knew was up to; the intricate details of their lives. How was work? How had they slept the night before? What did they have for breakfast? I sucked comfort out of hearing about day-to-day activities back home. Contrastingly, they didn't really want to talk about "boring city living" and wanted to hear about our adventures on the high seas.

It was a funny exercise in to-ing and fro-ing as we fought to gain control of the conversation: we settled for a pace where we'd ask one question and they'd ask one. To us, what we were doing felt routine and boring, but to the outsider it seemed riveting. We'd now been at sea for three weeks and they were fascinated about what living at sea in a kayak was really like.

They absorbed every word and you could sense them analysing the tone that might or might not have been hiding what we were really feeling. Then Mum said something that struck a chord.

"My little boy, I'm just so proud of you. You are doing so great – I can't even begin to imagine how tough you are doing it out there. You know how you wanted to inspire people? Well, you boys are splashed across newspapers in Australia and New Zealand every day and everyone – I mean everyone – knows about you guys. You're having more of an impact than you can imagine."

Wow, I thought. I smiled wryly and untactfully replied, "Mum, do you remember what you said to me two years ago?" I paused. "Do you remember saying, 'Stop wasting your time with this bullshit dream – it's completely selfish and you won't inspire anyone'?"

Mum was immediately apologetic. "I do remember that and I'm sorry. I'm just so proud of you now."

I felt guilty for rubbing Mum's nose in her own words, but I just couldn't help it. It was a childish reaction and I was immediately disappointed that I couldn't show more restraint.

DAY 23

After such a dismal forecast the night before, naturally we were expecting yet another cabin day, so we were excited, and amazed, to be greeted with paddleable conditions. The wind was meant to be 20–30 kilometres per hour from the east, but seemed much calmer. After doing a quick TV interview over the satellite phone, we jumped out into the pits and began paddling. I scribbled in my diary: "This favourable current is the work of God. Thank you."

After a couple of hours enjoying finally being on the move again, a spurt erupted 100 metres off our port bow, shattering a lengthy period of silent reflection. We eagerly scanned the horizon for another sign of life to confirm that we'd actually seen something, and that we weren't going crazy. There was nothing.

Then *boom*, it exploded into the air just 20 metres away, crashing on the water's surface rather ungracefully. Our first whale sighting! It spouted hundreds of litres of water into the air with each breath. These warm-blooded mammals surface occasionally to fill their lungs with air. Throughout the voyage, we wondered how they slept. Apparently, only one hemisphere of their brain sleeps at a time – that's why they're often said to sleep with one eye open!

Caught up in the magic of this intimate encounter, we forgot to pull the camera out until it was too late. We optimistically comforted each other by saying that we'd see plenty more. The improvement in morale that came with breaking the monotony of our routine never ceased to amaze us. For the rest of the day, we jubilantly paddled eastward, as huge gentle swells rolled beneath *Lot 41.*

14

BACK TO THE FUTURE

DAY 24

The forecast easterlies hit us hard. Throughout the night, *Lot 41* began to buck ever more violently as the wind and sea built aggressively. In a half-dazed state, I battened the hatches as water started pounding us from all sides. The constant bucking created quite an orchestra, as provisions and equipment worked themselves loose inside the cabin as we got tossed from side to side.

The hypnotic rattling had the consistency of a metronome, and it slowly became a kind of Chinese water torture. The ancient Chinese punishment drove its victim insane with the stress of water continually dripping on a part of the forehead, as, supposedly, the desire for the human brain to make a pattern of the timing between the drops caused insanity to eventually set in. Even the most subtle sound had a profound impact on me; Justin, on the other hand, was able to ignore it quite well – unfortunately.

A hanging toothbrush tapping, the inlet valve for the manual desal down the storage sides, or cords inside the charge box: the noise was usually worst when we were being buffeted around and, as a result, at those times I couldn't get much sleep. I think my mind associated not being able to sleep with the tapping caused by the aggressive sea state. Whenever I could hear even the most gentle sound, I'd search the kayak like a madman determined to find the source. Sometimes I'd go all night without finding it and by morning I'd vent my frustration with Jonesy, who'd often reply, "I couldn't hear anything."

Completely snapping on one occasion, I screamed, "*F**** this – what's making that tapping noise?"

"What noise, mate?" Justin groggily replied as he took out one of his earplugs. "I can't hear any tapping."

"*That* one," I insisted. Then a couple of seconds later: "There it goes again."

"Nah, mate, can't hear a thing. Just try and get some rest, Cas," he said sympathetically.

If the tapping hadn't driven me insane, Justin's reaction did. How could he not hear it? It wasn't like he was at the far end of the *QEII*.

Although the sounds in the cabin weren't annoying Jonesy too much, internally he was struggling. To me, he seemed upbeat, but he later confessed that at times he really battled to maintain a positive façade. Considering how naturally emotional Justin was, this must have been so hard for him. If he hadn't shown this strength, though, *Lot 41* would have been a sombre site.

I finally got *some* sleep, and as we woke up we knew that today we'd be stuck – once again – in the cabin. Without much debate, we decided to halve our rations on days we didn't paddle, in case we were out here for a little longer than expected. Besides, when we were holed up in the cabin we found it very difficult to consume 6000 calories worth of food – the equivalent of 21 pieces of KFC!

As Justin passed me half a protein bar later that morning, I realised the lights on the Comar Unit weren't flashing. With the Comar being a crucial defence against us being run over at sea, this was a bit of a worry – we were now almost invisible to passing ships.

We'd planned our route across the Tasman to avoid the major shipping channels, and as it turned out we only saw two container ships on our whole expedition. With our Comar out, we had to convince ourselves that due to our size and the fact that we weren't near any major shipping lanes, the risk of being bumped by a larger vessel was minute.

The traffic on the Tasman is nothing compared to, say, the Atlantic Ocean: we'd have been much more concerned if we'd been up there. Due to the minimal amount of traffic we were experiencing, we didn't instigate a "watch system" as ships at sea normally do. In all the offshore passages we'd done, there'd always been at least one person up on deck at all times to keep an eye on other vessels at sea.

DAY 25

Our bucking colt made sure we didn't get much sleep overnight. The wind in the morning had risen to above 55 kilometres per hour, accompanied by a 7-metre swell coming from the south-southeast. When out away from the coast, the size and direction of the sea is pretty much dictated by the wind. As it travels thousands of kilometres over the water, the wind's friction on the ocean surface causes the unpredictable sea state to form. That caused Lot 41 to lurch around like a drunken brawler, taking heavy hits but refusing to go down.

Out of sheer frustration with the weather, we gave Roger another call to get his thoughts. We knew what the answer was going to be, but just wanted to hear it from him: he was the gatekeeper to the weather. Reiterating our previous conversation, he told us these winds were being generated by a tropical cyclone north of Fiji. Always searching for the positive in a situation, the TC was heading east, so it posed a minimal threat. Again, at least there was a meagre gain to come out of a thoroughly depressing phone call.

DAY 26

> VIDEO DIARY, DAY 26 – JAMES
> "Who screwed up? Did we put too much faith in Roger? Did we not do enough research ourselves? Did we not design the kayak well enough? These headwinds are killing us. Normally Jonesy is the down one; the weaker one. Why am I the weaker one? I hate this seasickness."

Our third day stuck in the cabin. The wind continued to hammer us from the east, and to add salt to the wound – excuse the pun – we were now drifting back to Australia. We couldn't believe it – at this rate, we'd be floating into Sydney Harbour for Christmas. The weather began to abate in the late afternoon, but not enough to allow us to get in the pits and make up lost ground. By now, our heads were about to explode from lying on our backs for 60 hours plus. We managed to pump water for four hours, which was about the only benefit that came out of the day.

DAY 27

> VIDEO DIARY, DAY 27 – JAMES
> "Fourth f***ing day of shit locked up in the cabin. We've now lost close to half a degree [50 kilometres]. I'm getting over this pretty quickly. Every little thing is starting

to niggle now. Jonesy chewing loudly ... *every little thing.*
It's now been 27 days – 27 days of feeling like crap is
not fun. At least Jonesy is staying positive."

It was the fourth day now – we *had* to get out of the cabin. Even if
that meant going nowhere (which we ended up doing!). By 11am,
we began paddling into a cold 25-kilometre-per-hour breeze and
adverse current coming from the east-southeast. The sky was
covered in a gloomy dark shroud which reflected how we were
feeling about the whole situation.

We quickly realised that the paddle strokes were pretty futile.
We would have made more progress on the treadmill at the local
gym. We ended up going around in circles for an hour and a half
before our "workout" was complete.

Back in the cabin, we realised that we'd lost 42 kilometres
northwest over the previous four days of being cabin-bound. With
frayed nerves, we sat staring at the current overlay Pat had sent
through in the evening sked – it was a rude awakening. We were
being sucked into a giant anti-clockwise whirlpool. Our
immediate reaction, due to our utter frustration and disgust, was
to take it out on one another. It was as though we held each other
responsible. With neither of us able to storm out of the room to
blow off some steam, the rest of the evening was tense.

DAY 28

Conditions finally calmed to 10–15 kilometres per hour from the
east. Although progress was painfully slow as we were pushing
current, the sun was out, it was such a relief to be paddling again,
and we immersed ourselves in great conversation.

We made a pact that on our first dinner date back home with a
girl, we had to disguise a three-course meal comprising only the

cruddy rations we had on board *Lot 41*. We wondered how much our regal charm and class – as well as all the trimmings of a romantic candlelit dinner – could allow us to get away with in terms of serving up the crappiest meal our date had probably ever been subjected to. Admittedly, this is the kind of prank an eight year old might find slightly immature, but it did keep us amused at the time.

Running through the sked with Pat at 8pm, he told us that the Andrew McAuley inquest had started. We'd been dealing with Andrew's death every day since his disappearance: there hadn't been one day we'd been out paddling when we hadn't thought of how much he'd suffered in attempting to fulfil his Tasman dream.

My feelings towards Andrew had evolved torturously over the past five years. Initially we had deity-like respect for what he'd achieved and what he stood for. Towards the end of 2006, this had given way to anger and feeling betrayed, and on his fateful voyage, all the negative energy evolved into understanding and respect.

With its highs and lows, our experience with Andrew had taught me more about myself than any other single event in my life. Out here, our admiration for the suffering he'd been subjected to led to a deep admiration. We felt connected with him, and on some days we thought we could feel his presence urging us on, as if he too had let the negative energy dissipate. The three of us had shared something special that no-one else in the world could ever relate to – being in the middle of the Tasman Sea in a kayak.

DAY 29

VIDEO DIARY, DAY 29 – JUSTIN
"I'm frustrated as hell. While Cas was desaling, I managed to paddle 400 metres in 40 minutes. A toddler

could walk across the Tasman faster than that. I guess we
need to look at the positives … at least I'll lose some
weight and get skinnier. Maybe, just maybe, I might be
able to see my abs for the first time in my life."

We woke early to try and fight our way out of this current.
A gentle 10-kilometre-per-hour wind was coming from the
east, blowing rain on just the right angle to hit our faces. We
were baffled us as to why our progress was so slow. I struggled
through those first few hours because of acute pain that was
darting up my spine from my lower back – after a couple of
Nurofen started to take effect, though, the paddling became
more pleasant.

I began to get worried that my core muscles weren't supporting
my upper body. The core is your "transmission mechanism"
linking the strength of your lower body – where your stroke begins
– to the arms. Most people are surprised to hear that your legs
actually receive quite a decent workout when paddling. Often,
after a tough session on the water when you've been driving hard,
your legs are more sore than your upper body. Losing the driving
power from the lower body results in each paddle stroke becoming
significantly less effective.

I could tell from Jonesy's lack of conversation that he was
battling with his own world of pain. On days when steering was
difficult, his moods generally took a turn for the worse. There are
times on an expedition when you're better off not to mention the
pain or difficulty you're going through, and just get on with it.
Reflecting back on the time we left mainland Australia on our
journey across Bass Strait, as we paddled out of Refuge Cove on
the southern tip of Victoria we were incredibly intimidated by the
weather and the prospect of being so far away from land we

wouldn't be able to see it. If we'd discussed the situation as we pushed off the sand after we'd made our decision to leave, I think we would have paddled straight back to the refuge of the cove. However, this felt like one of those moments where it'd be better to have a chat about it.

"What's doing, mate?" I enquired, as tactfully as I could.

"I'm bloody tired, mate. I'm really not sleeping well at the moment," he said, sounding frustrated.

"How come? Have I been tossing at night?"

"Nah, mate, you've been fine. I'm not sure what it is."

Our pathetic progress, our difficulty sleeping, and the dreary weather were beginning to gnaw at our morale. We just couldn't figure out why we were going so slowly. When you're down, it seems everything is against you. My back was sore and I was paying more attention than normal to the chafe on my scrotum and bum. Every hour I'd lather Sudocrem on my backside, which provided temporary relief from the discomfort. But as the rain continued to fall, it caused salt water to trickle down my back, aggravating the chafe. In a 26-minute period, Justin counted that I tried to readjust my nuts 11 times.

To keep ourselves entertained, we talked about the perfect dinner date. Jonesy talked for half an hour about how he'd decorate his verandah with cushions and candles, and described in detail the 10 courses that were to follow. I joked that after the date she'd probably run to McDonald's to fill up, as the courses were so small – two mussels for entrée, one prawn for main and a strawberry for dessert! In spite of the chafing and the rain and everything else, and the fact that Jonesy himself would have vacuumed up such a tiny meal in less than 12 seconds, it was a funny conversation that picked up our morale.

DAY 30

VIDEO DIARY, DAY 30 – JAMES

"Six hours of brutal useless paddling, we find
ourselves absolutely no closer to New Zealand ...
tired, demoralised and shagged. Our balance is starting
to go – legs have lost a lot of strength. We just can't get
out of this thing. I'm getting over this. You can't beat the
sea – it's the boss. You just can't fight it ... it's too
powerful."

We paddled for six hours that day into both wind and rain and travelled 4.12 kilometres. At midday, we chucked out the para-anchor in defeat. Yet again, we drifted back to the 164 degree longitude. This "landmark" was turning into our holy grail. Like mercury, we'd grab at it, think we had it, and find it slipping out of our fingers.

Most of our food packs had been stored in the cabin, but we also had 40 packs (20 days' worth) in the bow. Supplies were starting to get low, so we moved some packs out of the bow and into the cabin, then jumped in the back. (As well as keeping us well equipped, shifting them also ensured that *Lot 41* was balanced in the water, even though we'd gone through 80 kilograms of food.)

As Jonesy pumped some water, I was just trying to get some sleep when – *bam* – a rogue wave smashed us on the beam, causing our Toughbook – which was designed to be water resistant, drop-proof, shake-proof, you-name-it-proof – to come flying out of its hidy hole and smack me on the head. *Brilliant*. Having an electronic brick pounding me on the skull, with a decent bump on the ol' noggin for a week to prove it, was a fitting conclusion to a horrible day.

DAY 31

"Slept like shit last night," I wrote in my diary. Between us we'd had an uncomfortable one hour's sleep. The fatigue was now starting to pierce past our gaunt, retracted eyes, through every muscle fibre and into our bones, which were beginning to ache. This deep-rooted exhaustion was taking us to places in our heads that we'd never been before. Sure, we'd been tired in the past – like in the three-day food and sleep deprivation exercise we'd done with the army. But no training or expedition had sucked the energy out of the marrow of our bones.

We were running on empty: life was becoming a matter of survival and fighting. By ourselves, I think either of us would have given up there and then on the morning of day 31. All we had was each other – and that was what we desperately clung to.

Waking in the morning, the first thing I'd routinely do was to switch on the GPS and wait for it to "acquire" (in other words, to locate) three satellites to give us a fix on our position. At the same time, I'd examine the direction the needle of the compass in the rear pit was pointing. Typically it was pointing west – that meant the prevailing conditions were coming from where we wanted to go. Not good. Confirming my suspicion, the GPS revealed that we'd drifted 20 kilometres northwest during the night. *Definitely* not good.

The situation was useless. Justin looked more-than-usually exhausted – he was constantly cross-eyed, which was somewhat disturbing.

We were trapped in this giant anti-clockwise current pulling us back towards Australia – we'd been going around in circles for 10 days. Staring at the ceiling of *Lot 41* I searched for answers and my mind entered an exhausted trance. I could sense Jonesy's fighting energy beginning to dwindle. We had to do *something* or this would be the end of our bid to cross the Tasman. A quote from the movie *Tin Cup* echoed in my head: "When a defining moment comes along, you define the moment ... or the moment defines you."

This was one of those moments. A lightbulb weakly flickered on and off in my hazy brain: "If we can't fight it, let's go with it. Let's use the wind and the current to break free of this god-awful whirlpool."

To this day I'm not sure whether this desperate thought was just a matter of staying sane and doing something that felt constructive, or whether it was a carefully planned out manoeuvre. Either way, paddling backwards at a reasonable rate seemed preferable to aimlessly drifting around in circles.

I discussed with Jonesy the concept of paddling back west towards Australia to break free of the current. We ran over the pros and cons, noting that we were extremely fatigued and therefore could not know how rational our reasoning was.

After we both decided it was viable, we rang Pat to talk him through our strategy – we knew we needed his advice on the strength of our reasoning. He discussed it with Roger and half an hour later we began paddling towards the afternoon sun with a following sea. How bizarre it was to see the compass needle pointing west and to paddle into the fading light. Even with a following sea, though, we were slightly concerned about the speed of our progress. What was slowing us down *now*?

That evening I had my weekly phone call with the family, but I wasn't in the mood to talk with them. Although we'd now decided on a strategy, we were far from being merrily on our way again, and every bit of positive encouragement my family sent us, I found hard to absorb. Our bodies were beginning to burn from our joint flame, and nothing else. Although it was understandable for them to say "just keep going" or "don't worry about it, the wind will change soon", it seemed as if no amount of external encouragement could pick our morale up – our families and friends sometimes felt too far abstracted from the realities of life on the Tasman.

15

RAIN, MORE RAIN, AND A PINK SCRUBBING BRUSH

DAY 32

I couldn't escape the stench. The sickening reek of urine. At some stage over the past couple of days, one of us had pissed all over my pillow and the stench now blanketed it. Tossing around from side to side, I tried to escape the smell by wrapping a thermal top round my head. It provided momentary relief, but the smell returned. To complete the ugly picture, *Lot 41* was starting to buck quite violently.

"Not again," I kept whispering to myself. I played my hypnotherapy tapes for hours, trying to escape into a trance. But my mind was fried. I couldn't evade the reality of the discomfort – it was engulfing me.

"I hate this shit," I yelled out, and at that moment I lost my mind – I began punching the wall of *Lot 41*. I swore and swore and – thinking about the gut-wrenching seasickness, and us going around in circles for days on end, getting further away from our destination by the hour; not to mention the piss-stained pillow – I suddenly wanted nothing more than for us to sink and for the whole ordeal to be over. I was defeated.

Jonesy seemed really worried. He pleaded with me to stop my ranting, concerned that I was going to break my hand.

I screamed, "I *want* to break it – then I can get off this bloody kayak."

Jonesy was desperate and really thought he might have to physically restrain me if I got too out of control. He was terrified that I might do something irrational and stupid like jumping into the ocean. I never thought of that as an option, but I did imagine other ways of aborting the mission. I fantasised about cutting one of my fingers off, and on a few occasions I pleaded to God for a debilitating illness to hit me, so I had an excuse to get rescued or die. I just wanted – *needed* – to be back on land.

Waking in the morning, I said to Jonesy, "I'm over this, mate, I need to get some rest. I don't give a rat's any more. I just don't care."

We drifted in and out of sleep for another half hour until Justin began to stir and get himself ready to paddle. I lay motionless, pretending not to be aware of his movements. He crawled over me, then said, "You had a really bad night last night, mate, try and get some more rest." My reply was a garbled groan.

He retrieved the para-anchor, and as he took his first couple of strokes an overwhelming sense of guilt juddered through me. I reflected on how we'd connected during the sleep deprivation training we'd done with the army. They'd tried to break us. They'd tried to pit us against each other and tear us apart. They'd failed. We were always there for one another, taking the other person's push-ups if they were battling, giving them a push when they needed it. But now I was letting Jonesy down – I was relying on him to carry us on. I wasn't contributing to morale or progress. I was becoming a whining burden.

"Get up, you fat shit," I yelled at myself. "Get up now. Your best mate is out there fighting for you, and what are you doing?"

I was angry for allowing this situation to occur. I swore to myself then that would be the last time I'd put the pressure on Jonesy to shoulder the brunt of the work. I rose and poked my head out of the cabin.

"Morning, mate," came his nonchalant greeting. "Wasn't expecting you out here till lunchtime."

Still disappointed about how I'd acted, I replied, "Sorry about last night, mate, I won't let that happen again."

Considering Jonesy must have been really worried about me – even wondered whether the expedition was going to continue – he was amazingly calm about me coming to my senses. Perhaps he just knew that, despite my outburst, I wouldn't let him down; not after what we'd been through to make it this far. We paddled on, plugged into our iPods.

Listening to some tunes, I thought about Colin Quincey's lone voyage across the Tasman. I remembered reading about how, during that expedition, he'd thrown vital equipment off the vessel, sworn at the ocean and kicked things. When I read this alarming detail, I vividly recall thinking that would never be me. Embarrassingly, though, I'd done the same – I'd "chucked a Quincey". I'd allowed the ocean to creep under my skin and infect my outlook. For the second time that day, I resolved to have the discipline to stay strong: "Kia kaha", as the Maori (and the All Blacks) would say.

During the afternoon, the wind turned south-southwest, which caught us off-guard. As I put it quite bluntly in my diary, "This inconsistent wind is really starting to screw us up." Our strategy to paddle backwards, to go forwards in the long run, was somewhat dependent on the weather forecast remaining static. We were planning on using the northeast winds to drive us southwest, then in a calm period that was to follow driving south, then southeast, to break free from the current. A combination of this odd wind direction and the current had us drifting northeast. *Damn.*

Normally, these westerlies would have been great but the last thing we wanted was to return to where we'd come from: back into the dreaded whirlpool. This confusion in the weather led to Jonesy's low point of the expedition. We were now in the same spot as we'd been 11 days ago.

As we continued south-southeast, surfing down 6-metre waves, we'd thought we were flying along – it felt fast and the paddling was truly exhilarating. Looking at the GPS each hour, though, we were horrified at the low mileage we were clocking up. How were we going to reach NZ – or, more pertinently, get out of the whirlpool – when even when we were using the wind and the current, we were plodding along like a fish through mud? Once again, we began questioning everything from our fatigue levels to our muscle atrophy. What was slowing us down? Indecision and uncertainty is what drives people mad at sea. It is one of the most powerful mind games that the ocean can play. Here was the Tasman once again testing our fortitude and resolve: if she was fighting us individually we would have been defeated long ago, but the two of us held strong and just kept plugging.

We slogged through the afternoon rain in the 6-metre seas that continued to pelt down on us. Water was everywhere: below us, above us, all around us. It felt like it was seeping into our bones. The incessant bullet spray on our Gore-Tex anoraks sounded like rain on a corrugated iron roof and instantly brought me back to Australia. Imagery of shearing sheds I'd slept in and mountain huts high up in the Snowy flooded through me. I wished I was tucked up in my sleeping bag, with my fingers curled around a nice warm mug of tea, my fleece jacket over my shoulders for extra warmth. I visualised sitting by the dirty window there, hypnotically staring at the water drops beading, then falling off the window sill.

A wave crashing over the top of us quickly brought me back to reality, prisoners fighting to break free of this god-awful whirlpool.

At the end of the day's paddle, I limply sat staring at the GPS, waiting for Jonesy to get inside the cabin. I examined the back of my hand: to be more precise, the knuckle of the middle finger on my left hand. It looked like the skin of a lychee. The dimples had been forming on the knuckle for days and they now completely engulfed it. They seemed to be spreading and we didn't know what they were. It appeared that they'd soon spread to the knuckle of my forefinger.

It was time for action. We took a photo and emailed it to Dr Glenn – who'd honed our suturing and IV drip skills before the expedition – for his analysis. Our email connection out on the Tasman was via a satellite phone that sent and received emails at 6 kilobytes per second. A mere 10 years earlier, every household had been jumping on the internet at these speeds. With the advances of modern technology, we not only expect transfer rates a thousand times faster, but we "need" them. At 6 kilobytes per second, it would take 10 minutes to transfer one image the size of a postcard. Due to the pitching and rolling of the kayak, we'd often find this connection dropping out as a "large" file was coming in or we were sending a photo. Some days, we could send five photos in 30 minutes without a glitch; other days we struggled to get a single photo through in less than two hours. The quality of our reception depended on where the satellites were sitting in their geostationary orbit. Fortunately, only once on the entire crossing did the phone not have enough satellites for us to make a call to land.

Dr Glenn got back to us shortly afterwards. His prognosis was that my skin condition was either genital herpes or warts – I was pleased it turned out to be the latter!

In the cabin that evening after another day's paddle towards Australia, we scoffed down our dehydrated meals and tried to raise Pat; but no reply. This was odd. For 32 days now he'd religiously been there to answer our 6am and 8pm skeds, and this was the first time he'd been AWOL.

Throughout the night we drifted another 20 kilometres northwest. Finally, as the piss-stained pillow had stopped worrying me so much and the seas were behaving, we caught up on some quality rest. More importantly, we had a strategy – a goal to work towards. Our scheduled westerly winds had been delayed a day, which bought us more time to paddle in that direction and get out of the whirlpool.

I'd had enough of rogue waves creeping through the open door and soaking me, so that night I spent a good couple of hours rigging our emergency canvas door cover, making sure it allowed a flow of fresh air into the cabin but still kept the ocean out. After a number of failures and design issues, I triumphantly showed off my rigging job to Jonesy, who was busy sending some emails off to Pat.

Unfortunately, he seemed only slightly impressed. "You know you're going to have to disassemble it in the morning, don't you, mate?"

I proudly sat there showing him the features of my amazing invention: the ventilation flaps, its incredible robustness. I must have sounded like a dodgy car salesman gone mad.

"Yeah, great, mate," he replied, like he was talking to someone with "special needs".

As I drifted off to sleep, still with a proud little smirk hidden under my bum-fluffy beard, I got kind of emotional about the prospect of destroying my masterpiece.

DAY 33

Not one wave entered the cabin all night. Tearing the cover away in the morning, I chuckled at the thought of what an alien looking down on us might have made of the scene – a naked hairy baby breaking the embryotic sac of *Lot 41* and crawling out of her womb. The constant spitting rain made sure I didn't laugh for too long as I fumbled to wring my thermals and lurch into them as quickly as possible.

Once we were in the pits, Jonesy and I talked about the next important decision facing us. With the loss of speed and paddling backwards, we had the potential to be out on the Tasman longer than we'd ever envisaged. So we didn't really have any choice: we decided to halve our food rations on paddling days, leaving us with one pack of food each day for the two of us.

It would take our bodies a few days to adjust to the new rationing, but we were determined to get to New Zealand with no outside assistance, and any food dropped to us would have compromised our voyage's "unsupported" integrity. Throughout the next few days our stomachs grumbled constantly, with every meal leaving us still half famished.

Justin is someone who loves his food. As a child, he acquired the nickname "Jaws" for his insatiable appetite for biting people, and although I'm not sure if there's a link, by his early 20s Jonesy had an undefeated record in eating competitions. He once challenged a mate to a 21-piece KFC feed-off (that's 250 grams of saturated fat), and won. In 2005, he ate 2½ kilograms of lamb shanks at a restaurant in Coffs Harbour and he smashed a 2-kilo roast for an afternoon snack prior to crossing the Tasman. As I said, the bloke doesn't mind his food.

Justin has always said the best part of any expedition is the breaks, and I honestly believe out on the Tasman he spent 60 per cent of his time dreaming about food, thinking about food, or talking about it. He designed numerous courses, made up dishes in his head and wrote four pages of cravings that he was determined to indulge in once we reached the shores of NZ. This was understandably a trying time for him, and he really had to fight over the next few days as his starving limbs became accustomed to less fuel.

With the reduced rations, we were much less selective – and much less fussy – about what we ate. By day 33, food that we'd dismissed at the beginning of the voyage as "disgusting" was in just as high demand as our favourite meals: choc-fudge protein bars and dehydrated curries were now shoved down our mouths without much thought. Taste was a luxury compared to the calories.

Just as fighter pilots have their name on the outside of their cockpits, we had our nicknames on the side of our pits – both were quite self-explanatory. The names our mates had given us were "Pieguts" – for Justin, of course – and "Boofhead". Our mates would joke: "Pieguts and Boofhead are off on their most excellent adventure!"

We were adapting to life at sea. Little discomforts – rain, chafe points, foggy sunglasses – all became part of the routine. However, one of the little niggles that drove me mental was losing sound in one of my waterproof earphones. Having sound blaring into one ear and a chaotic crackle piercing the other eardrum was mind-blowingly frustrating. It was an absolute privilege to have music out on the Tasman, but as is so often the case with "life privileges" they have the habit of becoming needs, and our iPods were no exception. By spending time in some of the most remote places on earth, Jonesy and I have been fortunate enough to learn valuable lessons about what's meaningful in life and what isn't … but I still would have *loved* that other earpiece to work.

In the past, Justin had always seemed to listen to music more than me – like when we'd run the Sydney Marathon. Ethically, I thought it was "weaker" to do exercise listening to music, and it was much more "pure" to do without. This was one of an endless list of things that changed on the Tasman. I found myself listening to music twice as often as Justin. Typically, I'd listen between 7am and 9am, have a one-hour break when we'd often talk, and then between 11am and 2pm most days, I'd listen to podcasts.

Paddling along at an agonisingly slow pace with a dud earphone, my frustration with the situation was increasing by the minute. Once again I broke. As I wrote in my diary: "F*** this rain, f*** the wind and f*** this stupid kayak!"

What could possibly be slowing us down? I asked Jonesy to grab the goggles from the cabin and pass them to me to take a look under the kayak. I thought the rudder might have snagged some seaweed and we might have been towing a string behind us. But I was wrong. Sticking my head under water, I was horrified to see the hull completely covered in barnacles the size of golf balls, measled on the underbelly of *Lot 41*.

"Mate, you're never going to believe what her belly looks like."

I passed Jonesy the goggles and he was equally staggered. "No wonder we're going so slow ..."

Right at the last minute before we'd left Forster, I'd bought a pink-handled scrubbing brush from the local Woolworths to clean our foil eating bags; and also for the minute possibility of us needing to scrub the hull. I remembered Justin saying prior to us leaving: "There's no way we're ever going to need that – I'm not planning on going for a swim out there."

Well (not that I'm gloating or anything), now we desperately needed that brush that had been dangling dormant from the ceiling for the previous month.

"Scissor, Paper, Rock," I blurted out. "And the loser has to go in and scrub the hull."

"Yeah, alright," Jonesy conceded, "that seems fair. Best of three? Or one round and whoever loses … loses?"

"One-shot rule."

"Okay, let's go. Scissor … paper … *rock*."

Imagining taking a dip with a hungry shark or two, our hands moved up and down like jackhammers as we contemplated the dire implications. To be fair, as when the para-anchor line got tangled, I secretly wanted to lose. I would have much preferred to be in the water myself than have my best mate in there.

I chose rock – which I seem to do about 70 per cent of the time (but don't tell Jonesy) – and Justin called paper. I lost and was ceremoniously handed the scrubbing brush: it was time to go in. Leaving all my clothes in the cockpit, I tied two safety lines around my belly as Jonesy nervously sat on both shark watch and camera duty. Slithering into the ocean, the warmth of the sea and the stunning clarity of the water were completely overwhelming.

Sunlight shimmered off small fish darting around the place in all directions as I got to work. Inhaling short, nervous breaths, I dived under the kayak and started scrubbing from midship, then made my way to the stern. I was somewhat comforted by having Justin nearby and being able to jump into the nearby pit in a second if I had to. The exposure was surreal, though, and with the translucent sea it was like floating through space in zero gravity. Dazzlingly blue, the water seemed to belong to some remote tropical island. If only there were bikini-clad girls and pina coladas waiting on the beach!

It had actually turned into a really pleasant afternoon. The sun was now shining for the first time in days, the sea had abated and the joy of going for a swim broke the monotony of our routine and was actually pretty enjoyable. Justin sensed how much fun I was having, and before long he left shark patrol and was in the water taking some amazing photos. For a short time we escaped the Tasman and felt like kids playing in a pool.

There were not only barnacles on the hull, but a decent smattering of algae as well; however, after about an hour in the balmy water we'd managed to remove all the major growth. The last job we did while in the water was to check the rudder lines and we observed that the port side had been quite badly chafed near the actual rudder, so Jonesy retied it past the chafe point. It took a lot longer than expected. But try to picture a 90-kilogram bloke straddling the back of a kayak, attempting to tie a knot with numb hands (naked too!). I think his fumbling display was understandable.

This maintenance on the Tasman had to happen when the weather gave us a chance – trying to fix a problem once it arose was never part of our strategy.

Drying quickly in the afternoon sun, we put our thermals on and resumed paddling. We were anxious about what difference having a barnacle-free hull would make. To our absolute delight, our speed doubled to 5 kilometres per hour. We were stoked. A combination of great hull speed, balmy weather and changing our routine by jumping in the water made our spirits the highest they'd been in weeks. For the rest of the afternoon, we merrily sang Christmas carols and a marching song we used to sing on bushwalks when we were kids.

DAY 34

We woke to a school of Mahimahi darting under the belly of *Lot 41*, feeding on baitfish tucked up under the kayak. Marine life seems to be attracted to any object in the water – whether it be a log, vessel or merely some debris – and *Lot 41* had adopted quite a maternal role in providing protection to these little fish. Her two favourite ocean children were Bruce and Larry, who soon became our best (and only) friends at sea. These two slimy mackerel had joined us in the second week of our voyage and were still "on board". As we progressed across the Tasman, these guys grew quite noticeably. By the end of the passage they'd reached such a size that they often bullied and ate other baitfish seeking refuge under *Lot 41*. Incredibly, these two intrepid baitfish stayed with us for over 1400 kilometres, providing many hours of company and companionship.

As the baitfish under the kayak were under attack by the Mahimahi, different emotions churned through my mind. We were excited by the frenzy but worried that Bruce and Larry might be taken by the onslaught. They were completely outnumbered, outsized and really didn't seem to have any chance of surviving the intentions of these hungry predators. As the sea bubbled and churned, we tried in vain to get a glimpse of our mates, but we couldn't see anything through the tangle of metre-long Mahimahi, who were executing perfectly timed fly-bys under the hull.

As we started to paddle, the excitement slowly died down and we were left feeling quite nervous about the outcome of the morning's onslaught. By 8am – 90 minutes after the bombardment began – the anticipation was killing me, so I grabbed the goggles and stuck my head under the water to have a look for our marine brothers.

At first, I saw nothing. My stomach knotted. Then, as I had a closer look, I saw Bruce and Larry tucked up on either side of the rudder right up against the hull. They'd cleverly realised they were safe there. My head burst out of the water and I eagerly spat out, "They're alive, mate!"

Both of us started laughing. The fact that our comrades had overcome seemingly insurmountable odds put us in a great mood. A lesson was there for the taking: if they could endure such an attack, we could at least continue to fight the Tasman. It may sound mad in hindsight, but their display of courage was really inspiring.

I was reminded of a scene from the film *Braveheart*, where William Wallace's uncle said: "First, learn to use this [pointing to William's forehead], then I will teach you how to use this [he lifted the sword]." Unless I was mistaken, Bruce and Larry had obviously watched the movie and put the ancient Scottish wisdom into practice.

Eating fish pie for dinner (no, not baitfish), I had a nice long chat to the family. Spirits were a little higher on board, now that we were making some progress, albeit still backwards. Once again, I was desperate to hear about their regular daily life, and – not for the first time – I found myself asking, "So what did you have for breakfast this morning?" We felt so alienated on the Tasman, we might as well have been on Pluto, and the thought of English Breakfast Tea with Vegemite on toast was somehow incredibly comforting. My brother Clary told me about his recent break-up with his girlfriend of three-and-a-half years: it felt bizarre to be bobbing around in the middle of the sea in a kayak, giving relationship counselling to someone back home.

DAY 35

When you're out for a drive in the country, you might marvel at the hills, trees, wildlife, or countless other distractions. For us, though, in the absence of anything else at all to keep us occupied, it was all about clouds.

There were heaps of different formations out there. Alto cumulus, which we called faglets, resembled the cotton-bud clouds out of the opening credits of *The Simpsons*. Often the whole spectrum of clouds, from below 5000 feet – cumulus – all the way above 25,000 feet – cirrus – were on display in the one vast portrait. Each layer intertwined with the other ones, forming a breathtaking display. Just as we did as kids, we'd watch the clouds mould into beautiful shapes – from teapots with weird tails to six-legged lions, we saw it all.

Paddling beneath a blanket of cloud, I couldn't help mulling over the fact that we'd been suspended under this greyish white for the previous nine days. As usual, trying to find the positives in every situation, I said to Jonesy that we were quite fortunate our electric water maker went down. He looked at me strangely.

"Please explain," he said, doing his best Pauline Hanson, but apparently quite perturbed.

"Well, if we'd been running the unit with all this cloud cover, the solar panels wouldn't have had a chance to properly charge the batteries, which could have led to our whole system going down."

"I guess so," Jonesy responded, sounding oddly unconvinced.

Later in the day, we ended up chatting about climbing. Apart from family and friends, it was one of the things I missed most out at sea, and Justin leveraged this effective tool throughout the voyage for picking up my mood. All he had to do was ask me about a climb I'd done in the past and, before long, I'd be rambling on about it move by move. To poor Jonesy's dismay, I'd sometimes drop my paddle and show him how each hand gripped the rock. People often tell me I have the memory of a goldfish (or maybe they don't – I forget now). However, it never ceased to amaze both of us how vividly I could remember the moves and the gear I'd used on particular climbs over the previous five years.

Some people say that many of the world's greatest adventures have been done, but to me adventures are all about growing as a human and having a mind-blowing experience you'll never forget. I remember climbing with a British bloke in New Zealand a few years back, and halfway up a snow-clad peak we were having a swig of water, when he said out of nowhere, "You know it's a bloody good adventure when 1. You come back alive; 2. You come back as friends; 3. You bag the summit."

That conversation ended up inspiring how I now look at adventure and make decisions in the outdoors. First and foremost, I try to make decisions that will keep me safe – there's always another mountain to climb and ocean to cross; the skill I've tried to learn is to make sure I get to see those other mountains.

I also try to value friendships above reaching the summit. Jonesy has always been one to put others' needs above his own – he always makes sure you've got the bigger portion of dinner, the earphones that work, etc.

Finally, having followed those two rules, it's time to bag the summit. It's so important not to let this overshadow the other two higher objectives, because when you start to prioritise the glory of the summit, you can find yourself in trouble.

Anyway, adventure doesn't have to be in the remotest place on earth. As a kid, adventure for me was about sneaking into the garden of that crazy old hermit across the road, or crawling up into the attic of my grandparents' place and finding old newspaper clippings from World War II. Wherever I'm at in my life, now and in the future, adventure will mean exploring, whether it's having a family, starting a business or whatever.

The conversation about future expeditions and the philosophy of adventure continued into the twilight. Justin talked about how he'd like to challenge himself in a landscape with waves similar to that of the ocean, but on land. Paddling along, he'd often imagine that the massive Tasman swells were not water but sand. He talked of wanting to explore deserts around the world. Ironically, the scenery in a desert and out at sea is so similar in so many ways – it's the wind that dictates the shape of the surface.

Towards the end of the day, we passed the 164 longitude for the fifth time in two weeks. Would it be the last?

16

THE ENDLESS NIGHT

DAY 36

Great. Strong southeasterly winds above 50 kilometres per hour had us holed up once again in the cabin. Laying to anchor feeling incredibly frustrated, we were desperate not to be blown back into the whirlpool – but all we could do was ride it out and wait for conditions to improve to make some progress.

We were only half-awake when we were suddenly shaken by an aggressive set of waves. *Lot 41* was dragged through a massive wall of water and dumped the other side. There was a horrible howling sound and when I looked outside to check out what it could be, I saw that the bridle had wrapped around the rudder (see the illustration on page 297) and the full force of the anchor was now loading it.

It was virtually dark now as we sorted through our options. We could either try to ride out the storm, hoping *Lot 41* could hold firm overnight; or one of us could get out there and try to untangle the mess. With the force and speed of the waves engulfing us, though, option B was incredibly dangerous. The rudder was crazily hammering up and down like an industrial sewing machine and for one of us to get in the water – in complete darkness – to try to fix it would be virtually suicidal. I'm so glad Jonesy talked me out of it ...

We decided to wait until the morning and hope that the seas had abated by then. As the screeching continued, we got into all our survival gear and prepared for the worst. We put our merino wool thermals on, our survival suits, our PFD Type 1 Lifejackets, made sure our 406 GPS EPIRBs (emergency beacons) were tied to each of us, and checked that the safety raft was ready to be deployed. We both each had an array of flares attached to us.

If the stern of *Lot 41* was ripped out, the cabin would flood in seconds. We could hear the quiver of fear in our voices as we ran through the situation with Pat. It was a night none of us would get any sleep, and it's branded in our memory as the scariest moment of our lives. (When we got back to Australia, a mate's uncle said it reminded him of what he'd been through in the trenches in World War II, waiting for an attack on enemy lines.)

Pat gave us the weather and indicated that the storm would build during the next few hours. With the worsening conditions, we all realised that this meant the force on the rudder would only increase.

As we lay down after sked, the god-awful screeching dulled the sound of the intensifying storm outside. Even by putting our earphones on to try and escape from the noise, it found a way of filtering into our eardrums. It sounded like *Lot 41* was being tortured – like a wounded animal about to be put down. *Screech, screech, screech.*

Making things worse, we quickly found we were beginning to overheat with all our survival gear on. When battened down, the condensation and heat inside the cabin became unbearable. Being covered in numerous layers of clothing designed to keep us alive in the bitterly cold Tasman water was proving to be horrendous, but we knew that if the back of *Lot 41* ripped out we wouldn't have the time to get into our survival gear. We had to have it on. There we lay, sweating from both fear and heat, trying to comfort each other by saying things like: "If she was going to go, she would have gone already."

Back home, the high alert made the media go crazy. Many of our friends, family and forumites stayed up all night with us. The forum on our website buzzed with activity and encouragement.

That night all we could cling to was each other, and our four years of rigorous preparation and planning. Our thoughts kept reverberating back to the structural work we'd done on the hull laminate and rudder layup and the worst-case training we'd done to prepare for an abandon-ship scenario. *This* scenario.

Lot 41 was designed to be positively buoyant. In other words, if every bulkhead and compartment filled with water, she'd still float on the top of the ocean. This was due to the amount of foam in the hull that was sandwiched between the two layers of fibreglass and the amount of foam added on the "bumps" on the side. This critical design consideration meant that *Lot 41* was supposed to be a safety raft in itself – it was designed to never sink. The models and theory had shown this was the case, but obviously we never wanted to be in a position to test this.

The screeching became lost in the howling winds, as sweat continued dripping from our faces. Our mouths were dry with a bitter taste like putting your tongue on the end of a battery, as we'd look at our watches every 10 minutes hoping an hour had passed. As the wind built, *Lot 41* started bucking ever more violently. Hour by hour ticked by – the night was lasting forever.

At 2am she kicked out the back of a massive wall of water. We were tossed from side to side, and as we careered down the face of the next big wave to hit us, there was no screeching. Same with the next wave – no screeching. It took another couple of minutes to register, but we slowly began to realise that the horrible noise had stopped. Our initial excitement that the bridle had – we thought – untangled itself soon turned to fears that the rudder had broken or the bridle had snapped under the load. With the sea staying angry and daylight a couple of hours off, we weren't going to be able to examine the damage until dawn broke.

Over the next few hours I convinced myself that the rudder would be bent beyond repair. We had an emergency replacement rudder on board, which would have been better than nothing but far from desirable. Even if the rudder was only slightly damaged, it would have played havoc with our steering. Because the force was now off the rudder, we were able to slither out of our survival suits and get some anxious sleep before dawn. What would the next day reveal?

DAY 37

We slept right through our 6am alarms – you can just imagine how worried our parents were back home. Pat had been getting nervous phone calls and emails from our families and friends for hours. He had to defuse the situation by saying that if there'd been an emergency during the night, both our EPIRBs would have been activated and our tracking would have made it clear that *Lot 41* was full of water.

As our family, friends and support crew grew increasingly anxious, we slept. I eventually half woke – feeling like the first time you open your eyes after a general anaesthetic. My lids rose heavily, then collapsed shut instantly. For that brief moment they were open, enough light flooded into my retina to register that the sun seemed higher than normal. Rolling over on one side and groaning, I opened my eyes and had a look at my watch – 8am.

"Shit, Jonesy, we've slept through our alarm," I shouted.

There was no movement.

This time I violently shook his leg. "Oi, Pieguts. Wake up, bro, we've slept in."

He sat up awkwardly, rubbing his eyes, and said matter-of-factly, "Bugger."

We quickly pulled the satellite phone out and called Pat. He picked up before it had time to ring through.

"Morning, Pat, it's Jonesy here."

Pat was obviously a bit freaked out. "What *happened?* Everyone back home is going nuts."

"Er … we accidentally slept in." It sounded incredibly lame, but Jonesy went on to explain we hadn't slept all night and when the bridle untangled itself, we'd crashed out. There was no time for idle chit-chat, though. We had to check the rudder and Pat had to alert the authorities that all was okay.

Sticking our heads out of the cabin we realised that we'd been so engrossed in getting on the phone to Pat, we hadn't observed the state of the sea. She'd calmed a little but was still furiously frothing – it didn't look like a paddle day and definitely looked too rough to carry out running repairs on the rudder if the need arose.

I put the goggles on and dunked my head into the water. It's amazing how angry the surface can look, but hidden beneath the surface, fish are swimming round in a serene environment. As I craned my neck to the right, I was expecting to see the rudder bent and half-mangled, but to my utter bewilderment, it looked absolutely fine; and unexpectedly Bruce and Larry were still there too! All five of us had made it through the night unscathed.

Jonesy smiled broadly as I yelled this great news to him, which he eagerly relayed to Pat. During the construction process, Justin had spent far too many hours working on the rudder. After that night, I didn't begrudge him one single second of it. It was still blowing 45 kilometres per hour from the southeast. We couldn't make any progress, so we had a great opportunity to catch up on some much-needed rest – we dozed all day as the seas around slowly began to abate.

DAY 38

The seas continued to die down, giving us the opportunity late in the afternoon to do some welcome paddling after having been holed up for two-and-a-half days in the cabin. We made some decent progress – 14 kilometres in four-and-a-half hours – far from the quickest we'd gone, but it was invigorating to be out in the pits paddling.

Although those extended periods in the cabin were a great opportunity for our muscles to repair and to catch up on some much-needed sleep, they also seemed to drain us. After each storm, we found the next few days harder and harder to paddle. It was as though the cabin time detuned our bodies – and our ability to poo – and it would take them a while to reacclimatise.

That night, we realised the laptop wasn't charging. Examining the wiring diagram, we traced the problem back to a heavily rusted terminal block. Pulling out a couple of spare blocks, we rewired the charger without issue.

These simple repairs at sea were frustratingly slow. It wasn't a matter of heading to the back shed, getting the tools and gear, then fixing it. To access our tools and spares beneath our cabin floor, we had to pack all our sleeping gear away, roll the mats up, pull out the relevant dry bay, empty all the contents, and locate the gear we were after. Once the gear was found, recrimping and rejoining wires was incredibly frustrating. Rogue waves would always hit right at the critical moment, resulting in one of us dropping the block or the nut, usually in the most difficult place to reach on the whole kayak. Time would then be spent trying to fish that gear out. Finally, the job would be complete and a couple of hours had been sucked into a void.

DAY 39

A welcome change of routine. Pat teed it up for us to chat with David Spence, the CEO of our platinum sponsor Unwired. David had been eagerly following our progress on the website and seemed just as excited to speak to us as we were to him.

However, after the initial "Hi, how are you?" and "It's so great to speak with you", we found it difficult to advance the conversation any further. We felt awkward. Both Justin and I are normally pretty good socially – we can talk for hours to anybody. But our lack of direct contact with the outside world, coupled with the primitive, survival-based existence we were leading, saw us totally unprepared for this conversation. We found it difficult to relate to David (or anyone else, probably). How do you honestly answer the question "How are you?" How do you say in a five-minute chat that at times you've been "completely exhausted, shit scared and want nothing more than to be back home"?

Despite the awkwardness, it had been great to hear from David, and with conditions not bad, we jumped into the pits and began paddling. Midway through the day we were greeted by a spectacular aerial show by a pod of dolphins. Darting round the kayak through the translucent water, they looked like supercharged mini-mini-subs. Every now and then, they'd launch themselves up to 2 metres in the air – you could tell they were having a blast. As with humans, the energy was infectious and we found ourselves having (almost) as much fun as they were.

I spent the afternoon listening to my favourite podcasts, Dr Karl on Triple J and Richard Fidler from ABC radio in Sydney and Brisbane. With Dr Karl answering questions like "Why are sunsets red?" and "Why are you warmer in a sleeping bag if you're naked?", and Richard having a fantastic ability to build a rapport with his guests that lets them feel comfortable telling their life stories, we were entertained for hours. It helped keep our minds off our growling stomachs – we'd been on half rations for over a week now. All in all, it was a good day – gaining 35 kilometres into a slight headwind.

Finally that evening, we received a forecast bringing some westerlies. Suckers for punishment that we were, Pat and Roger had dangled the westerly carrot in front of us on a few occasions, then stripped us of the anticipated pleasure a day or two later. Once again, we were excited by the prospect of having some prevailing conditions for a change. We didn't let our previous experiences get us down.

DAY 40

Preceding the westerlies, we were expecting a front bringing winds stronger than we'd experienced to date – 75 kilometres per hour; about the speed Lance Armstrong might reach hurtling down the Pyrenees. To prepare, the first thing we did on the morning of day 40 was dig out the series drogue – the heavy-weather anchor – from under the floor in the cabin, and carry out a couple of practice deployment and retrievals of this crucial piece of storm management gear.

Essentially, the purpose of all this gear in heavy weather is to keep the vessel perpendicular to the oncoming waves. This gives the boat a much better chance of riding through the storm without rolling down the face of waves. We deployed the drogue, which we only used in the severest conditions – fortunately, we only had to use it on three occasions – from the stern. It was a 50-metre line with a series of 40 cones along the length of the main line that were 150 millimetres in diameter. They had the effect of cupping a small portion of water and preventing the kayak from careering down the face of big waves. We soon learnt that this piece of gear would achieve its purpose incredibly well.

We spent most of the morning talking about binge drinking and the role it plays in society. I was taking the angle of the "good angel" and Justin was taking the "because it's fun" approach. Both of us partied quite hard in our first couple of years at uni, as most people do. We had a bit of a reputation for getting totally loose – my nickname when I was hitting the piss was Cass*aaaa* and Jonesy's was Random Man. I guess we were driven by insecurity about who we were, trying to shed our inhibitions in a social environment, as well as the whole fun of getting wild.

It seemed as if substance abuse was often a reflection of other issues people were having to deal with. I saw it all the time when I was working as an accountant. We spent 60 hours a week doing something we "had to", and come Friday night, the way so many of us would escape reality was to drink premium lagers on the company account. For me, the novelty had worn off pretty quickly and I'd escape at the end of the working week to the Blue Mountains.

Out on the water, Jonesy and I also talked about the similarity of the bond we felt with a fellow adventurer after, say, a challenging bushwalk, and the camaraderie of a huge night on the turps with your mates. You've probably heard it before that if life is a wild ride and you're having heaps of fun sober, where's the need to get pissed to magnify the experience? I don't think this had really struck me, though, until I started climbing with Dunc. He'd partied pretty hard when he was in his mid-teens, and he always reminded me that a day out climbing was infinitely more rewarding than being blotto.

As we slogged east for 11 hours that day, we passed the 800-kilometres-to-go mark, and although we only made 33 kilometres into the 25-kilometre-per-hour nor'easterly, our morale stayed positive all afternoon. With the forecast for winds up to 55 kilometres per hour from the east, we hadn't really been expecting a full day's paddle, but the front must have been delayed, so we pounced on the opportunity to scrounge a couple more miles.

It was quite tough, though. My lower back was beginning to be really painful and I'd had to take two Nurofen for the previous five days. Both sides of Jonesy's torso were cut and bleeding. Despite the padding, the constant paddling motion had caused the cockpit rim to saw into his flesh. We also realised that it had become much colder – most days we were now paddling in our cags.

Unfortunately, for dinner we ate two curries – our most-dreaded dehydrated meals. Earlier in the journey, we would have cheated the random-pluck system and swapped them for something a little more appealing for the palate, but now our ravenous hunger ensured we were licking the bags and trying to find a few more grains of hidden rice by the end of the meal.

DAY 41

Chaos. Through the night the storm gathered force and by morning we were being pummelled by 70–75 kilometres-per-hour winds from the north. We'd only managed one hour's sleep. We had the para-anchor deployed, knowing that at some stage during the day we'd have to swap to the series drogue. As the wave size grew through the morning, we started being pulled through the face of these mountainous walls of water. By lunchtime the waves were the size of a three-storey building. The ferocity of the wind continued to grow and we knew one of us had to get out of the cabin, pull the para-anchor in and deploy the drogue.

The massive swell was playing all sorts of nasty games with my inner-ear and I was feeling really queasy. Taking short sharp breaths, beads of sweat were forming on my face. My tanned-brown face was now green and I was choking down chunks of vomit that were about to burst from my mouth. Futilely, I tried to meditate.

The decision to exit the cabin was made for us in an instant. Completely submersed, we got pulled through the face of a particularly steep wave, and as we were spat out its back, we were greeted by that haunting screech of the bridle being caught again. F***.

Our hopes of it untangling itself were quickly dashed – we couldn't rely on luck out here – and Jonesy prepared himself to head outside. As he crawled over me, naked, there were no penis jokes this time – this was serious. He exited the cabin door, with waves constantly washing over the pits, and when he removed the cockpit cover to give himself room to pull in the para-anchor, the rear pit filled instantly with water. The broken bilge pump meant it was going to stay that way.

As soon as he began the para-anchor retrieval, *Lot 41* broached side-on. If one of these mountains of water broke on the kayak, we'd tumble down its face – with Justin outside. This was incredibly dangerous.

As the para-anchor neared the kayak, its lines tangled in the rudder and, without hesitating, Jonesy shouted above the wind, "Mate, I'm going in."

"Be safe, man," I forced out, trying to contain the vomit.

Jonesy put the goggles on, tied himself to the safety lines and slid into the tumultuous ocean. With the frothing seas slamming into *Lot 41*, he thought he'd entered hell. He struggled to the stern of the kayak and, even though he was on the leeward side, was being smacked against the hull as the waves crashed in. Initially, he was going to untangle the mess as fast as possible, but for some reason – and it possibly saved his life – he instinctively bobbed next to the kayak for a minute, familiarising himself with the wave patterns and the effect they were having on the kayak. Horrified, he stared at the rudder chopping up and down like a treelopper's axe. The whole 1.2-metre rudder was going from completely airborne to crashing through the water in seconds. Anyone caught underneath it would be killed with one blow.

Memorising the timing, J made a dash for the rudder, desperately untangled the bridle and swam frantically back to the rear cockpit, with waves engulfing him and *Lot 41*. He later described that moment as the most terrifying of his life. When dunking his head under the water's frothing surface, he couldn't help realise the stark contrast of the serenity lying below – Bruce and Larry were just cruising, blissfully unaware of the violent conditions above.

Coughing up litres of salt water, he jumped in the cockpit and finished retrieving the para-anchor. I opened the cabin door and began filming the unfolding drama, spurring him on with as much positive encouragement as I could muster. The para-anchor was now in and it was time to deploy the series drogue.

Justin was shaking terribly and his eyes were fixed open with fear. He bumbled with the D-clamp to attach the drogue for what seemed an eternity – his fingers had gone numb from the cold. Wave after wave crashed on top of him, threatening to tear him out of the kayak at any moment.

Just as he'd tied the drogue on, a rogue wave smashed us from the front quarter, flooding hundreds of litres of water into the cabin.

"Oh, f***," we both yelled as Jonesy slammed the door closed. Our sleeping bags were soaked and water was sloshing everywhere. As Justin deployed the drogue, I stuffed my head into the various compartments in the cabin and began the unenviable task of bilging the water manually out of each one. I couldn't believe our stupidity – having the cabin door open in these conditions. It was errors like this that would get us killed out on the Tasman. Until now, we'd been so sharp in not allowing issues like this to occur. We were disgusted at our performance. "Worst bit of seamanship this trip," I wrote in my diary, although maybe I summed it up better in the video diary: "We're f***ing idiots."

Justin was outside for another 20 minutes as I vigorously tried to drain all of the water. The cabin was our safe haven – it was where we could hide to escape being wet and scared. Lady Tasman had now stepped over the line and her entry into our cabin was rude and unwelcomed. It was as though we'd been violated – like having our house broken into. As Jonesy re-entered the cabin, we were pissed that all our personal belongings had been soaked. It'd take two days for our sleeping bags and our cabin thermals to dry. Water even sloshed around in the power distribution box, which had deliberately been mounted high on the cabin wall.

Fortunately, the series drogue made the rollercoaster much more comfortable than the battering we'd been taking with the anchor deployed. As we lay down in the late afternoon, it was the first opportunity we'd had to mull over the events of the previous few hours. I hadn't realised how close Jonesy was to being smashed to pieces by the rudder. It sounded incredibly full on. We tossed and turned all afternoon while riding the largest swell either of us had ever encountered. Prior to leaving Australia, we'd talked to numerous crusty sailors who tried to paint a picture of what it was like to weather a mid-Tasman blow. But words can't describe the chaos.

Just as we were going to sleep, Justin called his family – which really got under my skin. We'd been sitting listening to our iPods for hours; then when it was time to sleep, he decided to get on the phone. When he finished the call, I blurted out untactfully, "That was a bit selfish, mate, you could've made the call when we were both awake."

He'd just been through one of the most traumatic moments of his life and, understandably, he needed some comfort. I should have been more in tune with his needs, but a character trait I've always had is to say exactly what I'm feeling. Justin, on the other hand, is much more tolerant, and when there's something to be said, he delivers his message quite subtly. Throughout the voyage we had numerous debates about whether we should just say it or be tolerant and hold it in. The conclusion was that I should be more careful of my wording and Justin needed to speak up more often if there was something I was doing that was bugging him.

DAY 42

By now we were more fatigued than we'd ever thought possible, we'd had a few encounters over the past week in which we were fearful for our lives, and our bodies had wasted considerably. Despite all this, Jonesy made a comment on the video diary about the joy we experienced getting out of the cabin and doing some exercise. We were in the pits again and our goal seemed to be drawing closer.

During the storm of the previous day, the baby wipes we used for wiping the zinc off our face – which were stored in the pouch on the outside of the cabin door – had been ripped out and thrown into the Tasman. To our amazement, after an hour of paddling, we saw something bobbing right in front of our bow. It was the baby wipes! What are the chances of losing something overboard some 12 hours earlier in the middle of a raging sea, and coming across it again?

17

SHARK BAIT

Christmas in the Castrission house has always been a particularly special time. Throughout the year we all seem so busy, but it's one occasion we always get together and really enjoy each other's company. Out on the Tasman, we felt alone. There were no presents this year – we hadn't brought any for each other (we'd optimistically assumed we'd be sitting in the family dining room on the day).

DAY 43

Christmas Day – *ho ho*. The fatigue levels had now ventured past the stage where our eyes wanted to shut, to the level that we plainly felt sick – quite similar to being badly hungover, really.

I had to wake through the night numerous times to see whether the westerlies had blown in. We wanted to maximise our drift by using these favourable winds as much as possible. As soon as they arrived, the para-anchor stayed in its bag till the much-loved westerlies left us. Unfortunately, a combination of waking every hour and the increasingly bumpy sea state resulted in me not getting back to sleep from 2.30am onwards – which was so frustrating.

Moving out into the cockpits that morning, I took note that the combination of the fatigue and the time bunkered up in the cabin had rendered my bowels useless – they hadn't moved for three days. It really felt like my body was beginning to shut down. Every now and then the stomach would rumble and I'd try and push something out, but nothing was happening. I knew a few days in the pits would help make me regular again.

Paddling along in the rain, with the seas building, I listened to Christmas carols. Slowly, I began to weep. I thought of my family back home, unwrapping their presents, with our family dog Max playing with the wrapping paper. I then imagined them having a nice big lunch and the masses of food that would be chucked away at the end of the day – pure decadence. As tears trickled down my face, they got lost in the rainwater.

The closest we'd got to a Christmas present was a dice-size piece of Christmas cake made by Justin's sister, Louisa. She'd wrapped the cake in foil and had drawn various symbols on the outside – Christmas trees, holly, bells. It made me think of home. We'd rationed our dehydrated meals over the past week to ensure we could both have a roast chicken meal with added mince at dinner. Throughout the day we salivated over the thought of being tucked up in the cabin, enjoying these special rations.

As we kept paddling, we began to sing Christmas carols. These songs were good fun, taking our minds off the fatigue, but the paddling that afternoon was nothing short of wild – 55–60-kilometre-per-hour winds from the southwest with massive swells rolling in. Waves broke all around and on top of us. It was a Christmas Day neither of us will ever forget. During the evening we drifted past the devil's number – 666 kilometres to go. It spooked me but not Justin, who was much more sensible; not allowing superstition to create negative energy on the kayak. We made 107 kilometres fast.

DAY 44

Justin has never been a morning person. But these first five minutes of the day were proving harder and harder for him. He'd often set his alarm up to 10 minutes before our official get-up time, just so he could slowly get the cogs moving when the proper alarm went off.

The prevailing swell and wind kindly kicked us 40 kilometres eastward during the night. Take away the fatigue and we would have been laughing, but unfortunately, the rough seas had made sure we couldn't sleep. That now made three virtually sleepless nights in a row.

Waking in the morning to see the bow pointing east was a welcome change. It was critical that we pounced on these favourable conditions, but our bodies were pleading otherwise. We were exhausted beyond reason, with constant throbbing from the pain that severe fatigue brings. I wanted to lie in the cabin and just close my eyes, and if I'd been by myself, I probably would have. Mustering all the energy we could find, we lumbered out and made our way into the pits.

Boxing Day brought the most terrifying yet exhilarating paddling of our lives. There was a 6–7-metre swell rumbling from the southwest, and each time we crested one of these giants it felt like staring down from a two-storey building. Normally, in these conditions, we'd ride them out in the cabin, but after a month and a half at the reins of *Lot 41*, we'd grown confident in her ability to handle the conditions. Knowing there was a very real risk of us being torn out by a breaking wave, we both had our PFDs on and were doubly clipped into the safety line. We realised that getting separated from *Lot 41* was a death sentence. One of us would have no chance of being able to locate the man overboard and paddle a 1-tonne kayak back to rescue him.

As we bobbed up and down through these mountainous waves, our nerves were becoming more and more frayed. Despite being in our Gore-Tex cags, we were completely sodden by the spray and splashing of these waves as they rolled underneath us. It was only a matter of time before one of these walls of water crashed on top of us. As the anticipation built, we tried to dabble in conversation but our words would get lost in the howling wind, so for most of the day we paddled in silence.

Finally, at 2pm we started climbing the side of one of these monsters. As we were lifted up, it seemed to get steeper and steeper, rearing for an attack. We stopped paddling and braced, fear charging through our bodies. Staring in awe at the 3-metre vertical crest of the wave, I was struck by a disturbing thought – had we pushed too hard? Within seconds, it started to curl menacingly over us. There was no escaping this one.

Bam. It crashed down on the kayak. We were immediately engulfed by whitewash as we found ourselves smashed on our side and careering down the bottom 5 metres of the wave. I was certain the rudder would catch and we'd begin to roll, and was terrified by the thought that the safety lines might tangle, trapping us under water.

Glimpses from the entire journey flashed through my mind as we surfed down the side for what seemed like hours. Then as we slowed down and approached the trough of the wave, the surrounding white water dissipated and we were gasping for a breath of air. *Lot 41* was flung violently back upright and we sat in the calm water of this trough between two giant walls of water.

I turned round to Justin, his face pale with fear, and said, "Mate, this would be so much fun if it wasn't so bloody scary."

"Touche," he replied, then repeated it for extra emphasis. "Touche."

After emptying the water that had filled our cag hoods and all our pockets, we resumed paddling, with 10 pounds of adrenaline stabbed straight into our arteries. We might have been exhausted, but there was no need for caffeine for the rest of the afternoon, or the rest of the expedition, really – we were completely wired!

On day 44, we'd just had the ride of our lives; but I'll also remember it for the furry nut disaster. Opening up our nut rations for the day, we realised most of them were covered with mould. After a quick debate about the feasibility of chucking them, we realised that our bodies needed the calories. For the rest of the voyage, a lot of the nuts were furry, and instead of that nice white flesh on the inside they were yellow. We had to dust the fur off on our shoulders, then toss the nuts in our mouths. Delicious. But food was fuel – without the calories from these fur balls, there'd be no reaching the elusive shores of New Zealand.

Once we entered the cabin, there was no escaping the violent bucking. It shook us hard, making sleep impossible. Embarrassingly, even though I'd promised Jonesy I wouldn't "lose it" again, at 1am I started punching the walls, screaming hysterically, "I want this f***ing kayak to sink – I'm going to sink it."

Justin was once again scared I was going to do something dangerous and irrational. At the time, I didn't care.

DAY 45

Finally, as the wind abated, we were able to get some sleep. We woke at 6am to calm seas gently rocking *Lot 41* like a baby – the abruptness of the change in conditions amazed us every time. As I started passing Jonesy back the dry bags from the pits, I saw a plume of water erupt less than 50 metres from the kayak.

"Jonesy, there's a whale out here."

"Whatever, mate."

"No seriously," I insisted. "Stick your head out and take a look."

Justin peered out the window and was instantly dumbfounded. I was too – I couldn't have been more awestruck if I'd run into Wolfgang Gullich at the local milk bar. (Don't tell me you've never heard of the greatest rock climber of all time?!) The whale cruised by, passing a mere 20 metres to our port side. It was so close, we could feel it breathing.

The water around the body of the whale moved in perfect rhythm with this magnificent creature. In fact, for that brief moment it was as if the breathing of the whale was the lungs of the Tasman. As its ribcage expanded and contracted, we were mesmerised by being in the shadow of a mammal the size of an aircraft carrier with the grace of a dolphin. Seeing sharks, tuna, albatrosses – and dolphins – had all been cool, but this intimate encounter was almost spiritual. It glided through the water, exuding an aura of supreme confidence and grandeur – we were just stunned by how beautiful it was.

Captivated by our whale experience, we had the slightly more mundane task of rewiring the electric bilge pump in the rear pit. The previous week since it had malfunctioned, it had been really frustrating manually pumping the pit as we got ourselves ready for the cabin each night. Justin did a great job cutting out the float and switch to simplify the system, and we were quite chuffed with ourselves after successfully combating this frustrating niggle.

We paddled on in calm conditions quite silently for the day, mulling over our humbling encounter with the whale. Towards the end of the day we saw the first container ship we'd seen on the horizon while out on the Tasman. It was there one moment, gone the next.

Before jumping into the cabin, Justin started recording something for the video diary: "End of day 46 today."

Just as he was about to review the day's events, I interrupted, "No it's not, mate, it's day 45."

We continued to argue the point for several minutes, until finally we had the common sense to open one of our diaries and take a look. Day 45 had drawn to a close. Even though each day had its own unique challenges, in our exhaustion they'd begun to fuse together. We'd both truly believed the other was dead wrong.

DAY 46

For the first time on the expedition (or our lives, for that matter), we started taking sleeping tablets the previous night. In all my previous adventures I'd never been a fan of anti-inflammatory drugs, sleeping tablets, caffeine tablets or the like. I felt it detracted from the experience and clouded your judgement in understanding how your body was dealing with the stress of expedition life. It was now different – we were taking our bodies to places they'd never been before. My daily dose was two No-Doz, two Nurofen, two Anzemet (the anti-nausea medication given to chemo patients), two Phenergan (also anti-nausea) and, now, one sleeping tablet. We often speculated about how many caffeine tablets were needed to cancel out the effects of a sleeping tablet.

We gradually began to see our mental aptitude fade as we progressed – slowly – towards the Land of the Long White Cloud. Each extra day we were out there, the worse our alertness became. We were now at the level where we couldn't recall the details from the previous evening's sked or weather forecasts. More worryingly, neither of us was able to remember hourly mileages. Every day we'd been playing a game of guessing how far we'd travelled by turning the GPS on each hour. But we couldn't play it any more, as we could never remember what the distance we'd travelled was an hour earlier.

We now constantly confused east and west, kilometres travelled – amazingly, we'd paddled 450 kilometres in the last five days (I think!) – versus kilometres to go, port and starboard, left and right, and people's names: the list went on. We tried to stay patient with each other, though, often laughing off the confusion. Our saving grace was having a waterproof notebook tied round our necks at all times. The salt-encrusted lanyard rubbed viciously on our skin causing quite bad chafing, but at least we were able to write down anything that needed remembering.

And with the absence of bowel movements, it wasn't just our minds that seemed to be drying up. This was caused by the gnawing hunger in our empty stomachs. Our bodies were trying to suck every last calorie out of our dwindling food supplies.

Crawling out of the cabin that morning, I stupidly made a comment to Justin: "Mate, we've just about ticked every 'box' in terms of experiencing life at sea. I mean, we've seen storms, we've seen the ocean at its best and worst, we've seen almost all the sea creatures we were expecting to see out here – heaps of whales, dolphins, Mahimahi, tuna and baitfish. The one box left to tick is to see a shark – I guess we'll probably see them as we approach the coast of New Zealand."

"I've been thinking the same thing," Justin replied cautiously "but didn't want to say it in case it jinxed us."

It was a good point. "I must admit, I've been thinking it for a few days but haven't said so for that very reason."

"Just don't bring it up again until we reach shore."

"Alright, mate."

Throughout the day we got increasingly frustrated at our apparent slow speed. Like a couple of weeks earlier, we pulled the goggles out and took a look at the hull. Sure enough, it was measled once again with barnacles and algae – one of us would have to go in.

We both knew the routine. "*Scissor, Paper, Rock.*" This time, though, we realised the implications were a little more serious, as the water was now much colder than the temperatures experienced in the EAC. Whoever went in would come out almost hypothermic.

Justin lost and again I wished I could take his place out there. He plunged over the side and began scrubbing the hull. As soon as he entered the water his head shot up and he shouted out, "It's f***ing freezing in here, mate; I don't think I'm going to last long." His skin instantly goose-bumped and went vibrant red.

With the ample layer of fat on his body of one who had rarely said "no" to second helpings, Justin had always been able to handle the cold water of canyons and the like quite well. During his later school days, he hadn't been nicknamed "the Dugong" – a sea cow – for nothing. For him to complain so quickly about the temperature, it really must have been freezing.

After he'd vigorously scrubbed the rear half of the kayak, he swam towards the pits and lumbered out of the water. "I just need a couple of minutes to warm up," he chattered between his quivering lips.

He was shivering violently and I thought that might be my cue to complete the task. "You've done a great job, mate, I'll finish her off," I said hesitantly, knowing that if I went in, I'd come out frozen too.

But Justin was adamant. "No way, Cas, I lost – it's my responsibility to finish what I started."

"But, Jonesy, you're almost hypothermic – I'll do it."

"I said no. I just need five minutes."

End of discussion. I knew there was no stopping him – that's why I was out here with Justin; for his ability to endure amazing punishment and keep fronting up for more. True to his word, after five minutes he re-entered the water and finished the hull off. After the job was done, we immediately began paddling to try to warm him up. His teeth continued to chatter for another half hour as his body vibrated like a tuning fork.

At 7pm we stopped paddling and started preparing *Her Majesty* – our latest nickname for *Lot 41* – for the evening. Justin washed himself and jumped in the cabin, and as I was packing the pits, I noticed something unfamiliar. It looked like a fin. A *shark* fin. It couldn't be – could it? It disappeared and I assumed it was my mind playing tricks on me; but suddenly, it reappeared.

Hardly believing my eyes, I yelled out, "Jonesy, there's a bloody shark out here, mate."

"Bullshit, Cas."

Bam. It torpedoed into the side of the cabin and *Lot 41* lurched to one side. I scampered back to the rear cockpit, stripped my clothes off – part of my daily routine – and leapt inside. We sat staring out the door in utter amazement at this giant predator as it continued to circle us. It was hard to take it in; *there was a shark out there.*

After a while, though, we calmed down a bit, and as our familiarity with the situation grew, Justin said playfully, "Hey, mate, I dare you to touch its fin."

A mad glint entered my eye. For a brief moment, I thought that would have been kind of cool. After all, it was this type of inquisitiveness that had us out here in the first place. Then, fortunately, I came to my senses. "Jonesy, how could we ring our parents up and say that we lost a hand because we were trying to pat a shark?"

On the off-chance the victim didn't bleed to death, the grief our mates would have given us for our stupidity – as we returned to Australia missing a finger or two, if not much worse – would have left us wishing that the shark *had* killed us ...

Justin didn't have the chance to reply before we realised simultaneously that there wasn't one, but two fins out there. Oh God, *two* sharks – were we the aquatic version of meals on wheels? We kept staring out the wide-open door, eyes fixed, completely naked and ... well, it was difficult trying to pinpoint the exact emotion we were feeling. Was it fear or excitement? Or both?

As the sharks continued to circle us – and the second one was about two-thirds the length of *Lot 41* – we were becoming more blasé about their company, as we felt safe inside the kayak. We both remembered that when she was being constructed, our boat builder Graham had given us a hammer and a cut-out of the hull laminates, saying, "Bet you can't put a hole in it." On either side of an 8-millimetre foam core sandwich were two layers of fibreglass and Kevlar (the stuff they use in bulletproof vests). We'd gone to work beating this panel and it didn't even fracture.

The sharks seemed pretty curious about Graham's handiwork. Every now and then, they'd rub themselves against the length of the kayak. Their skin both sounded and felt like sandpaper – it was surprisingly rough and textured. Going to sleep that night was bizarre, to say the least. Having the teeth of a couple of sharks barely a centimetre away as the two of them continued to swim underneath us was unforgettable.

18

ACHING JOINTS AND
GRUMBLING STOMACHS

DAY 47

DIARY, DAY 47 – JAMES

"Woke 0600 [6am]. Sharks now gone. Each morning is
getting harder and harder, both constantly hungry; bum
very sore today, can't do squats any more – legs can no
longer support body weight."

Talking to the two cameras on board – Mr Camera (okay, so it's a
slightly *Play School*-ish name) – became like talking to a third
person. Each camera had its own personality, and although it
didn't ever talk back to us (obviously), we enjoyed the one-way
dialogue with these inanimate objects.

Mr Camera became one of those friends you could trust
completely and spill the beans about exactly what you were
thinking. It was a private conversation, though, and even if Justin
was well within earshot, I'd talk to Mr Camera as if he wasn't

there. Occasionally, we'd be whining about the other person, but it was unspoken etiquette not to interrupt a conversation with our quiet mate. Funnily enough, I'd sometimes say something directed at Jonesy, but he wasn't allowed to blow up at me because he knew I wasn't talking to him!

Pushing another westerly current, we found *Lot 41* making pitifully slow progress on a calm sea, which had us wanting to tear our hair out. In these conditions, we should have been making great progress. It felt like the Tasman's long delicate fingers were clawing at us from the depths of the sea. She wanted to keep us out there for a little longer – it seemed she was enjoying our company.

Once again, we found ourselves increasingly frustrated at Pat, Roger and the whirling currents we couldn't understand. With the data our support team were receiving, they were providing the best possible information that they had access to, but unfortunately we were now finding the current charts on the eastern side of the Tasman painfully inaccurate. Our support team was seeing one thing and we were experiencing currents doing the exact opposite.

After a few very slow hours, we called Clouds on the satphone to see if he had any idea about what was going on. After some to-ing and fro-ing, we decided to head south and see if we could punch out of the current. Roger's only advice was: "Whenever you find yourselves pushing a current, the only way you can make any progress is to head perpendicular to it." In other words, stubbornly beating your head against a wall often gets you nowhere.

Paddling in that direction took us further from our initial goal of Manukau Harbour – Auckland – and was drawing us away from our closest landfall, the northern tip of the North Island – Hokianga Harbour (a mere 400 kilometres away). Our speed didn't seem to improve, though, which baffled us completely.

Once again we felt trapped – we couldn't head east or south – and yet again we found ourselves questioning Roger, Pat, the weather bureau etc. And for the first time we began to wonder how much fight we had left.

After another hour of futile paddling, we retired to the cabin and enjoyed a relatively calm afternoon. Later, I sat in pit 2 and desalinated a good 10 litres of water, while Justin was inside reading some forum posts out loud. Obviously we were feeling pretty dispirited, but these boosted our morale enormously:

> Sergio: "Come on, boys, you are the strongest guys I
> know. If anyone is capable of this, it's you. Push on, push
> on, paddle and paddle, and a break will come."

DAY 48

Sleeping through our alarms, we were greeted by our GPS telling us we'd drifted south-southwest through the night. We continued to push on south-southeast through this fortress of swirling currents around the NZ coast which seemed hell-bent on barring our entry. Progressing a painfully slow 8.5 kilometres in seven hours' paddling, we again stopped early afternoon, immersing ourselves in one of the most serious chats we'd had in the voyage so far, asking the straightforward, but incredibly complex, question: "Why are we still out here? What's motivating us to go on?"

Our situation was starting to feel desperate. We were now far more exhausted than we'd ever been (both during the expedition and in our whole lives), our bodies were constantly aching, our food supplies were dwindling and we were, of course, once again stuck in some god-awful current. So what was at the core of this adventure?

We discovered that afternoon that there was far more to us being out there than to be the first people to cross the Tasman Sea by kayak. We realised that we'd wanted to prove something to ourselves and the world. Mediocrity and conformity freaked us out: we wanted to be different. It might sound a bit dramatic, but we wanted to explore the extremities of our being and define what we were capable of. It was like those people who live in the suburbs, driving massive 4WDs around the city that never see an unsealed road. We didn't want our lives to be like that. We wanted to push our minds and bodies down those dirt tracks; to take our 4WD and see if we could redefine its limits.

The danger of playing this game is going beyond your limits and ending up dead; but for us, adventure has never been about playing Russian roulette with the objective dangers of nature. Crossing the ditch was an exercise in setting up *Lot 41* and all our processes so we could take our souls to undiscovered places – to expose those inner demons. We'd now done this. So again, we prodded – why go on?

Were we being motivated by the fear of failure or the fact that we hadn't given the Tasman our all? Maybe a bit of both. The bottom line, though, was that for all the pain it brought, we knew we could still take one more paddle stroke.

Our insurance policy against being out there forever was our food running out – we'd then have to be rescued. We calculated that with further rationing, and supplementing our diet with fish, we could last out close to 90 days unsupported. At that point I felt it would be time to abort the mission, but Justin, on the other hand, was keen to make it to NZ regardless of needing a food drop. I saw a drop as completely destroying our mission of an unsupported crossing and thought that if we needed that kind of help, we might as well have taken a support boat the whole way across and paddled the ditch in our regular kayaks. But Jonesy saw it as something we'd started and needed to finish, however long it took.

But while we had our shared motivation for persisting with the expedition, both Justin and I had very personal reasons to keep on going. As we retired to the cabin, Justin did a video diary: "I continually let Cas down big-time the last two years – he's shouldered heaps more of the work than me. This is my time to give something back to him. He's stayed outside an extra two hours to pump water 'cause he can't do it in the cabin – it's made me feel really guilty."

It was typical Jonesy – on our adventures, he always felt uncomfortable if someone else was working while he had some downtime.

Sometimes when we'd bitch to Mr Camera about the other one, we'd hope the other person would take note. On this particular occasion, though, I think Jonesy was trying to make me feel better. He'd heard me say earlier in the day: "I'm really lucky to be out here with Justin – no-one in the world would have put up with how useless I've been in the cabin and not have a tiny feeling of resentment."

DAY 49

DIARY, DAY 49 – JAMES
"Frustrated/pissed off with the slow progress, these unknown currents and new meso scale overlays [a map showing *Lot 41*'s position in relation to the currents]. No favourable currents towards NZ now. Wasted energy paddling down south. Auckland (500km) or New Plymouth (450km)? Who knows. Not far now, but oh so far."

The sea remained relatively benign today, but we weren't able to make any progress, as a 30–40 kilometre-per-hour southeast headwind made sure we were cabin-bound the whole day. The biggest morale booster we'd had in the previous couple of days was when we unwrapped the spare iPod and found a whole set of new videos on it, and these absorbed our attention as we continued to drift west back to Australia.

There was a pile of climbing movies I'd forgotten I'd put on there, which transported me back to some of my favourite climbing spots around the world. I paid particular attention to the rock formations, valleys, waterfalls and, I guess, the essence of being on land. I swore to myself that I'd never take the beauty of land for granted again.

DAY 50

New Year's Day. We celebrated extravagantly by polishing off the last of Louisa's Anzac biscuits. Once again the weather was stunning but, once again, we were drifting back towards Australia. After a quick TV interview over the satellite phone, we had a "crisis sked" with Pat. It appeared that the Rescue Coordination Centre (RCC) in NZ were deeply concerned with the length of time we'd been out on the Tasman and, judging by our recent progress, wanted to initiate a rescue ASAP.

They had to be kidding. We were angry that the authorities wanted to take our fate in their hands without even consulting us about how we were doing and what the reason was for our apparently slow progress. They had this image that we were totally decrepit, painfully weak and not making progress because our bodies were too wasted.

They also believed – wrongly, as it turned out – that we only had 20 days of food remaining on the current rationing. We alerted Pat that we could quite easily have got out to 90 days if we had to and that our food provisions were nothing to be concerned about.

As this was happening and RCC were in the early stages of mobilising a rescue, we received word that our families were flying across to New Zealand to meet us on our arrival. That afternoon as we slowly slogged on, we could see vapour trails from the planes above. We couldn't help but feel the energy of our families being within few kilometres of us. What would it be like seeing them again – I could almost feel Dad's grey beard bristling against my neck as I hugged him. Then a horrible thought entered my mind which I should have bitten my tongue and not told Jonesy about – but I couldn't help myself.

"Hey, Jonesy."

"Yeah, mate," said Justin through his blistered lips.

"I've just had the most awful thought, which I don't really want to tell you about, but I feel I have to."

"I really hope it's not what I'm thinking."

"Mate, can you imagine if the plane crashed, killing our whole family? How could we ever live with ourselves – the guilt would be crippling."

"Geez, Cas, how did I know you were going to say that? I was thinking the same thing."

We'd now spent so long together that we could almost pre-empt what the other was thinking or about to say. The stress of the past month and a half was now starting to show in that stupid scenarios like this one would get me quite emotional. My mind wouldn't leave the idea alone, and for the next hour I continued to explore this horrible vivid picture.

A 15-minute drift test broke this thought pattern. It revealed we were moving at approximately 2 kilometres per hour west-southwest. Although we weren't making progress towards New Zealand, the scenery was stunning. The sea was relatively calm, and with the vibrant light dancing above our heads, it was, as I wrote in my diary, "one of those days that we will always dream of … these are the days we will remember". Needless to say, I was overwhelmed by relief that evening when the sked revealed that our families had arrived safely in NZ.

DAY 51

Throughout the night, the ache in my joints and my grumbling stomach woke me several times. Both shoulders and my back were the worst. I could no longer sleep on either side – my favourite sleeping position – as it would send the whole arm numb. It wasn't an acute injury but one caused by overuse.

We woke to a beautifully calm day. The previous three days, my bowels had been completely congested and blocked, but enhancing the morning's enjoyment was my first decent bowel movement in 72 hours. I couldn't believe how something so simple improved my morale and outlook!

Mid-morning we saw an albatross chillin' in the water. To our amazement, it just stayed there. We decided to paddle over to it, half expecting it to fly away as we approached. Having spent heaps of time talking and thinking about albatrosses since the expedition had begun, it was fantastic for us to get so close to one. Graceful in the air, we were impressed with the power of its big flipper feet that would effortlessly propel it through the water faster than we could paddle.

The personality of the albatrosses on the eastern Tasman was vastly different from those closer to the Australian coast. We found the "western albatrosses" weren't interested in us at all – they'd fly past us without even a glance. Initially quite put off by their arrogance, we found it difficult to build any rapport with these graceful giants.

But as we neared NZ, there was a stark change in their personality and they began to be more personable and inquisitive, often coming back for a second and sometimes even a third fly-by. We couldn't figure out what it was about the New Zealand albatross – had the bush telegraph spread through the bird world to go and check out those two crazy dudes in that funny looking kayak? An ornithologist would probably say it's pretty stupid to say that the birds were getting more inquisitive and friendly – but that was what we observed.

We knew these birds can fly big distances – up to 510 kilometres per day, in fact – and are known to travel from a breeding ground on the southern tip of NZ (Stewart Island) to Tasmania, pick up food for their young, then fly all the way back!

With their strong muscular covering, we could understand how seafarers could be tempted to eat them – if it wasn't for the "myth of the albatross". Among sailors, and in the poem "The Rime of the Ancient Mariner", this large seabird is considered a harbinger of good luck, and capturing or killing it, whether deliberate or accidental, is thought to bring misfortune and woe to the ship and its crew, and death or curse to the sailor who kills it. Although starving, we never even considered capturing one of these birds.

As the albatrosses got bored with our company, we were greeted by a pod of dolphins energetically leaping into the air – it had to be a good sign. Up until the Tasman, neither Justin nor I had given much thought to superstition – as far as we were concerned, tarot cards, star signs and palm readings were only for the gullible and people reading trashy magazines. Now, it was amazing how we'd look for the hidden meaning of *everything* – a shooting star, a glimpse of wildlife, even a slight change in the breath of a wind. Each encounter with the natural world provided a break from the monotony of life at sea and started to take on a deeper meaning. We were asking ourselves, "I wonder what that means" or "What is God trying to tell us here?" It was like some "greater spirit" was conversing with us.

Paddling along late afternoon, a large brown fin effortlessly cruised in front of the bow. Alarm bells rang immediately – this could only be a tiger shark, known for their intrusive, aggressive nature. They have a reputation for munching on just about anything. Then as a small wave washed over the bow, it stealthily submersed itself like a submarine and was gone. Nervously paddling on, we checked behind the kayak every now and then to see if it was tailing us. We tried to be as robotic as possible and not to send "fear waves" out, as we'd been told that sharks can sense them.

It had been a day in which we'd seen an incredible display of Tasman creatures. It reminded us that she was bubbling with life – and it was only going to increase as we approached the shores of New Zealand.

There were also signs that we were getting nearer to land. In places, oil streaks and rubbish floated on the surface, and although we were outraged to see this pollution, we were glad about what it represented. Civilisation was drawing closer.

DAY 52

The sea was dead calm, but we still found ourselves pushing current. Four hundred kilometres to go. The formations in the sky were now different – a good sign that we were approaching land. The thick, moist, mid-ocean clouds had given way to high wisps of cirrus – like peroxide-white fairy floss hurled out a car window – that only formed above the high mountains of New Zealand.

They were familiar, reminding me of the months I'd spent mountaineering in the South Island, where cold air would be forced up to 40,000 feet high off the mountains causing clouds to form.

Plugging along at a painfully slow rate, we did a 15-minute drift test that revealed a current was pushing us 1.6 kilometres per hour northwest (towards Queensland). These circular currents barring our entry into New Zealand were starting to fray both our nerves, and Justin's elbow had started to drastically flare up with bursitis, which caused him a lot of pain.

We weren't in a disastrously bad mood, though. At the end of the day – the same as most other days – I sang out "Quittin' time! Quittin' time!", imitating the foreman in the film *Gone with the Wind*. It was our version of the Flintstones' "Yabba dabba doo!" and Jonesy seemed to enjoy the moment as much as me. Then, while he got the para-anchor ready to deploy, I immersed myself in a video diary and whinged that I was finding holding the camera up hard work.

DAY 53

> VIDEO DIARY, DAY 53 – JUSTIN
> "Beautiful morning, calm seas, but probably the ugliest
> mood we've had on the kayak."

Our support team was sending us the most up-to-date current charts available. On the eastern Tasman, these overlays were surprisingly accurate; now, they had no relevance to our position. The frustration was getting under our skin. The Tasman was finally beginning to succeed in its mission – it knew it had no chance if we stuck together, but once we began squabbling, reaching NZ would be so much more difficult.

"Mate, you're taking too bloody long getting ready in the mornings," I aggressively spat out after waiting in the pits for him for 20 minutes.

"Give me a break – there's a lot I've got to do in getting the cabin ready every morning," Justin replied defensively (he'd had an atrocious night's sleep, which didn't help his diplomatic skills).

"Stop being so f***ing smug. You can never take any objective feedback. You're always right. You never apologise when you make a mistake. You always get defensive," I said, almost looking for a fight.

Jonesy jumped in immediately. "I get defensive because whenever you address me with feedback, it seems like you're attacking me."

"I say it the way it is. C'mon, mate, surely I don't need to carefully craft what I'm saying – you're not that bloody sensitive, are you?"

"I'm not saying that. Can you just work on the way you deliver your feedback?"

"Yeah, okay, but only if you're more open to it."

"Deal."

As we paddled on in uncomfortable silence, an object appeared 100 metres off our port bow. Justin was the first to speak. "Cool, what is it?" he called out.

"Not sure, mate, it looks like a traffic cone – let's go and investigate."

As we got a little closer to it – about 30 metres – I reaffirmed my initial thoughts. "Yeah, it definitely looks like a cone of some sort – a big black cone. Hey, mate, have you changed bearing?"

"No, why?"

"It's almost on our beam now. Quick," I directed him, "turn left before we miss it."

"That's weird." He seemed quite perplexed. "It seems to be drifting up into the wind."

As we got to within 10 metres of it, we realised it wasn't a cone at all – it was a giant fin gliding in circles. The apex of the fin stood at least one-and-a-half feet out of the water. We immediately realised our stupidity. Our childish inquisitiveness was once again biting us on the arse – this time we were sure it was a great white shark. We quickly altered course and again tried to employ our "robo-paddling" technique, eager not to send out any bad energy.

The next half an hour of paddling was terrifying. These sharks are the lions of the ocean, with a formidable reputation for destruction – even in the shark world, they're well up the food chain. We briefly discussed the viability of bunkering down in the cabin but decided that this wouldn't alleviate the problem, as it would keep us in the vicinity of the shark. It was best to paddle on.

After we arrived on land, I learnt that Justin had felt horrible that I was in the front pit. He had the protection of the cabin if the shark came up for a chomp, while being in the front pit I was completely exposed and couldn't hide if it came from below. I'd futilely held my paddle like a lance, ready to spear it, knowing that the blade wouldn't even slow its momentum.

As we slogged on, we could feel land was approaching. As well as the clouds, the birds were noticeably different and the amount of rubbish in the water had increased. The Tasman had lost its sparkling clarity and was becoming murky and cloudy.

DAY 54

We (in other words, Justin) started the day by replacing all the corroded battery terminals. This took over an hour, resulting in us having a shorter day in the pits – a tad over 10 hours. I'd been saving and saving *The Power of One* audio book by Bryce Courtenay the entire voyage. Finally, it was time to delve into this classic I'd been so looking forward to listening to, as all my music playlists and podcasts had been exhausted and I needed a morale injection. The pain resonating from our bones through every muscle fibre was now almost unbearable, and listening to this audio book allowed my mind to drift to a fantasy world and seek some kind of solace.

Packing up at the end of the day had become more difficult as I could no longer stand up in the pits. As Justin would pass dry bags out, I'd find myself having to keep one hand holding on to the cockpit rim as I constantly collapsed. Inching back into the cabin, I felt like an invalid. It was the first time in my life I'd begged my body to carry out simple functions and it had failed to respond.

DAY 55

In my diary, I wrote, "250km to go. As the days go on, clarity of thought seems to get more and more vivid. The understanding of our past makes more sense now and the visualisation of our future seems so sharp." It was an interesting contradiction. We were struggling to articulate left and right, east and west, but our inner thoughts seemed more vivid than ever before in our lives.

DAY 56

The wind had begun shifting to the northwest – a welcome relief. Although it was predominantly behind us, we needed to remain cautious that it didn't blow us south of New Plymouth, one of our possible landing points, towards the Cook Strait. This narrow stretch of water between the North and South Islands of NZ was notorious for funnelling water through on the ebb tide at an extraordinarily fast pace – up to 15 kilometres per hour.

The nor'westerly brought with it an overcast angry sky that resulted in wet, cold paddling. We had to weigh up whether to wear our Gore-Tex cags and spray skirts to trap the warmth or go without – the barrier gear made the paddling more enjoyable as we stayed warmer, but resulted in severe attacks of prickly heat on going indoors. The other option was not to wear these barriers, be cold the *entire* day, then be much more comfortable in the cabin. Each day now we fluctuated between the two, with the option we hadn't chosen always seeming like the more attractive one. Yes, it really is always greener on the other side.

As I recorded in my diary later in the day, even when we weren't cocooned in our cags and spray skirts we were both feeling like "prisoners of freedom". The ideology of pursuing our dreams and trying to break the shackles of society was what drove us to be out here; but ironically, by pursuing this freedom we found ourselves surrounded by a desolate landscape and in a situation seemingly becoming more and more hopeless.

Any escape from the Tasman was failure. We couldn't bail so close to land, or "just have a rest for a few days", as the NZ authorities would come and pick us up for sure. We were also too far from the shore to be able to let ourselves relax. Our actions were now being driven by the momentum created. We were trapped. The main difference from my days as an accountant was that Justin and I owned this dream – or nightmare; sometimes I wasn't sure which. It was all ours and to make it happen we had no choice. If we'd been forced on this mission by an employer or an army officer, we would have collapsed from exhaustion and mental breakdown long ago.

19

AOTEAROA WHISPERS –
A DANDELION FLOATS BY

The rawness of life at sea was a simple matter of survival; however, once this was taken care of, our minds had the chance to roam and explore almost endlessly – to dream about the future and anything else that drifted into our thoughts. The expedition had given us close to two months for reflecting on our lives.

Our relatively simple existence on *Lot 41* meant that we didn't have to filter the truckloads of information usually dumped on us every day. In fact, the smoke had cleared so much that the most basic childlike questions began to occur to us. "Why is the ocean blue?", "Why is the whitewash from waves more powerful than fully formed non-breaking waves?", "Are all bubbles white?", "How does a tug boat pull oil rigs around the world under constant load up and down waves?" (One of the forumites provided the answer to that one – thanks, Ol Oiler!) Back in the "real world", if we'd had such an inquisitive state of mind, our brains would probably have exploded with the overload.

DAY 57

The wind built a little overnight, but fortunately nowhere near as much as the 70-kilometre-per-hour blast Pat had predicted in last night's sked. We woke to a gentle 10-kilometre-per-hour breeze from the north – maybe the trough had been delayed? We scampered out into the pits to try and notch some mileage under our belt before we got hit. Although it was cold and rainy, we were buoyed by our average speeds of 4.5 kilometres per hour.

As waves of hunger focused our thoughts, I asked Justin whether he thought Scott of the Antarctic had ever considered eating other members of his party on that fateful journey. It might sound a bit ghoulish, but I told Jonesy that if I were to die now and we were out of food, I'd want him to eat me – I was sure I'd be tasty – and arrive in New Zealand carrying the flag for us both. He was the same. Before departing, we'd been undecided on this scenario, but now that we were in the situation, the answer was clear. We'd become so psychotically single-minded about finishing what we'd started, nothing would block our success.

From the safety of base camp, it's always been easy to say that those unfortunate souls who died going for the summit, or any other objective, should have turned back. In the past, I've turned back on many summits, knowing that the mountains would always be there to climb. But this was different. The only way we could push ourselves to reach the land of the long white cloud – or Aotearoa, as the Maori call it – was to convince ourselves that there was no other option. Never in my life had I had such clarity for an objective. The risk of death, pain to family and friends and long-term damage to my body no longer registered in the decision-making process. These were all distant distractions with hardly any impact.

The Tasman was encouraging something other than our childlike inquisitiveness. Another beautiful aspect of being out there was the amount of time we had to visualise the future and where we could see our lives going. Before leaving Forster, we were so driven by our desire to cross the Tasman that life afterwards didn't exist. We'd deal with it when we got there. Now on the water, we could spend hours and days dreaming about anything that crossed our minds. These meandering conversations planted all sorts of seeds that might eventually blossom when we hit dry land. But this dreamtime didn't happen overnight, or even in the first week or fortnight – it took us over a month to get any kind of clarity. Looking back on it now, we're grateful we had so much time and space.

That evening, we had the longest sked of the expedition so far – 90 minutes. Everyone back home was beginning to get very excited, and the media was starting to go crazy. Pat tried to paint a picture of the reach and impact our expedition was having. We were averaging over 15,000 visitors a day to the website, all major papers in Australia were running daily articles and there seemed to be a heap of people wanting to be there for our arrival. We found it hard to break our mid-Tasman mindset and realise that we were actually bearing in on our arrival.

DAY 58

DIARY, DAY 58 – JAMES

"A plane! First people we have seen in 40 days since *Aquarelle*. We could see their faces and what the pilot was wearing – a red striped vest. They hung around for two hours. Awesome to have some company out here."

155 kilometres to go. We started the morning with three TV interviews: with the *Sunrise* program on Channel Seven, Channel Nine's *Today* show and 2GB radio. Frustratingly, these interviews

delayed us getting into the pits till 8.30am. We had to remain focused. The memory of Andrew McAuley was ever present and we knew we couldn't let our guard down for one minute. We'd defined entry into New Zealand as being the most dangerous phase of the expedition – similar to climbers returning from a summit.

We were mentally and physically wasted and facing a hazardous stretch of ocean that potentially threatened our survival. Approximately 80 kilometres off the NZ coast, the ocean floor of the Tasman rises steeply from 4 kilometres deep to 100 metres in just a few kilometres. This can play havoc with both currents and swell height. In the right sea state (or not), steep monstrous walls of water up to 20 metres high can form in these areas. They have a reputation for sinking container ships and frightening sailors all around the world. We'd decided to "sit off" the shelf if there was a big blow expected and only cross it when the weather forecast remained tranquil.

Once past barrier number one, we'd be faced with a changed sea state where the waves would be much more steep and choppy. As we'd found, this felt like dragging *Lot 41* through knee-deep mud – she hated it. Each wave would stop our momentum, resulting in excruciatingly difficult paddling that burned more calories than we had available. Additionally, the currents round the coast of NZ are renowned for their strength and power. We'd experienced "mild" currents and the enormous impact they had on our progress all the way across, and dreaded having to deal with more powerful currents so near the coast.

The problem with being so close to shore is that we couldn't just chuck out the anchor or drogue and let the ocean chuck us around. We'd run out of sea room and run the risk of being smashed up on the rugged coastline. Equally, we dreaded the prospect of landing on one of the wild beaches of NZ. It would be ugly, and the chances of both *Lot 41* and us being smashed up were high. It was a high priority to reach a harbour. Unfortunately, there are only a handful of suitable ports on the West Coast.

Pat was well aware of these risks as were RCC NZ and Terry Wise, who'd escorted us out of the heads in his yacht *Brindabella* at the beginning of our first sea trial and who was going to supervise our passage the last few days. Our family, friends and the wider public stayed somewhat oblivious to these hazards, which made balancing the expectations of the media, our sponsors and our supporters quite difficult. Often the media would get frustrated when we made it clear we only had x amount of time for an interview. But we had to stay switched on to our primary objective, which was to get to land safely. With the wind coming from the north, we'd now decided that New Plymouth would be our landfall.

New Plymouth is a lively small city on the stunning southwest coast of New Zealand's North Island. With a population of just under 70,000 people, it is nestled between the rugged coast and the flanks of Mount Taranaki. The locals proudly boast that it's by far the best place to live in NZ; with the ability to go for a surf in the morning and then ski in the afternoon, while being surrounded by one of the most stunning landscapes around. We couldn't have chosen a better landfall.

About this time, we sadly farewelled Bruce and Larry. There was increased fish activity as we were approaching New Zealand, and our two intrepid friends had obviously decided it was too dangerous to stick around. We were surprisingly lonely without them.

Paddling along early in the afternoon, the long-awaited trough – from Pat's sked a couple of days earlier – sailed through without too much puff. We were able to remain in the pits as it passed, then were greeted by glorious paddling conditions. It seemed that the news crews had been waiting for this moment, and before long we had a number of helicopters and fixed-wing aircraft buzzing overhead.

Initially, we just stared at them, astonished. We could clearly make out that the first pilot was clean-shaven, with a red woollen vest hiding his small pot belly. A wave of relief washed over me: at least if the shit hit the fan we were within chopper distance of NZ – helicopters could only fly 350 kilometres from the coast.

The initial wave of relief unexpectedly gave way to a feeling that they were both outsiders and intruders; like they didn't belong out here. Weirdly, like an only child suddenly confronted with a brother or sister, we felt a twinge of jealousy at having to share the sea with anyone else. We'd been waiting so long for this moment of human contact, but we were soon urging them to leave us alone with the Tasman – "our Tasman" – a little bit longer. Over the next couple of days, quiet paddling with just the sounds of the ocean would become a distant memory. Land was now near.

When the aircraft left us, we began to focus on some of the realities facing us on arrival. During the voyage, our minds had wandered endlessly through the infinite possibilities of the future, but ironically we'd overlooked a lot of life's practical details. Where would I live when I got back to Australia? How would we *get* back to Australia (we hadn't even thought about booking a flight)? And even the most mundane thing – it looked like we'd be walking the streets of NZ barefoot, because we'd forgotten to pack a pair of shoes.

Mulling over these issues, four birds in perfect line formation passed over us, headed directly for the nearest landfall. Realising that our winged buddies would probably arrive before sunset, we were instantly envious. We might miss the tranquillity of the sea, but we were still desperate to get to New Zealand. *Only a couple more days now … only a couple more days*, I whispered to myself.

DAY 59

130 kilometres to go. As the sea had built through the night, it made sure we didn't get any more than four hours' sleep. We woke to 45-kilometre-per-hour winds from the south, a similar feel to those conditions we'd paddled in over the festive season, but smaller.

Crawling out of the cabin, we gaffa-taped the video camera onto the solar panels, hoping to capture some exciting paddling. We hoped that the cabin would act like a sail and we'd fly through the 5–7-metre swell that had developed. We believed the opportunity would present and we had to be ready for it.

Mid-morning we were greeted by our first tangible sign of land that must have blown from the South Island – a dandelion (although, with our minds as fuzzy as they were, we couldn't recall the name at the time!). I remembered blowing on these white balls of fluff as a kid and making a wish, but I guess it was pretty obvious – even to a dandelion – what I was wishing for at this stage.

Maybe it was just tiredness, but I had a general feeling of uneasiness all day. I was getting frustrated with Jonesy falling into the trap of summit fever. In the past, I'd climbed mountains with people who'd stopped following decision-making processes, precautions and rules, because the summit was "just over there". Complacency would get us killed.

I was determined for us to keep everything the same – it wasn't the time for us to change any of our systems. One month earlier, there was no chance in the world that we would have been out paddling in these conditions. Now that there was such a short distance to go, though, we were tempted to start altering our eating, paddling and desalinating patterns.

We'd rigorously established a routine that was keeping us alive, and in these final stages, I was putting an exaggerated emphasis on keeping this routine. I didn't want us to change anything – keen to ensure we could survive out here for another month if we had to. To that effect, it felt a tad odd pumping three hours each day when land was only a maximum of four days away. Was it a waste of energy?

It was around this distance from shore that Andrew McAuley had got into trouble, and his spirit seemed to engulf us. We couldn't escape this feeling that was everywhere and everything. I've never believed in ghosts or the like, but there was *something* there. At times, I got pangs of uneasiness but generally it was a feeling of acceptance and approval. Obviously I can't know for sure, but it felt like he was there, tapping us on the shoulder and saying, "Well done, boys, you've done good." It did feel, in a way, as if all three of us were sharing in the journey.

There was more sadness in the air when we learnt that Sir Edmund Hillary had just passed away. Apparently, there'd been the possibility that he'd be on the beach at New Plymouth to welcome us in. Sir Ed had inspired us so much throughout our adventures.

Based on the weather forecasts, we weren't expecting to be out here any more than three to four days. In hindsight, it seems a little irrational, but my anal stubbornness only 10 hours earlier to stick to our processes had eased a bit, and finishing up for the afternoon, we decided it was time to get stuck into the remaining food provisions. We'd deprived our bodies long enough – meagre rations were now a thing of the past.

As I wrote in my diary, we pillaged the "food stores in bow this arvo – took all the Snickers bars, dehydrated food – we're coming in to land, baby." Our minds had shifted outlook. There was no holding us back.

DAY 60

DIARY, DAY 60 – JAMES

"Terry looks like a madman! Don't know who is more excited – him or us?"

The sea built through the night to 55 kilometres per hour from the southeast. Adding to the frustration of being so close was our northwesterly drift of 1.5 kilometres per hour. We kept drumming into ourselves that it was no different from being mid-Tasman. We stayed in the cabin in the morning and the seas gave way to a stunning afternoon as we hit the sticks. Although we were still pushing current, the conditions were perfect without a cloud in sight.

We gave a couple of friends a call in the morning – we needed some morale boosting. Both Wade – a friend who I'd boxed with at uni – and Ben were excited to hear our voices but a bit concerned about our lack of mental aptitude. I asked Wade how he was going with a book he'd been reading over two years earlier; then at the end of the conversation, I said, "I'll just pass you on to Mum now," and handed the phone to Jonesy.

Mid-afternoon, paddling along under a brilliant sky, I was listening to the last seven hours of *The Power of One* when we spotted a large aluminium-hulled fishing vessel approaching our port side. As we tried to work out exactly who was on board, we saw the well-built silhouette of Terry Wise, standing on the cabin roof waving his hands frantically back and forth.

A large-framed, seasoned sailor, his childlike enthusiasm as he waved in crazed semaphore epitomised his personality. As he and the rest of the crew approached us, we were awash with nervous excitement. We were about to have our first proper interaction with someone apart from each other in nearly seven weeks. How would we react?

It was hard to sum up 60 days of the most vivid highs and lows of my life in a half-hour conversation. Fortunately, Terry had spent years sailing around the world and had gone through similar experiences, so even if we weren't making much sense he understood us.

When we resumed paddling, our cadence was noticeably faster and our speed through the water had increased. Jonesy and I both revel in being isolated from "civilisation", but the whole way across, there was a clear correlation between our contact with the outside world, our morale and the progress we made. For example, two days earlier, when we'd initially seen the choppers and planes buzzing round, and again today with Terry, our stroke rate had picked up significantly.

Although we hadn't had regular, direct contact with people on the Tasman, the online forum had provided a similar boost. The forum let everyone involved, including us, experience something special. Take one of the forum regulars, Ol Oiler, for instance. Every couple of days he'd post incredibly entertaining and well-written short stories on his life working on tug boats. His yarns provided us with hours of entertainment and gave him the chance to be part of a community as he battled with cancer. (Sadly, Ol Oiler passed away a couple of months after our return. At his funeral, he had a photo of Lot 41 on top of his coffin – we'd never had the opportunity to meet him.)

It was fantastic being able to share our experience with Ol Oiler, and, in a similar vein, I think in the future the impact that human contact can have in the most extreme environments will push adventurers beyond previous boundaries. This communication is going to be one of the defining elements of adventure through this period in history. If Scott or Mallory had had constant contact with their loved ones, could they have pushed that little harder? Could Scott have returned to One Ton Depot and Mallory to High Camp?

Explorers of yesteryear took photos and letters of loved ones to help them through difficult times. The thought of having live video conferencing when clinging to the side of a mountain or being rolled in mountainous seas is mind-blowing. And this technology isn't far off.

Of course, there's also the question of whether all this takes away from the purity of the adventure. As I said one day on the video diary, "Gone are the days when 30 staunch blokes go down to Antarctica and return in five years, if they're lucky. If our tracking beacon goes down for five minutes, the world (well, parts of the world) panics. The dynamics of adventure are changing. It's fascinating to be a part of it. Is it a good thing?"

Does technology aid adventure or does it crush the romanticism of it? I strongly believe it will provide the tools to push the remotest frontier even further. Adventure will only be dead when people stop dreaming and stop growing.

When Terry left us, we paddled on for another couple of hours, and couldn't help the feeling of comfort beginning to glow inside us. We were now within aerial access of New Zealand and fishing boats could get out to us with a short three-hour jaunt from the coast. TracPlus (the NZ company which was providing the beacon on the front of *Lot 41* that transmitted our position every six minutes back to our website) had changed our tracking patterns, and was now updating every 30 seconds. We were closing in on our objective and, given the sharp rise in the floor of the Tasman close to shore, our whole support team were nervous about the dangers of re-entry. They were focused on keeping us alive all the way in.

Late afternoon, 114 kilometres from solid ground, we were paddling along in silence on a glassy calm ocean and could feel it breathing as a gentle swell bobbed us up and down. On our starboard side was a fiery mosaic of reds, oranges and yellows dancing through the sky. On our port side to the east, it was more peaceful, with pastel purples and blues softly giving way to one another, preparing for another night. Suddenly an outline formed in front of us. It was a pyramid peeking out above the clouds in front of us.

"Hey, Jonesy," I said quietly, choking as I tried to hold back tears.

"Yeah, mate," he replied, concentrating on the next stroke, blissfully unaware of the little piece of information I was about to tell him.

"Look up there – I can see Mount Taranaki," I said calmly, as relief soaked through my veins.

We both stopped paddling and stared in amazement – it was the most beautiful sight we had ever seen. *Land.* For the first time in 60 days. I slowly turned round in my pit and our eyes locked for a brief moment. Jonesy had taken his sunglasses off. His eyes were welling up – first the capillaries went red, then tears started washing down his face. Uncontrollably, I followed suit. Sticking my hand out, we embraced each other and wept. Justin, who was usually a bit more emotional than me, had done a brilliant job all expedition in forbidding himself to cry, but at that moment it was too much. We bawled and bawled.

Our reaction was starkly different from when we'd seen

mainland Tasmania after paddling across Bass Strait. Back then, we'd been young, naïve and had no idea what we were getting ourselves into. The Tasman journey had taught us so much. Instead of the childish yelling, screaming and singing of "Amazing Grace", "Waltzing Matilda" and our old school song, we sat in silence, quietly sobbing, and reflected. My mind raced through the previous two months, as well as the four years of preparation that had led to us being out on the Tasman. Vivid memories of our journey flashed through my mind as I stayed fixated on the pyramid in front of us.

We gathered ourselves and resumed paddling, guided now by land. I was on a completely different train of thought now, though, as I couldn't help thinking about Andrew and how close he'd been to reaching the shore. He would have witnessed a similar scene – the welcoming but still-too-distant New Zealand coast.

After he'd been separated from his kayak, it must have been horrible – indescribably – for him sitting in the water, the lifejacket keeping him bobbing on the surface, probably knowing he wasn't going to make it through the night. Every now and then, my eyes looked down from the horizon to the black water all around. Remembering my recurring nightmares in which I'd seen Andrew's ghostly pale face staring at the mountains as tears began to flood down his cheek, I shivered, imagining myself in his position. If I found myself in the water, would I have the energy to battle or would I have to give in? I've always been a fighter, but looking down at the ocean with the cloak of darkness approaching, by now I don't think I was in any state to resist. And I could see myself asking the question, "Was it worth it?"

The remaining light in the sky slowly washed away, handing over duties to the night god. On cue, the Southern Cross began to rise right behind Mount Taranaki. Darkness veiled the slopes of the mountain, leaving the Southern Cross to guide us in.

We continued to paddle together, intent on breaking free of the northwest current. Pushing until midnight, Jonesy then retired to the cabin to get two hours' kip. Prior to him drifting off to sleep, he had a one-hour sked with Pat, who refused to give us a weather forecast beyond Monday – two days away.

"Boys, you have to arrive on Sunday," he told us. "I've got faith in you – I know you can do it. If there are any anti-inflams or No-Doz on board when you arrive, you haven't pushed hard enough."

Pat wanted to get us in to New Zealand on the weekend for two reasons. There was another front approaching in a few days' time and we didn't want to be near the coast when it was due to blow in. Also, he thought we'd attract a bit more attention in the media on a Sunday than a weekday – something which hadn't even occurred to us.

As Jonesy had on the fourth night of the voyage, I similarly experienced a moment of nirvana as I paddled along by myself that evening. A blanket of stars overhead twinkled on the calm sea, keeping me amused every now and then with a shooting star. At 1.30am I was deep into visualising what it was going to be like embracing our families, when a spurt of water erupted a mere 10 metres in front of the kayak.

I was in such a deep trance that it took a couple of moments for the abnormality to register. As my mind laboriously tried to digest this information, another spurt erupted. Then another, and another. Some whales had come up to have a look and keep me company. The events of the previous few hours had amazed me. First seeing land, then the Southern Cross rising behind Mount Taranaki, and now these whales. It was a really spiritual experience, as if there was more to the moment than pure coincidence – it felt like a deeper force was in play.

I was enjoying the moment so much, I hardly noticed our swapover time drifting by. I'd been paddling strongly and was really getting into my stride, so I thought I might as well continue and allow Jonesy to catch up on some sleep. The hours flew by as our speed began to pick up – we were escaping this northwest current and edging closer to our goal.

2 0

THE SMELL OF PERFUME

DAY 61

> DIARY, DAY 61 – JAMES
> "It's all been worth it … It feels like we could reach out
> and touch Mount Taranaki … Magic moment of life."

As the darkness slowly gave way to the dull morning light at 5am, I felt chuffed with my effort – I'd been out in the pits for 15 hours straight. Waking Jonesy up, he seemed a little dazed and confused that he'd slept right through the night. After realising the mileage I'd put in, he patted me on the back and got ready for his shift. I inserted my earplugs and crashed out for the next three-and-a-half hours as Jonesy took the reins.

Without me realising, a media vessel had come out while I was paddling and apparently they were a little disappointed they hadn't got shots of us both in action. One of the two cameramen politely asked, "Do you reckon you could wake James up so we can get the two of you?"

Justin almost started laughing, replying, "Not a chance in the world, buddy. He's just done a huge stint and he's earned a couple of hours' kip."

While I was asleep, Jonesy put in a fantastic shift. I wrote in my diary the next day that my effort that night had probably been "the proudest paddle I've ever done in my life", adding that it had geed Justin up to match it, "which, of course, he did!" I hope he didn't mind me taking some credit for his efforts …

Both of us were paddling again at 10.15am. Around lunchtime, David Spence, the CEO of Unwired, came out to see us in a coastguard boat. Another familiar face! David had believed in us right from the start, backed us the whole way, and had now made the effort to come out and greet us. He'd played a huge role in making this journey happen. We weren't quite at our conversational best, but it didn't matter. As the boat was about to depart, David yelled out some advice we'll never forget. It was one of those vivid moments where the clouds seemed to part, and an angel with a halo poetically announced, "Remember – humility, guys … humility. Remain humble."

At the time, it seemed completely out of context and we didn't have any idea what he was talking about. Had we begun to come across as arrogant in our media interviews or podcasts? We'd learn later that he was referring to the reception he knew was brewing in New Plymouth and the reaction our arrival was going to generate around the world.

After David and the coastguard had left, other boats began to mill around us. As they did, we felt quite awkward making small talk with our visitors. We were fine answering "media questions", but when the cameras were off and we had to just have a conversation, we found it difficult. What do you say? "So … how was your Christmas and festive season?" was one question we started asking, in an attempt to help us break the nervous tension that flooded the air.

We felt like an exhibit at the world's wettest science museum as everyone stared at us in awe. You could see them analysing our every comment and gesture, examining us like lab rats. And, to be fair, we probably would have done the same thing in their situation.

When the boats – and choppers – left towards dusk, we immediately felt comfortable with the isolation and quiet. Because of previous problems I'd had settling back into city life after an expedition, I was becoming a little apprehensive, bordering on scared, of being around lots of people again. After shorter jaunts into the bush or out to sea, I'd struggled big-time, so what would my reaction be like after the Tasman? I knew Jonesy would be alright – he always has been on re-entry. But after Bass Strait, for instance, I'd suffered from post-expedition depression.

I guess any adventure that detaches you from so-called day-to-day life, pushes your mind and body to the edge and then plants you back in the real world is always going to be difficult to digest. Not that I'm comparing myself to Apollo astronauts (moonwalking will never have the glamour of kayaking … sorry, Neil), but after their once-in-a-lifetime experience, they suffered a high percentage of depression and drug and alcohol abuse, and some committed suicide.

The conditions remained perfect as we drew ever closer to New Zealand. Fighting fatigue and numbness, I wrote in my diary: "We really have beaten any sense out of our brains to listen to the body – stop/rest isn't a part of our vocabulary any more."

We were now on full rations and made the decision to stop pumping our fresh water. It was so much fun to be able to eat as much as we wanted at each break. Interestingly, though, within a day we'd got used to this luxury and it no longer brought the enjoyment that it did the day before. It was a micro lesson in materialism and standard of living. The human mind adapts really quickly to higher standards of living and makes that the new benchmark. Gorging ourselves, as well as other luxuries, became a necessity almost instantly.

At 4.40pm, we had 46 kilometres to go. We were now closer than anyone had ever been to crossing the Tasman by kayak. Before we'd allow ourselves to go to sleep on what we hoped would be our final night at sea, we wanted to be close enough to the coast to ensure that nothing would stop our arrival on Sunday. Our fatigue was almost unbearable as we paddled towards the lights of New Plymouth, which dotted the horizon.

On the final night, it was a shame that our nerves were completely frayed and we bickered over lots of little things. Justin wanted to stop and rest, while I was keen to get our distance-to-go down to 20 kilometres before we called it a day. He began to complain that we always did what I wanted and our disagreement started from there.

We compromised, paddling on to 1am, then captured a precious four hours' sleep. We were so exhausted that our alarms didn't wake us. Uncannily, we woke up after Justin had a dream that Terry Wise was tapping him on the shoulder, trying to wake him for our final day's paddle in to shore.

DAY 62

This was it. It would be the last time we'd have to put on wet, shredded thermals, listen to music out of one earphone, and be tethered to *Lot 41*. We enjoyed the detail of each and every ritual on the morning of day 62. Because of our "sleep-in", we were caught by some choppers in the morning as we tried to don the thermals, stark naked. Being beyond caring what they thought, we had a job to do and weren't going to let them influence our routine.

As those choppers left we saw a boat flying towards us, but couldn't identify who was on board. The first thing that struck me was the stunning aroma of female perfume; from 30 metres away, it was like an atomic blast. I was instantly aroused and was slightly embarrassed then to discover the scent belonged to the 60 *Minutes* reporter Liz Hayes. (It wasn't that you'd laid it on too thick, Liz! It was just that I'd smelt nothing but salt, Jonesy and salt for the previous two months.) If I was going into sensory overload from perfume wafting in from metres away, though, I wondered how I'd react once we got to land.

We were soon engulfed by motorboats coming to accompany us in for our final 20 kilometres. Then, on the calm sea, we saw what looked like a platoon of Navy Seals approaching. We had no idea what they were. Suddenly, we realised it was 30 kayakers paddling out to welcome us. Just like when we'd left Forster, we instantly felt more comfortable being surrounded by kayaks, rather than much larger vessels. And as a bonus, Terry had taken on the policeman role to ensure that they didn't come too close to us. To maintain our voyage's unsupported status, it was crucial that we didn't touch another boat.

Among the other visitors, a wild-looking middle-aged man with a healthy beer belly came charging towards us. He was in a 5-horsepower tinnie no larger than a bathtub. As soon as he got close to us, he stood and screamed out, "Rob Browning from the forum. Rat 1 and Rat 2, God bless you bloody legends. God bless you!" he yelled euphorically. We both thought he was absolutely mad being 10 kilometres off the coast in a tiny boat. This was possibly a bit rich, coming from two people who'd paddled 3000 kilometres ...

The last couple of days had been a dream. The sea was breathing gently, with only a soft breeze coming from behind us and a favourable current willing us to shore. The Tasman had finally opened the gateway – it seemed to be her way of congratulating us and telling us to enjoy the day. No, we hadn't tamed her, far from it, but maybe soothed her just a little.

With these great conditions, and surrounded by fellow kayakers and other boats, our hull speed improved to 5 kilometres per hour through the water. We talked with our fellow kayakers, and every now and then gave a friendly wave to a chopper or media boat. *Less than one hour to go.*

At these moments you never think of basic bodily needs – like peeing! I wondered how many wedding couples had been at the altar, needing to hang a pee? Apparently, that was the first thing Hillary had done when he reached the summit of Everest. From our point of view, we'd become so used to just peeing and stooling over the side whenever the need arose, we just did it. I guess we'd unconsciously become like animals in more ways than we'd realised. We no longer had that freedom with all these people all around. Where could I go? I asked Justin, but all I got was an unsympathetic laugh.

After holding on and holding on, it felt like my internals were about to erupt – I'd always imagined this triumphant moment a bit differently. I just couldn't keep it in any more – I started peeing in my pit, the spray skirt providing an excellent toilet lid. The perfect crime! Bilging out as much urine as possible, I prepared to just put up with the stench.

With 14 kilometres to go – the distance of a Sydney City-to-Surf – we were greeted by the smell of land, which immediately swamped the aroma of bodily fluids. Just like the waft of perfume a few kilometres beforehand, the scent of grasses, plants, flowers and dirt was overwhelming. The air seemed to have a thickness that's only carried by land. As we passed an oil freighter moored 2 kilometres off the coast, it blew its ginormous horns a few times as the crew lined the gunwales, cheering and waving. Justin pulled out our rusty aerosol equivalent and honked it back in acknowledgement. The huge difference between the bellow from the ship and our *tweek-tweek* really brought it home – *Lot 41* had just been so small out there.

Paddling into the port of New Plymouth, we approached the beach and couldn't make out any humans. Justin called out, "I think there are a whole heap of funny coloured rocks up there, mate."

"They're not rocks, Jonesy, they're people!" I yelled.

Peering through eyes beginning to well up, he replied, "Holy shit, they are too."

We were stunned – the shore was lined with thousands of people cheering as madly as if the All Blacks had won the World Cup (like that will ever happen!). Pat had told us to be ready for something huge, but never in our craziest dreams did we expect a reception like this.

The beach was covered with over 25,000 well-wishers and supporters – it was mind-blowing. We paddled on, completely absorbed in the moment (and, thankfully, not being distracted by the need to pee), slowing our cadence down as a traditional Maori outrigger canoe came to escort us through the harbour. One hundred metres from land we gingerly stood up and waved to the crowd, who roared with excitement.

Our legs were weak and standing was difficult – we needed to hold on to our cockpit rims to support our weight: the wash from other vessels was enough to knock us over. As we dipped our paddles in slowly, I instantly made out the red, teary faces of Mum and Lil (they'd always been good at getting to the front of crowds) as they jumped madly up and down. For one brief moment, my eyes locked with Mum's and we were both oblivious to the hysterical commotion.

As the bow of *Lot 41* rubbed up on the sand, I had to refocus one last time on the expedition. It was important for us to reach land completely unassisted so critics would never say that our voyage across the Tasman was aided (it was all incredibly pedantic, I know). Terry remained as the policeman, shepherding the crowd away from us. We took our legionnaire hats and sunglasses off and ceremoniously removed the dog collars – which had held our knives, journals and cameras throughout the expedition – from our chafed necks, carefully stashing them in the bow of the kayak.

Standing up, we both pumped our fists in the air, tore our spray skirts off and untied our safety lines from round our stomachs. This was so symbolic: we were now free from the sea, free from *Lot 41*.

On the count of three, we threw ourselves into the waist-deep water, our feet connecting with the earth for the first time in two months and 3318 kilometres. It was a fantastic, completely indescribable moment – we'd done it. We'd *done* it!

There was just one minor problem: we could hardly stand up. Immediately realising how weak our legs had become, it was lucky there was a little water around to stabilise us as we lumbered about, trying to find each other for support. Arm in arm we embraced and staggered towards the beach. My legs collapsed after a few steps, but Justin picked me up and kept us going. Our friendship had survived and our support for one another had continued right to the end. We'd stayed friends *and* made it to NZ – what more could you want?

As soon as my feet left the water, I looked down at them covered in fine dark sand – they felt detached from the rest of my body. It was a strange thought in the middle of the mayhem, and it was quickly overwhelmed as our families tearily embraced us. Although Mum was lathered in sweat, it didn't stop me from burying my face into her neck. She'd never held me so tight. She didn't want to let me go – I was one of her little boys.

Lil nuzzled her way in between Mum and me, and as I picked her up and our cheeks touched, our tears fused together. Dad, being Dad, had held back briefly until he was shoved into my arms. Underneath his prickly grey beard, choked in tears, he whispered, "I'm so proud of you, son." It was the most special moment of my life.

I looked across at Jonesy, who was engrossed in a similar moment with his family. His mother was crying hysterically, repeating his name over and over.

Everyone, including some news reporters and cameramen, seemed to be welling up. It was completely unbelievable to think we were the cause of all this emotion.

After the initial family hugs, David Spence and Pat emerged and embraced us too. All we could say was "thank you" over and over – they were the ones who'd made this dream a reality. Then out of the crowd, one by one, burst our closest mates who'd flown over to New Zealand for our arrival – first came Uncle H, Tom, Lach, Tink, Aidan … and good old Jen. Our families and Pat had kept this brilliant secret from us.

Wow … what was Jen doing there? Up to that point, I think she'd been the only girl I'd ever loved. In the intensity of the moment, I wanted to say something to her, but I couldn't conjure the strength. Imagine that – we'd just kayaked all the way across the Tasman and when it came to expressing raw human feelings, I hid behind the buzzing commotion.

By this stage, Jonesy and I were both a whimpering mess – and the commotion was continuing. In front of us, the crowd parted and we were greeted by eight Maori in traditional clothing, adorned with facepaint and performing a haka. How appropriate, as we'd left the shores of Australia to the chant of "Waltzing Matilda".

After we'd hugged everyone, and after David had sprayed a bottle of champagne over us all, Tink, Jonesy's brother Andy, and Clary lifted us onto their shoulders and carried us up to a stage that seemed to have been constructed to celebrate our arrival. At shoulder height, I was once again blown away by the number of people there. My eyes briefly focused on a large sign peeping behind an Australian flag: "Where the bloody hell have you been?"

As Tink, Clary and Andy deposited us on stage, we were officially greeted by the mayor and the people of New Plymouth. Mayor Pete was a human mountain of a man, and his passion for the Taranaki area was even bigger. If it wasn't for his remarkable energy, our arrival wouldn't have been anywhere near as unforgettable as it was. Then, after the formalities, we conducted a few media interviews, where I'm certain we didn't make much sense.

Later, we were whisked away in an ambulance for a full blood test and medical check-up. Sitting in the relative quiet of the ambulance with Pat and a nurse, we were able to gather our thoughts a little and allow him to brief us on what was to come.

Our connection with Pat now meant much more than mere friendship or a "business relationship" – through our time with him out on the Tasman, we'd developed a deep bond. It was more of a paternal relationship he had with us: he'd always been there for our skeds and phone calls and been our voice to the outside world. He'd lived our harrowing moments and often found himself sleepless as he managed the expectations of family, friends, the media, and us out there. In the peacefulness of the ambulance, we locked eyes and shook our heads. We'd made it. I think we were all still in a little shock – had we really just kayaked from Australia to New Zealand?

I felt giddy at the speed we were travelling – literally. The fastest we'd gone in the previous 62 days was possibly 15 kilometres per hour down the face of a wave in a storm – now the trees and buildings seemed to be flying past our windows. As the nurse took my blood pressure and temperature, I looked down at my limp, sandy feet again. There was a stark contrast between my raggedy clothes and dirty feet and the fresh white sheets of the ambulance bed; my feet still felt alienated from the rest of my body.

Out on the Tasman, I'd thought we'd looked quite normal, but now, surrounded by showered and well-groomed people, I realised we were a ghastly mess. There was zinc cream lathered all over our faces and Justin's ratty whiskers were bleached white from exposure to the sun, while with my beard and ragged hair, I knew I didn't exactly look like Pierce Brosnan right now.

Lying in the ambulance beds, we passed fresh cherries to each other which had been shoved in our hands – what a great gift! – by a local farmer back at the port. The fresh fruit tasted amazing. As we were wheeled out of the ambulance into the hospital, with the fluorescent lights whizzing overhead, doctors, nurses and patients all poked their heads around to see the two nutty kayakers. After an examination by the doctor, blood samples were taken and we were given the green light to leave. The doctor's parting words were: "Your bodies have been through an incredibly traumatic experience. Don't eat too much meat or drink too much alcohol over the next few days." Justin and I looked at each other wryly and smiled. Whatever made him think we might want to do something like that?

Reaching our boutique bed and breakfast smack-bang in the middle of town, we were greeted by the friendliest staff imaginable (as well as our friends Zoran and Gordana, who, to their horror, had arrived in New Plymouth two hours after our landing). After everything we'd seen and done, the biggest challenge of the day was actually trying to get up a single flight of steps to our rooms – our legs were so wasted, we needed a person under either arm. When we opened the doors, our eyes almost blew out of our heads: the beds were larger and, we soon discovered, softer than anything we'd seen in our lives! Out on the veranda was a massive basket of fresh fruit and nuts and, as I closed my eyes and bit into the sweetest strawberry of my life, Justin went straight for a can of whipped cream, shaking it and triggering a mouthful. Pieguts – what could you expect?

After we'd gorged ourselves and jumped on our beds, the 60 *Minutes* crew – who'd been with us every moment since we left the hospital – left us to have a spa and shower in our rooms. I stood in my thermals, staring into the mirror, and confirmed what I'd been thinking in the ambulance. What a disgusting sight! My beard was mangly and my tattered thermals hung limply on a frame that resembled a coat hanger – there wasn't an ounce of muscle or fat left.

Tearing my clothes off, I carefully examined my naked body: it looked different through the eyes of a mirror and in a marble-white bathroom (compared to what I'd been seeing the last couple of months). I was starkly out of place and felt like an impostor. There was just too much contrast between this stunning room and my ragged animal appearance – I belonged outside.

Sinking into the larger-than-life spa with bath gel frothing bubbles almost felt the same as sliding into my cockpit. I gazed at my weather-beaten hands, where multi-storey blisters had formed, and repeated to myself, "We made it, you're safe now. We made it, mate." I was really having trouble getting it to sink in.

As I swam around in the spa, scrubbing the zinc and Sudocrem off my skin, every now and then I plunged my face into the water, allowing my long hair to float on the surface. Turning the spa off, the bubbles dissipated quickly and, to my horror, left behind a browny soup with bits and pieces of skin, hair, pubes and strapping tape floating around.

I stood up and turned on the shower for phase two of the cleaning process. Pulling the plug, I saw much more than just dirt, grime and salt crystals flow down the pipes. We'd left the ocean and a part of us would always remain out there. Life was going to move on now and it would never be the same.

We met our family and friends downstairs for a drink, then made our way to a Lone Star restaurant, where the biggest stack of ribs and steak were waiting. We'd had plenty of cravings out on the Tasman, but the most powerful was for juicy, succulent pork ribs. A local Speight's beer was energetically shoved in our hands and two mountains of ribs immediately followed. The chefs looked on as we separated the meat with our steak knives with surgical precision. The flavour flooded my taste buds in every sense of the word – it felt as if the volume of appreciation had been tweaked up in every facet of my life in the hours since we'd returned to land.

That's one of the beautiful aspects of adventure – it's taught me true appreciation in every sense of the word. Mastery will come (I imagine) when I can continue to operate at that level of appreciation for the rest of my life. In the past, I've found it so easy to swing quickly back into my old habits, forgetting how good that steak really is, or for that matter my family, or even that flower I walk by on my way to work. Deprivation seems to be the key.

I peered through the tower of ribs between Jonesy and me, struggling to make a dent in this monolithic pile of pig. I was amazed that J had devoured his whole stack and moved on to his sister's and mother's plates. He'd written down four pages of cravings during the journey and was apparently now on a mission to satisfy each one of them. Within 10 days of being back on land, he'd put on 6 kilograms – nice one, Pieguts.

Completely exhausted, we made our way back to our B&B for an early night. Our two rooms were on either side of the corridor, and before going in, we stood at our doors and stared at one another.

"Mate," I said feebly.

"Yeah, Cas."

"If you need anything tonight, or you can't sleep, just come on in – I'll leave my door unlocked."

"Me too, Cas. Me too. Thanks for an incredible journey."

I couldn't believe the amazing transformation Jonesy had undergone over the previous four years. Sure, it had been slow, but he had really progressed so far as a mate from those early days when he was constantly pissing his time against the wall. The expedition had forced responsibility upon him, mainly because of the problems I'd experienced with seasickness, and he had pulled through. He'd become the captain of *Lot 41* through his constant loyalty, unselfishness and unwavering commitment to the mission at hand. The expedition had strengthened our bond so much that calling him a mate doesn't sum it up at all – he had become, and will be forever, much more than that to me. Through the Tasman becoming our surrogate mother, by default we had become brothers. There is now an iron-clad bond that can never be broken.

We embraced and patted one another on the back. Finally in my room, I expected to crash out immediately and not wake for the next week, but strangely I found myself staring at the ceiling for the entire night, only capturing about 15 minutes' sleep. The incredible energy from all the people at our arrival and the events of the day turned that ceiling into a plasma screen on repeat. It was one of those moments in my life I'll never forget – as they say, life is not about the number of breaths that you take, but the number of moments that take your breath away. Our arrival – no, the journey over the past four years – had been one of those moments, and my body was way too wired to get any sleep.

At midnight, I flicked the TV on to see our story on BBC World News and CNN. (Media coverage of our expedition even made it as far as the Niagara Cafe in Gundagai. The current owners temporarily plastered over the photos of Prime Minister John Curtin with clippings of our arrival – which was pretty cool.) Already, it didn't feel like us. Switching the telly off, the scenes playing in my head were even more vivid.

I woke at 3am and started writing. During the last couple of days of the expedition, Jonesy and I had talked about what life might have in store for us after the ditch and I now started writing down post-Tasman goals, thoughts and feelings. I was already feeling a little restless about not having a goal to aim for or channel my energy towards. I guess this is one of the inherent weaknesses of being a goal-oriented person – what happens once you achieve your goal?

If there is one thing the Tasman taught us, it's that dreams are possible to be realised … but unfortunately we've had to work bloody hard for them. For J and me, life has never been about what we've done or achieved in the past, but using that experience to provide the skills and knowledge to tackle larger objectives in the future. It's a continual journey of self discovery and growth – if we achieve these out of an experience, it's been a success.

I did know, though, that for us the Tasman was just the beginning, the first rung on a ladder that provided plenty of lessons for the future. The question we then faced was what those future adventures and dreams might be. There was no gravity weighing down our expectations – we'd proved to ourselves that we could do whatever we wanted to do.

I started brainstorming each facet of my life and excitedly channelled that energy through the wee hours. Meanwhile, dazed and confused, Justin jumped up out of bed at 5.30am and looked around for his paddling gear and paddle.

After breakfast, the 60 Minutes producer reminded us that we'd signed an exclusive agreement with them, and that if we spoke to any other media, they'd have to cancel the contract. Understandably he was trying to protect his asset, but for the next couple of days we felt like we were confined to a straitjacket by the fear he instilled in us. In a way, our minds were on a different planet and we found it hard to reject interviews from people who'd followed our journey from Forster and who we'd spoken to via satellite linkups while out on the Tasman.

Unfortunately, Pat – rather prematurely – left New Zealand that day. We wanted to share the "mission" success with him, and assumed that he'd be there to look after us as he'd done when we were out at sea. However, his wife was back in Sydney looking after their baby boy, so understandably he couldn't stick around.

It was at this time that one of our best friends, Tom Mitchell, our only good-looking mate, stood up to fill the role of our "manager".

Since we'd left Australia, he'd done an outstanding job running the media side of things. Tom had always been a great talker and we would have found those first few days back on land pretty difficult without him. We latched on to him to make decisions for us and provide a buffer from the now-foreign outside world.

As we were beginning to discover, there were numerous people pushing and pulling us in different directions – everyone from our friends and family to sport managers, media and the public seemed to be trying to mould us into what they wanted or expected of us. Everybody had their two bobs' worth on how we should be acting in public and in the media, what we should wear, how we should carry ourselves etc. But we were Justin and James – the same two mates who'd left Forster two months before, and as the days progressed, we found the pressure quite difficult to deal with.

The first morning on dry land, we sat down with Liz Hayes and the crew for a gruelling five hours of interviews, conducted at the local sailing club. She was incredibly friendly and after a while it felt like just having a chat with someone over a coffee – the cameras were all but forgotten.

On our arrival the day before, we hadn't had much of a chance to mingle with the locals, who'd flooded both our families and ourselves with warmth and hospitality. Everything had happened pretty quickly before we'd been stuffed into an ambulance and whisked away. Fortunately, that afternoon Mayor Pete put on another public function so we had a little more time to meet the people of New Plymouth, sign a few autographs – over 600! (which took four hours) – and display our majestic, but stinky kayak. For a couple of months, we thought she'd smelt quite welcoming, but all of a sudden I was just as appalled as onlookers seemed to be. The occasion had a fantastic vibe to it and we were just so grateful for how welcome the town made us feel.

That evening, a local bar put on a "welcome back" party for us. For the previous two years, I'd controlled myself with my alcohol intake, knowing that being hungover would hinder my training. That night, though, was one of the wildest, loosest nights of our lives. We consumed stupid amounts of alcohol and found ourselves unashamedly stripping down to our undies on the dance floor to "It's Raining Men" by Geri Halliwell! All-up, it was four years of pressure released in one night. Both of us ended up taking a local girl back to our rooms that evening, which isn't something we're particularly proud of – but after spending two months in a kayak with another hairy, smelly bloke, we were ridiculously horny.

At 7.30 the following morning, after two hours' sleep, we found ourselves conducting our final 60 *Minutes* interview in NZ. We reeked and felt like crap – nothing different from cabin-bound life in a mid-Tasman storm then.

Four days after our arrival in NZ, we flew back home to Sydney – it was the first time I'd ever flown business class. Looking down at the sea 40,000 feet below, Justin and I toasted crossing the ditch with a gin and tonic in hand. Every now and then, the cabin crew would tell us the exact latitude and longitude of our position and our minds would instantly be transported back to life on the Tasman at that location. Again, I kept asking the question: had we really spent two months in a kayak out there? Blasting along in the opposite direction at 800 kilometres per hour, I was struggling to come to grips with how *far* it actually was.

At Sydney airport there was another media scrum and a couple of hundred mates and bystanders to welcome us home. A new beer label had sent the face of their new campaign, "Miss Bondi Blonde", and some other models to the airport to escort us to a limousine. That night, they launched the beer at a ritzy bar and asked us to throw on our penguin suits and join them. It was obviously incredibly confronting being face-to-face with my idols from the Sydney glitterati, not to mention my heroes from *Home and Away* – and to think we were being paid for the privilege!

We milked these experiences for what they were, but knew it was ridiculous to think of ourselves as celebrities. It was so weird having women throw themselves at us – it seemed insane that picking up had never been so easy. In the past, if we'd succeeded in our feeble attempts to woo a girl with our charms, she'd usually had a couple too many or we'd been plain lucky.

The fickleness of human behaviour struck a chord that we couldn't stop thinking about. Over the ensuing weeks, we had girls who we'd liked in the past flinging themselves at us with love letters, texts and just *having* to see us. Trying to make sense of all this was quite confusing – we were still exactly the same two blokes as when we'd left. Although we had a great time and enjoyed the company of those people we hadn't seen for years, our close friends were the ones who'd been in it for the long haul, and they were the ones we felt most comfortable with.

Within a couple of days of being back in Sydney, we booked in to have our post-expedition DEXA scan. This was done on a machine that looks somewhat similar to an MRI unit, which scans up and down your body compiling information on muscle, fat and bone density of each limb of the body.

The results were fascinating: over the course of the expedition, Justin had lost approximately 10 kilograms, of which 5 kilograms was muscle and five fat. I'd lost approximately 6.5 kilograms, but 90 per cent of that weight loss was muscle and only 10 per cent fat. My percentage body fat actually went up through the expedition as I lost proportionally more muscle than fat. Apparently, I should either have had a higher fat percentage going into the expedition (Jonesy kept telling me I should have been supersizing each and every meal – maybe he was right!), or my diet should have had a higher percentage of protein. This would have prevented my body from cannibalising muscle stores when it got hungry.

Many expeditioners over the years have argued on both sides of the fence as to the benefits of pre-expedition bulking up. From our experience, we're definitely on the side that it's beneficial to bulk up both fat and muscle stores. Back in the 1970s, in Kathmandu on the way to Mount Everest, the famous British mountaineer Don Whillans was given grief about his excess weight compared to his lean counterparts. His reply to this nay-sayer was: "In three months' time I'll look like them and they'll probably be dead." Science has progressed since that time, but the principles remain the same.

The human body is incredibly resilient and, in the case of Jonesy and me, it had bounced back quite quickly. The muscle rejuvenated and blood tests revealed that internally we were healthier than we'd ever been. The biggest lag in our recovery was exhaustion.

When we finally got back home in front of a computer, over 1500 emails were sitting in our inbox. We made sure we eventually responded to each one – that took us six months! – but initially we felt under more pressure to deal with emails from prospective managers, book publishers, companies wanting us to endorse their products and more.

Mentally, we were still out at sea and because of the exhaustion we found it difficult to keep our concentration and make decisions. We knew we needed a manager to deal with these requests. But which one? Although Tom had done a great job looking after us in the early days, he was about to head over to

England to pursue his dream to be an actor – watch out, Hugh Jackman!

For the first six months we engaged celebrity management agency The Fordham Company to secure commercial opportunities and to capitalise on what we'd achieved. They were fantastic at negotiating on our behalf, quick to snap up deals and offered great advice. However, as our bodies slowly recovered, we were reminded of a lesson we'd learnt in preparing for the Tasman. The only people who'd make our dreams and goals a reality were ourselves. This was supported by Nick Fordham, who also encouraged us to take over some areas of our commercial affairs and treat them like running our own business.

I didn't want to go back to life as an accountant – there were heaps of valuable lessons that Jonesy and I had learnt which we felt passionate about sharing with others. So far, our post-Tasman career has consisted of writing this book you've just read, getting a documentary off the ground, sharing our story with thousands of people round the world with a keynote presentation about crossing the ditch, and of course … dreaming of our next adventure.

We've really enjoyed presenting our Tasman experiences to the public, even though at school I found it difficult to stand up in class and read a simple passage from a book. I've always had a bit of a lisp and at an all-boys school, my classmates gave me endless grief about my diction. It's funny, but both Justin and I now have such a great time up on stages around the world sharing our journey. Some people have been critical of us making a living out of our Tasman experience, but why can't your work be something that provides you with so much enjoyment?

After leaving school eight years ago, I'd become a chronic diary writer. In 2008, I forced out just four quite-short entries, when in the past they'd flowed effortlessly. Why? I think it's because I've now found what makes me happy. Diaries had provided a release for me when I was confused and unsure of my place in this world. It was the lessons that the outdoors kept drilling home that taught me the true roots of motivation – personal growth and love (of yourself as much as anyone else).

It was in this discovery that I learnt the first stage was to love myself. Through my early 20s, I found it difficult to find love in my life – I abused my body and very nearly killed myself climbing on numerous occasions. On returning from the Tasman, I found myself in a beautiful relationship. Waking up each day with Mia has become as exciting as climbing any mountain or any ocean adventure. When I share the outdoors with her (or just normal life), the experience seems to explode 10-fold with enjoyment. To me, it adds saturation to the picture – making each day just that much more vivid. I feel like love really is the essence of my soul – without it, I'm constantly searching; with it, I'm happy. By depriving myself of this basic human need, I made it impossible to find true happiness.

Adventure is relative. By no means can I see myself pushing the limits of my own endurance for the rest of my life. Although I love what I do now, I can see how the framework Justin and I learnt in putting together the Tasman expedition could be applied to other life experiences – from preparing for a day cragging up in the Blue Mountains to buying my first home.

The two best things that came out of the Tasman were that we arrived in New Zealand better mates than we left and we still enjoy our paddling. They were the super important objectives in defining what was meant by a "successful expedition". In 2008, neither of us did much paddling – I live in the Blue Mountains these days, climbing as much rock as possible. I'm now climbing harder than ever before.

This has been less to do with my physical strength or technique improving, and more to do with my motivation and focus – lessons that the Tasman taught me. A large source of my motivation for climbing in the past was the ego boost I received from climbing hard, bold routes. These days, I climb for other reasons – trying to learn something new about myself. At the end of a day's climbing, I love to reflect on how I've dealt with things like fear, pushing myself physically to the limit or how I've managed to channel my focus. Interestingly, this shift in motivation has led to me climbing dramatically harder grades.

Justin, on the other hand, has enjoyed being back in Sydney – catching up with friends, doing the odd bushwalk, and going out. He's been spending some of his spare time finishing off his Masters of Commerce and taken a keen interest in the post-production of the footage we captured on the Tasman.

And as for our dear friend *Lot 41*, who looked after us for 62 days on one of the wildest and most unpredictable seas in the world, we felt deeply obliged to find her a good stable to rest in. We donated her to the Australian National Maritime Museum, where they'll do a great job of nurturing and caring for her.

21

HEADING FOR THE CHOCOLATE FACTORY

Within weeks of returning to Sydney, the adventure bug began nibbling away at me again – I needed a project to sink my teeth into and I knew what it had to be. It was a place that had always held a starry-eyed fascination for me – it was the factory of adventure and home to some of the most inhospitable beauty on the planet. Stunning landscapes, masses of animals you only ever saw in documentaries, combined with fierce weather and a long history of exploration – all of this had captivated me since I'd first started reading books for fun. When the idea hit me about going there, excitement just flowed through my blood, generating the same energy as when I first began to dream of the Tasman. To me, this was the closest thing to Willy Wonka's Chocolate Factory that I could think of.

With that in mind, in April 2008, a couple of months after returning from the Tasman, I felt ready for another trip to Wonka Land with Jonesy (who, ironically, was beginning to bear a faint resemblance to Augustus Gloop).

I was heading up to the Blue Mountains for a weekend's climbing when I made the call. I was a bit surprised by how nervous I felt. As with the Tasman, I knew I couldn't do this expedition without Justin. "Hey, J, what's been happening?"

"Not much, mate, since I saw you a couple of hours ago."

He had me there. I decided to move on quickly to my romantic proposal. "How'd you like to catch up for dinner?" I asked.

"You're not really my kind of guy," he chuckled. "Anyway, this sounds ominous – I'm sensing déjà vu."

"There's nothing to worry about – but I do need to talk to you about something."

Jonesy could see right through me. "That's *exactly* what I'm worried about. I told my parents that the Tasman was going to be my last big adventure …"

We arranged to have dinner a few days later at the same pizzeria where I asked Justin about paddling to New Zealand. There was the same big barrel-chested man with the same moustache making the same pizzas. There was no Libby this time, but her "successor" looked strikingly similar. It's funny how, coming back from an adventure, I always seemed to be more aware of people doing the same job year in, year out, which I think I'd struggle to do. Occasionally I wish (and so does my poor mother) that I wasn't as restless as I am. At times, life would be so much easier.

I could tell Jonesy had had a couple of big nights. There were bags under his eyes and the normally chalk-white sclera were a dirty yellow in colour.

"Don't ask," he said before I had time to question him. "Had a coupla massive nights."

We couldn't stop laughing – we're the same people we've always been.

We spent a few minutes chatting about what we'd done the previous weekend, but before long Justin said, "Tell me what you're thinking, Cas."

There was a brief silence. I wondered how I was going to bring the subject up. I decided to launch straight in.

"Antarctica, mate," I excitedly belted out. "How 'bout it? I've got this idea to do something truly amazing down there."

His face lit up and, without hesitating, he smiled. "I'm in – let's do it!"

Signalling to the waitress to bring us a pen, we looked down at the paper tablecloth and started scribbling. The energy of the Tasman began to flow through us as the ideas hit the table. Once again, we felt alive.

APPENDIX

CROSSING THE DITCH – HOW WE APPROACHED IT

1. RISK MANAGEMENT APPROACH

After we first had the idea to cross the Tasman, we began to ask as many questions as possible that we'd need to answer before deciding whether or not it could be done. Over a 13-month period, asking and answering these questions, as well as our subsequent research, led to the creation of our risk management document – a 50-page blueprint on how to cross the Tasman. It was initially designed for ourselves, but it proved to be a really useful document in convincing other stakeholders that it was possible to cross the Tasman, unsupported and in a kayak.

2. EQUIPMENT

The risk management research gave us an indication of the equipment we'd need to safely cross the Tasman. Our equipment needs were similar to the rowers of the Woodvale Atlantic Challenge, Sydney to Hobart and round-the-world sailors. There had only been a handful of transoceanic kayak crossings in the previous hundred years. Although each of these voyages was closely examined and scrutinised, in terms of equipment, not much was learnt from these voyages.

Description	Weight	Quantity	Total Weight (kgs)
PADDLERS			
James	85	1	85
Justin	95	1	95
Lot 41 hull			200
Clothing (wet and dry) Icebreaker Bodyfit Kokotat Gore-Tex cag and drysuit	10	2	20
Personal effects	7	2	14
Bedding – Synthetic Roman Sleeping bags	4	2	8
iPod and H2O Audio Waterproof casing	1	2	2
LOGISTICAL SUPPLIES			
Water	80	1	80
Food	1.6	100	160
Medical supplies (basically a Cat 0 kit)	8	1	8
PADDLING EQUIPMENT			
Paddles (Solution flat-bladed snap down paddles)	1	2	2
Spare paddles	1	2	2
Splash decks and night covers	1	4	4
Sunglasses (Rudy Project)	3		
ELECTRICAL EQUIPMENT			
Power distribution box/ Battery charge box/PV	8	1	8
Electrics i.e. lights, wiring, etc	10	1	10
Deep cycle batteries	24	3	72

Description	Weight	Quantity	Total Weight (kgs)
ELECTRICAL EQUIPMENT (cont.)			
Solar panels	2	2	4
Bilge pumps	0.92	1	0.92
Water pumps and extract	2	1	2
EMERGENCY EQUIPMENT			
RFD liferaft	20	1	20
Emergency supplies for raft	6	1	6
Aquafix Personal 406 EPIRBs	0.3	2	0.6
Life jackets – Type 2 PFD	1	2	1
WATER DESALINATION			
Katadyn Power Survivor 40E	11.3	1	11.3
Katadyn Survivor 35	3.2	1	3.2
COMMUNICATIONS			
Iridium satellite handset	0.3	2	0.6
Satellite aerial	0.13	1	0.13
VHF radio system	1.3	1	1.3
Panasonic Toughbook	1.2	1	1.2
TracPlus – Daestra	1.6	1	1.6
NAVIGATION			
Garmin GPS	0.3	2	0.6
GPS aerial	0.13	1	0.13
WEATHER			
Series drogue and rope	10	1	10
Para-anchor (and retrieval set-up)	5	1	5
TOTAL			**830**

3. HEAVY WEATHER

Facing heavy weather in a small craft is daunting, to say the least. Large seas can be broken up into two categories: breaking and non-breaking waves. In his book *Heavy Weather Sailing*, Peter Bruce noted about the latter: "a conventional yacht's stability is such that it cannot be capsized by even the combined action of wind and waves, no matter how high and steep, if they are not breaking." Breaking waves are the primary concern of heavy weather.

The US Coast Guard states that: "It is important to note that most storms do not create dangerous breaking waves"; however, it is breaking waves that cause offshore vessels to capsize, which generally occurs when the vessel is caught beam on (side on) to breaking waves. Tests have shown that breaking waves with a wave height of 30 per cent of the hull length could capsize some vessels. All boats tested capsized when the height of the wave was 60 per cent of the vessel's hull length.

After speaking with numerous sailors and conducting our own research, the manner in which we prepared for this heavy weather out on the Tasman was to:

- *Before we left*: Construct a vessel with the structural integrity to handle 20-metre breaking waves
- *Before the storm*: We were well prepared for the heavy weather before it arrived. The first stage of this was being aware of the conditions expected. Our weather forecasts and warnings came from: Roger Badham and on-sea observations of cloud type, wind/swell direction, barometric pressure etc.

    A major part of our strategy was to: have the series drogue deployed; be in the cabin, all safety gear checked and ready to be deployed if need be; and ensure both of us were prepared – i.e. well fed, hydrated and strapped in – before the weather hit.

- *Ride it out*: Ensure the appropriate drogue/sea anchor was deployed. Of the 62 nights we were at sea, we deployed the parachute anchor 51 times (fouled twice), series drogue twice and rode with general conditions on six nights. The series drogue handled the roughest weather we encountered much better than the parachute anchor. We deployed both pieces of equipment off a bridle attached to a five-point anchor system on the stern of the kayak. Both retrieval and deployment were done from the rear cockpit. Note the close cell foam wrapped around the bridle in order to prevent it fouling with the rudder. We designed the system so that the main line to the storm gear deployed would snap before the bridle and the attachment points to the kayak.

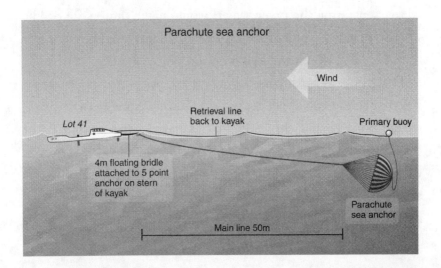

Parachute sea anchor

Wind

Lot 41

Retrieval line back to kayak

Primary buoy

4m floating bridle attached to 5 point anchor on stern of kayak

Parachute sea anchor

Main line 50m

4. DESIGN OF KAYAK

The design of the kayak evolved around the provisions and safety gear that would be needed. We tossed up a multitude of designs including:

- Using the room of the cockpits to sleep in with a cover that came over the cockpits at night;
- Small cabin in the middle of the kayak separating the two cockpits;
- Rear cabin.

Design A was avoided, as life in the cockpit – of any kayak – is constantly wet. There would be no escaping the salt water. This would increase the risk of skin infections, damage to vital communications gear, and result in a much colder voyage, thus increasing the risk of hypothermia and poor judgement from lack of quality sleep.

Design B wasn't chosen, as paddling a double kayak with 1.5 metres separating the two paddlers would make timing the paddle strokes incredibly difficult and the rear paddle would be staring at the cabin rear, which would not be all that pleasant!

Design C was agreed upon, but still was not perfect. Because we were expecting 60–70 per cent of the wind to come from the west, we did not feel that either the vertical face of the cabin door, or the profile of the cabin, would be that much of an issue. However, we paddled into headwinds for 90 per cent of the voyage, which caught the cabin face constantly. In hindsight, we would have reduced the profile of the cabin.

Two critical design considerations of *Lot 41* were:

- The kayak had to be positively buoyant, i.e. if every bulkhead filled with water, she would still float;

- The stern of the kayak had to blow up into the wind when the kayak was drifting. This ensured relatively dry entry into the cabin and that the bulk of weather would roll over the sleek profile of the stern.

5. KAYAK CONSTRUCTION

The budgeted time-frame was 12 weeks to complete the basic hull. This was completely inadequate, and as with all unique designs, the time line blew out to close to double what we'd anticipated. The boat builder, Graham Chapman, believed the delay was caused by several factors, including the use of epoxy resin (which has a long cure time compared with Vinyl Ester resin – the designer was adamant about using this) and the constant changes to the design due to perceived flaws in the CAD design, i.e. not enough storage room in the cabin, and size of the water tanks on board. The fit-out of the bilging, wiring and portholes, etc, took another six weeks.

Basic hull laminate:
  Outerside layer:
  Eglass 300 weight twill weave
  Kevlar 285 weight plain weave
  Double Bias 450 weight fibreglass
  Core:
  Klegecell foam core 8 millimetre
  Inside layer:
  Double Bias 450 weight fibreglass
  Kevlar 285 weight plain weave
  Eglass 300 weight twill weave

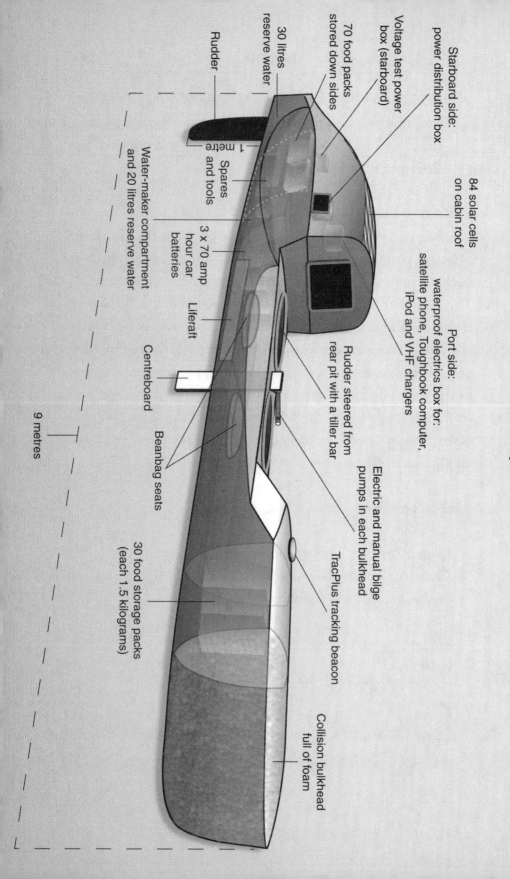

'Lot 41' layout

Starboard side:
power distribution box

Voltage test power
box (starboard)

70 food packs
stored down sides

30 litres
reserve water

Rudder

1 metre

Spares
and tools

3 x 70 amp
hour car
batteries

Liferaft

Centreboard

Beanbag seats

Water-maker compartment
and 20 litres reserve water

9 metres

84 solar cells
on cabin roof

Port side:
waterproof electrics box for:
satellite phone, Toughbook computer,
iPod and VHF chargers

Rudder steered from
rear pit with a tiller bar

Electric and manual bilge
pumps in each bulkhead

TracPlus tracking beacon

30 food storage packs
(each 1.5 kilograms)

Collision bulkhead
full of foam

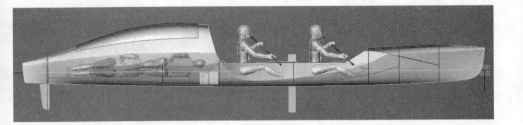

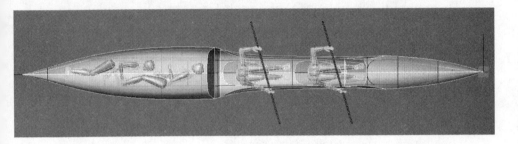

SLEEPING AND PADDLING POSITIONS IN *LOT 41*

Justin was in the rear cockpit (steering the rudder) and slept in the tight end of the cabin. I paddled in the front cockpit and slept with my head next to the cabin door: the fresh air helped enormously with seasickness.

6. ELECTRICAL SYSTEMS

Craig Thomsen from Solar Sailor/Enlog Sytems both designed and built the electrical system on board *Lot 41*. With a basic brief of what power needs we had, Craig designed a system that was far more extensive and robust than any other system designed for a small boat voyage to date. The main power drainages were:

- Desalinator
- Satellite phone
- Laptop (for marine charts and email)
- TracPlus transmitter

- Comar Class B AIS transponder
- Electric bilge systems
- Video and still camera charge
- Electric fan
- iPod charge

There were two stand-alone solar charge systems on board *Lot 41*, and three separate power storage/supply systems. This gave us redundancy in the event of a system going down. Craig drilled into us that the crossing was an exercise in maintenance and patience, rather than paddling. So long as we maintained our bodies, the craft and our electrics, there was no reason why we couldn't cross the Tasman. He was right.

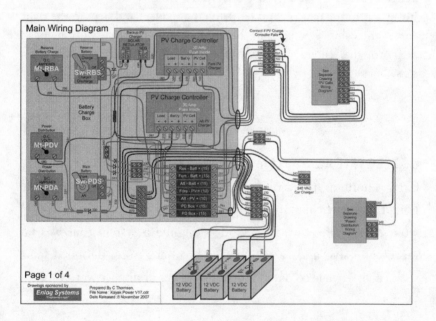

7. SPONSORSHIP/BRANDING

As two relatively young blokes, we found it crucial to show a high level of professionalism right from the start. After we'd completed our risk management document, and on paper knew we could paddle a kayak across the Tasman, we then spent all our effort designing our "image". Ben Barin's invaluable input in this phase was critical in ensuring we were able to get funding and sponsorship. This included:

- logo and brand design – "Crossing the Ditch"
- business cards
- website
- letterhead
- elaborate and tailored sponsorship proposals

We soon learnt that sponsorship from a company is not a charity donation. It was crucial that "Crossing the Ditch" would provide a tangible return to each of our sponsors. Before we sent any proposal to a prospective sponsor, we'd ask ourselves: "What's in it for them?" We'd only proceed if we felt that we'd accept the offer if it was sent to us. It was important to keep in mind that each potential sponsor had different measures of quantifying a return on investment. Finally, product support is infinitely easier to source than cash. Everything from our hull laminates to the 20 kilograms of almonds we ate out there was sourced from sponsors.

8. TRAINING

Coach Steve Vermay from Race Recon helped design our training regime. On average, we trained 25–30 hours per week from July 2006–Oct 2007. We rotated through the following cycle to achieve our goals:

- Foundation building: 4–6 weeks
- Power training: 3–4 weeks
- Cardio-power endurance: 4–6 weeks
- Cardio and muscular endurance training: 3–4 weeks
- Rest: 1 week

The primary goal of training was to make our bodies as indestructible as possible. This meant bulking up both fat and muscle stores while building our endurance. See below, a sample of a weekly training schedule:

CROSSING THE DITCH

Week Beginning: Mon 04-11-06 (Week R - Micro 2)
Training Phase: Base 2

	AM		PM	
Monday	Rest		Recovery Beach/pool 1 hour swim and water running Core work	
				1 hour swim
Tuesday	Paddling (K1) river Intervals 10 min warm up, 25 x 4 min ~80% 90 sec rest 10 min cool down Core work		Paddle (K2) ocean 2 hour paddle	
		2 hours		2 hours
				12/5/09
Wednesday	Paddling (K1) river Crossing pace Weighted boat, as you feel Core work		See weights2 30 min run/ride	
		4 hours		30 min
Thursday	Swimming		Paddling (K2) ocean Crossing pace, 80% on the lifts 30sec lifts every 10min Core work	
		1-2 hours		2-4 hour
Friday	Paddling (K1) river Crossing pace Weighted boat Core work BOAT DELIVERY		Weights See weights2 30-45 min run/ride steady BOAT DELIVERY	
		4 hours		30-45 min
Saturday	Bike and paddle (K1) flat Test and adjust the boat Core work		Paddle (K2) ocean or river Test and adjust the boat	
		2 & 2 hours		2 hours
Sunday	5-7 Long paddle (Ocean) In Lot 41 if possible Core work		Rest	
		7 hours		

"Getting Ugly" weekends, where we'd push our boundaries hard, played a big part in helping us prepare for the Tasman. Extreme exercise with both food and sleep deprivation was the goal. This was perhaps the most valuable training we did prior to the Tasman expedition. It taught us how to suffer, but more importantly how to keep moving when our bodies were begging us to stop.

9. EXPEDITION NUTRITION

Food is a critical aspect of any expedition. It provides both the fuel (duh!) and motivation to keep going. We based our meal plan on both Antarctic/Arctic sled-hauling expeditions and the meal plans followed by participants in the annual Woodvale Atlantic Rowing Race. We found 6000 calories sufficient for the energy we were expending. When we had to cut to half rations on day 33, significant weight loss occurred.

CROSSING THE DITCH
Sample Food Plan

Objective:
To establish a plan for a sustainable diet for a period of 50 days at sea that will provide the following:

1. Between 5000- 6000 Calories/ Day
2. Diet consists of approx. 45% Carbohydrates
3. Diet consists of approx. 15% Protein
4. Diet consists of approx. 40% Fats
5. Total food weight per person per day
   <1.5kg =>1.5kg x 2 persons x 50 days = 150kg

Here's a one-day food sample from out on the Tasman:

Here's a one-day food sample from out on the Tasman:

BREAKFAST

"150g Muesli, 50g powdered milk, 60g Sustagen, Fibre Plus bar, 500ml water"

	Muesli	Powdered Milk	Sustagen	Powdered Milk	Bar – Kellogg's K-time bar
	Per Serve 150g	Per Serve 50g	Per Serve 60g	Per Serve 50g	Per Serve 33.4g
Energy – Cal	650	108	64.8	108	120.00
Protein – grams	13.65	5.26	15	5.26	1.67
Fat – grams	20.1	6	0.4	6	0.63
Carbohydrates – grams	97.05	8.4	40	8.4	25.67

MID MORN / LUNCH

"Protein Bar, Scroggin and Sports Drink" / "Dehydrated meal, tuna (foil pack)"

	Protein Bar	"Scroggin- seeds (40%) (sunflower seeds and Pepitas), Fruit (40%) (Sultanas, dried apricots)	Sports drink	Sample Honey Soy Chicken (Back Country Cuisine)	Tuna
	Per Serve 65g	Per Serve 200g	Per Serve 25g	Per Serve 175g	Per Serve 100g
Energy – Cal	260	915	90	393.88	117.83
Protein – grams	20.2	32.5	0	17.5	25.1
Fat- grams	6	100	0	11.9	1.8
Carbohydrates – grams	31.5	75	15	55.6	0.1

MID ARVO / DINNER

	"Power Bar, Scroggin"		Dehydrated meal		
			Main Meal		Dessert
	Protein Bar	Scroggin	Sample: Honey Soy Chicken	Olive Oil Supplement	Snickers Bar
	Per Serve 65g	Per Serve 200g	Per Serve 175g	Serve 100g	Serve 60g
Energy – Cal	255	915	393.88	885	280
Protein – grams	20.1	32.5	17.5	0	4
Fat – grams	5.1	100	11.9	100	14
Carbohydrates – grams	28.9	75	55.6	0	35

	TOTAL	TOTAL WEIGHT= 1508G	
			Percentage of PFC
Serve size	Total weight	1508.40	
Energy — Cal	Total calories	5556.39	
Protein — grams	Total protein	210.24	0.19
Fat — grams	Total fat	383.83	0.34
Carbohydrates — grams	Total carbs	536.22	0.47

10. HOW DID WE RECORD THE EXPEDITION?

At all times we both had a waterproof notebook around our necks and an Olympus SW725 shock and waterproof camera as well.

We had two free roaming cameras on board: a Sony SD Handycam and a Sanyo Xacti Waterproof Camera. If there was one regret we had on the Tasman, it was not investing in some HD lipstick cameras built into the hull.

11. MUST-READ BOOKS

If you're planning a small boat voyage, I think the 10 must-read books would be:

Alone at Sea, Dr Hannes Lindemann

A Speck on the Sea, William H. Longyard

Captain Bligh and Mr Christian: The Men and the Mutiny,
        Richard Hough

The Rock Warrior's Way, Arno Ilgner

Extreme Alpinism, Mark Twight

Lionheart, Jesse Martin

Shackleton's Boat Journey, F.A. (Frank) Worsley

The Long Way, Bernard Moitessier

Kayak across the Atlantic, Peter Bray

Sailing Alone around the World, Joshua Slocum

For more info, please check out:
www.crossingtheditch.com.au

ACKNOWLEDGEMENTS

A real special thanks has got to go out to every single person who helped make this dream a reality. Justin and I are the first people to admit we weren't the best kayakers or adventurers out there ... in fact we're not the best at anything! If it wasn't for a vast support team spanning 16 different countries, we would still be stuck in Sydney Harbour.

First and foremost, I want to thank Jonesy for an incredible adventure. He's my best mate and always will be. He kept me alive out there on the Tasman and I'm looking forward to sharing a number of great adventures with him.

Thanks to my family – Mum, Dad, Lil and Clary – for putting up with me through some pretty difficult times, letting us take over the garage for a full year and sorry in advance for the upcoming expeditions ...

Same said for Justin's family – Rod, Chintra, Louisa and Andrew – thanks for your support (both financial and emotional) and understanding. Louisa – thanks also for the Christmas cake!

Without Patrick Brothers (Captain Pat) running the support of the expedition and the website, the expedition would not have been anywhere near the success that it was.

Tom Mitchell, apart from being an amazing mate, the way you handled the media and Jonesy and me when we got back from the Tasman was incredible.

To our major sponsor Unwired, a big thank you to David Spence and Linda Mak for believing in us and providing a major chunk of the funding to make it happen.

Rob Feloy, your design of *Lot 41* was brilliant. A big thank you as well to Graham Chapman up at Adventure Marine for the thousands of man-hours spent in the construction of *Lot 41*.

Our other sponsors, thank you so much for your support, we look forward to building long-term relationships with each of you: Eptec, FGI, Pretorius, Solar Sailor, Panasonic Toughbook, Rush Digital, TracPlus, Resi Mortgage Corporation, AWE Ltd, Australian Geographic, S-Direct, Activate Outdoors, Icebreaker, Pacific Sailing School, CDTL, Rudy Project, Kokatat, Garmin, Suunto, Pittarak, Solution Paddles, Pains Wessex, Day Two, Gatorade, Back Country Cuisine, Aussie Bodies, Oceantalk, Climb Fit, Gear Shop NZ, Series Drogue, Para Anchors, Marlin Trailers, H20 Audio, Skwoosh, Boroughs Australia.

A special thanks to Mel Cain and Patrick Mangan at HarperCollins, who made this book possible.

Sorry if I missed anyone out, but to the following people, Justin and I are indebted to your countless hours spent working on *Lot 41*: Roger Badham, Craig Thomsen, Ben Barin, Bruce Richards, Hugh Anderson, Phil Harmer, Anthony Gordon, Brad Gordon, Steve Vermay, Nicole Browne, Terry Wise, Warwick Burton, Greg Quail, Carl Dumbrell, Uncle Colin Raftos, Nick Fordham, Alan Cooper, Margaret Dreyer, Dr Glenn Singleman, Nick Edwards, Lach Whittaker, Peter FitzSimons, Lincoln Hall, Jesse Martin,

Strath Gordon, Larry Gray, Uncle H, Andy Worth, Harry Potter, James Smealle, Jay Cooper, John Leece, Tom Richardson, Ian Lowe, Andrew Mathers, Rod McClure, Alby McCracken, Duncan Hunter, Jen Cooper, Tony Mowbray, Rex Pemberton, Mayor Peter Tennant, Mike Hanning, Geoff Grut, Barry from Adventure Marine, Sean Griffin, Daniel Millar, Simon Blundell, Zoran Mitreski, David Johnston, Bryan Glover, Ben Hurdis, Paul Fenn, David Marsh, Alex Symes, Aidan Kerr, James Hammond, Hugh Porter, Colin Barr.

And all the countless mates who donated their time and therefore their nights' sleeps – fibreglass is infuriatingly itchy and doesn't come off for days …